Planning and the Rural Environment

PERGAMON URBAN AND REGIONAL PLANNING
ADVISORY COMMITTEE

G. F. CHADWICK, PhD, MA, BScTech, FRTPI, FILA (Chairman),
Planning Consultant,
Sometime Professor of Town and Country Planning,
University of Newcastle upon Tyne

D. R. DIAMOND, MA, MSc,
Reader in Regional Planning,
London School of Economics

A. K. F. FALUDI, Dipl-Ing, Dr techn,
Professor of Planning Theory,
Delft University of Technology

J. K. FRIEND, MA,
Institute for Operational Research

D. C. GILL, BA, MRTPI,
Director of Planning,
Humberside County Council

B. GOODEY, BA, MA,
Senior Lecturer in Urban Analysis and Perception,
Urban Design, Department of Town Planning,
Oxford Polytechnic

D. N. M. STARKIE, BSc(Econ), MSc(Econ),
Department of Geography,
University of Reading

B. STYLES, BA, MCD, MRTPI,
Divisional Planning Officer,
City of Birmingham Planning Department

Planning and the Rural Environment

by

JOAN DAVIDSON M.A., M.Sc.
and
GERALD WIBBERLEY C.B.E., BSc., M.S., PhD.

PERGAMON PRESS

OXFORD · NEW YORK · TORONTO
SYDNEY · PARIS · FRANKFURT

U.K.	Pergamon Press Ltd., Headington Hill Hall, Oxford OX3 0BW, England
U.S.A.	Pergamon Press Inc., Maxwell House, Fairview Park, Elmsford, New York 10523, U.S.A.
CANADA	Pergamon of Canada Ltd., 75 The East Mall, Toronto, Ontario, Canada
AUSTRALIA	Pergamon Press (Aust.) Pty. Ltd., 19a Boundary Street, Rushcutters Bay, N.S.W. 2011, Australia
FRANCE	Pergamon Press, SARL, 24 rue des Ecoles, 75240 Paris, Cedex 05, France
WEST GERMANY	Pergamon Press GmbH, 6242 Kronberg-Taunus, Pferdstrasse 1, Frankfurt-am-Main, West Germany

First edition 1977

Library of Congress Cataloging in Publication Data

Davidson, Joan.
Planning and the rural environment.

(Urban and regional planning series; v. 18)
1. Regional planning – Great Britain. 2. Land use, Rural – Great Britain – Planning. I. Wibberley, Gerald, joint author. II. Title. III. Series.
HT395.G7D34 1977   309.2′63′0941   76-54311
ISBN 0-08-020527-5 (Hardcover)
ISBN 0-08-020526-7 (Flexicover)

56,848

Printed in Great Britain by A. Wheaton & Co. Exeter

Contents

vi   *Contents*

List of Tables

List of Figures

List of Plates

1 Lowland countryside: the North Downs in Kent; well farmed and well wooded, but how long will it last? (Photo: John Topham)

2 Alderley Edge, Cheshire. Well managed, accessible woodland is an important, and often neglected, amenity asset. (Photo: Countryside Commission)

3 Leisure in the countryside. Clumber Park: cars, picnics, family groups — have we too readily accepted a stereotype? (Photo: Countryside Commission)

4 Crook o' Lune in the Forest of Bowland. Informal recreation in natural surroundings is a central theme of country park policies. (Photo: Lancashire County Planning Department)

5 Exciting opportunities for children: an adventure playground at Knebworth Country Park. (Photo: Countryside Commission)

6 Cycling for pleasure during an experiment at Clumber Park. (Photo: *Daily Express*)

7 The life of the countryside has its own attractions: an open day at Houghall Farm, Durham. (Photo: R. G. Woolmore)

8 A new agricultural landscape: the South Downs in Sussex. The hedges have been replaced by post and wire fencing; permanent pasture and scrub have been lost. The New Agricultural Landscapes Study suggests that cover can be retained and planted along the boundaries of holdings and on land too difficult to farm. (Photo: L. and M. Gayton)

9 Ripening wheat: beauty in efficiency. The New Agricultural Landscapes Study showed that farmers' attitudes to the landscape differ from those of many visitors to the countryside. (Photo: John Topham)

10 Beauty in diversity: waste land on farms may be untidy but ecologically rich; new planting could disturb established habitats. (Photo: John Topham)

11 Town and country: the environment of the urban fringe in North Kent. (Photo: John Topham)

12 The landscape of the fringe: Green Belt land in Hillingdon once worked for gravel, then used for waste tipping, now derelict. (Photo: Joan Davidson)

13 Access to the fringe: the Green Belt in Hillingdon, an uninviting entrance to a local open space. (Photo: Joan Davidson)

14 Amsterdamse Bos on the fringe of the Dutch capital: 'man-made wild'. (Photo: Joan Davidson)

15 Farming in the uplands: a precarious living from a harsh environment. Sheep grazing in South Uist. (Photo: John Topham)

Preface

The concept of countryside is elusive. As an environmental entity it cannot be rigidly defined, although we may see it as an assemblage of resources (many of them natural) and activities concerned with extensive uses of land. The countryside is also a powerful social entity, involving not only those whose business is the handling and planning of rural resources, but also those who value them in other, often quite intangible ways, and whose livelihood is based upon activities in the town. The popularity of the countryside is growing — both as an environment to enjoy and one to study. Its planning, for so long the cinderella of professional interest and practice, shows signs of increasing respectability.

In 1970, the first Chair of Countryside Planning was established at University College London with funds from the Ernest Cook Trust and since that time the authors have been developing a course on rural planning for postgraduate students reading for an M.Phil. degree in Planning. It is out of the context and discussions of the course that this book has emerged. It is a very selective one, reflecting not only our special interests and viewpoints, but the inadequacies of experience. Our concern is with the look and feel of the open countryside, with the function and appearance of the rural environment, rather than with the problems of its people and the settlements in which they live. It would clearly be misleading to suggest that environmental issues are the only or the most important components of countryside planning; this must embrace many other social and economic problems which we do not discuss. But our experience in government agencies, in teaching and research has led us to think that although many rural problems — in housing, employment and transport — are far from solved, issues of the built countryside are not neglected fields of study. Indeed they have, at times, so preoccupied research workers and policymakers that the rest of the countryside (and more than 80% of Britain) may have received rather less attention than it deserves, especially among town and country planners. The open countryside, no less than the town, is changing rapidly; it harbours divisive interests, and it, too, experiences the repercussions of restructuring in the patterns of national and local administration.

Our central theme is the conflict of interest generated between some of the major planning systems concerned with the development of rural activities and the protection of rural resources. We look at the repercussions of changing actions and attitudes for the fabric of the countryside but we have not sought to be comprehensive. The planning systems we discuss in Parts I and II reflect our view of how the emerging range of environmental problems and opportunities in rural planning can best be illustrated. We could have taken other examples: dealing in greater detail with other planning systems, like water conservation or mineral development, which we discuss mainly in the context of upland problems. In the uplands and the urban fringe, the subjects of Part III, we explore some of the ways in which rural interests interact in two very different areas. Lastly, in Part IV, we review the development of rural planning and speculate on a variety of issues which will shape the countryside of the future.

We make no apologies for our concern with attitudes as much as with facts. It has been our intention not only to report but also to comment, and inevitably values and prejudices emerge. But the countryside is dominated by such issues; to exclude them from any discussion of how it might develop would be as unreal as it would probably be impossible.

We have gained much from our discussions with the postgraduates who helped to shape the course: our thanks go to a large number of them who, over four years, challenged both our facts and our interpretation of them. Many specialists in various fields of countryside planning — in local and central government, farmers' organisations and private practice — came to debate rural problems with us. Our thanks go to them, and in particular to Arnold Grayson (of the Forestry Commission), Max Hooper (of the Institute of Terrestrial Ecology), and Andrew McLellan (of the Sunderland and South Shields Water Company) for their stimulating seminars which provoked so many ideas.

One of us (J. D.) is especially grateful to Reg Hookway (Director of the Countryside Commission) for introducing her to the subject and continuing to encourage the necessary blend of enthusiasm and scepticism about rural problems.

Many busy people made valuable comments on the draft: Reg Hookway, John Davidson, Arnold Grayson and Roger Sidaway read the whole text; Adrian Phillips, John Zetter, M. L. Lawson and R. G. Brown commented on particular chapters. For tireless typing we must thank Cathy Mills, Susan Hope, Roseanne Kyriakides and Sheila Kingsnorth. But most of all we are grateful to those who helped in other ways: to Ursula Branfield who gave a small child many happy hours while this book was written, and to John and Peggy for their understanding and encouragement.

J. D.

G. P. W.

January 1976

CHAPTER 1

The Countryside and Conflict

The countryside has a special place in the minds of most people, whether or not they live in it. To many, the rural environment appears discrete and recognisable, changeless — even though we will argue that it is not — and by its contrast with the town, offers peace and naturalness. Rural life harbours activities and values which are revered, traditions which are seen to be quite alien to the impermanence and frivolity of urban living.

But although most people might subscribe to this collective view of the rural heritage, their particular interpretation of it is very different. Attitudes to the countryside, to the use of rural resources and to the operation of rural activities are strongly polarised. In recent years, many different interest groups, within government and outside it, have emerged with a stake in country matters. Rural pressure groups survive and multiply.

Expressed in a much simplified but convenient way, their preoccupations can be classified as follows. There are those whose dominant concern is the production of more food more efficiently, both in technical and economic terms. There are others, essentially preservationists, who wish to retain the countryside pattern and activities of their youth. Many people like to live in, or just visit, rural settlements which, though they retain a pleasing historic character, have dramatically changed their function in the rural economy. Yet other individuals and organised groups work for the protection and improvement of the biological diversity of rural areas. Many people see the countryside as their playground and feel strongly that they have the right so to use it. Land use planners[1] working on behalf of those living in inadequate urban environments, are concerned with the redevelopment of old cities, and the creation of new ones in pleasant rural surroundings. Likewise, other professional groups are involved in the improvement of communications through country areas, the exploitation of mineral reserves, and the conservation of water resources. For each of these groups, different attributes of the rural environment are significant; few would agree on how the rural environment and economy functions; all have very different conceptions of how a countryside of the future should develop and the degree of control and direction that should take place.[2]

The Countryside and Planning

The case for urban planning is largely accepted; to many people the idea of planning the countryside is not only anathema, but a contradiction in terms. For them, the countryside *is* the countryside only because it is assumed to be natural and unplanned, and in terms of physical planning, this is, in many ways, still largely true.

1

The 1947 Town and Country Planning Act, which followed various earlier legislative attempts to impose controls, in a piecemeal way, upon physical change introduced, for the first time in Britain, a comprehensive system of land use planning.[3] The two principal components of the 1947 system (which was consolidated in 1962) were development planning and development control. Development plans, prepared by local authorities in the fifties and sixties now cover the whole country, zoning all land for the particular use or assemblage of uses thought most appropriate to it. They describe existing conditions, outline proposals for action by public agencies and show those areas to be protected from various kinds of development. Development plans thus provide a framework of land uses against which day-to-day developments can be considered and, if necessary, controlled.[4]

The merits and defects of this planning system have been discussed by many critics, notably the Planning Advisory Group,[5] but most agree that, for its time, the 1947 legislation was a fairly successful example of public intervention in the use of land. It remains, despite substantial modifications introduced by the 1968 Town and Country Planning Act, the basis of the planning system operated by most local authorities today. In the urban environment, the Act has been, and still is, a major influence on the nature and scale of physical change. In the countryside, especially the open countryside the effects have been less obvious, for in its objectives and methods, the orientation of the physical planning system has been overwhelmingly urban in emphasis.

In theory as well as in practice, rural planning has been preoccupied with the question of where, and where not to build. In the circumstances of the 1940's there was ample justification for this view: the planners' approach, like the national outlook, was inevitably conditioned by the pre- and immediate post-war experience. Certain aspects of it were particularly important in shaping the form of planning legislation that came in 1947 – not only in terms of planning *objectives*, but (and this is important) in the *means* of achieving them. In retrospect, four issues seem especially important.

First, planners and public alike had inherited a fear of uncontrolled urban expansion and a determination to resist the ugly, inefficient, straggling development of the thirties about which the Scott Committee, among others, was so concerned.[6] The 1947 planning act rightly emphasised the control of building development as a means of achieving this goal. Secondly, there was a determination that agriculture should never again suffer the kind of depression that occurred in the thirties; politicians and planners were convinced that Britain should aim to minimise her dependence on imports of foreign food and timber. Building up an efficient agricultural system, producing cheap food for a war-weary nation was seen as a major objective in the use of the countryside, and this policy was spelt out in the Agriculture Act of 1947. It was altogether understandable that agriculture and forestry should have been exempt from planning control: virtually none of their operations counted as development for the purposes of the 1947 Town and Country Planning Act. Moreover, a major – and only recently modified – component of planning was the protection of agricultural land against all forms of urban development.[7] Even if these arguments had been contested in 1947, and land planners had sought to intervene more in agricultural affairs, their political strength was limited. Foster argues that the new Ministry of Town and Country Planning, despite its wide responsibilities, was heavily dominated by long-established and more powerful government departments.[8]

Thirdly, there was little pressure for physical planners to be involved in the countryside in a positive way, by, for example, acquisition of rural land for a public or protective purpose. There was little use of the countryside for leisure. Provision for what there was, and protection of the landscape in those areas of finest scenery (then a more important concern) was handled in the National Parks legislation of 1949. Likewise, provision for wildlife conservation in the countryside had been made in the establishment of a separate public agency (the Nature Conservancy) with its own legislative remit to set up nature reserves and carry out research in them.[9] There was another and separate system for the conservation of water resources. In most of these rural activities the physical planner had no role to play.

Finally, perhaps the most important factor in minimising this involvement in countryside matters at this time was that the obvious problems, in urgency and magnitude, were in the towns, and in the need to reconstruct bombed city centres. Moreover, most planners, in their training and interests, were strongly oriented to the built environment; they defined much of their task in architectural or engineering terms and they were unfamiliar with the rural disciplines of resource and estate management.

The role of planners in the countryside has thus been an indirect one of protection against urban developments, but in this their efforts have undoubtedly been successful. The expansion of agriculture after 1947 on land safeguarded from urban uses, allowed British farmers to increase their contribution to the total home food market to above 50 per cent. The countryside of today would certainly be less extensive, less beautiful and probably less accessible if building development had been less rigidly controlled. But this function, vital though it was, effectively masked other problems. Planners, who dealt with rural issues at all, were trying to maintain a *status quo* which they felt to be inherently changeless. In this, Green and others have argued that:

" . . . the . . . years since the Town and Country Planning Act of 1947 represent two decades of wasted opportunity for *positive* rural planning".[10]

But the countryside did not go unplanned. Despite the lack of involvement of physical planners, powerful *resource* planning agencies, with their own systems of legislation and finance, have shaped the use and appearance of the countryside since the war. The Ministry of Agriculture, for example, with its persuasive planning system of guaranteed prices, grants and advisory services has guided the development of a highly efficient agricultural industry in technical and economic terms. The Forestry Commission has also used persuasive means of achieving afforestation objectives by providing advice and grants to private owners under various woodland management schemes. Substantial financial incentives exist in the fiscal system which benefit landowners who invest in commercial forestry. The Nature Conservancy Council now owns many National Nature Reserves but it has also achieved wildlife conservation goals by persuading landowners to enter into special management arrangements which will ensure the retention of valued species and their habitats.

All these and other public programmes for the support of rural activities and the protection of rural resources have been pursued outside the statutory Town and Country Planning system and with rather more positive goals for the countryside and methods of achieving them than would be familiar to most planners. Yet these programmes add up to a significant amount of rural planning in the widest sense. Hookway and Hartley consider that, far from being a neglected subject, rural resource planning, involving not only the public sector, but also private landowners, estate managers, and their representative organisations, has been highly successful since the war. They argue, in passing, that the approach to planning in urban and rural environments has been fundamentally different:

"Planning the countryside of Britain is . . . a matter of the conservation of natural resources. Planning our towns, on the other hand is . . . concerned with the development of land resources."[11]

The resource planning programmes are concerned with the manipulation of natural or semi-natural systems such as the soil, drainage basins or wildlife habitats. Their primary goal is to protect and enhance the resources of these systems to ensure that they continue to yield what is wanted: crops, or drinking water, or a particular plant species. Superficially, the approach and the philosophy of this kind of planning seems very different from the work of urban planners concerned with the regulation of human activity and the control of building development. As thinking in urban and rural areas focusses increasingly on environmental *management* the distinction now begins to blur, but the situation of the post-war years could be seen in a neat and simple way: with *resource* planning in the countryside and *development* planning in the towns, each conducted independently of the other.

The Development of Rural Conflict

But this view of a countryside guarded from the excesses of urban growth, with its resources protected for many uses in a controlled, harmonious way does not reflect the reality of present conflict.[12] Differences exist not simply between urban and rural activities and ideologies but, perhaps more severely, *within* the countryside, between the agencies of rural change. They arise from social and economic changes which were not anticipated in the immediate post-war years when planning legislation was framed. With hindsight, we can see that the attitudes of physical planners to the countryside were not simply the product of past experience, but were reinforced by what the future was thought to hold. Most analysts of the weaknesses of post-war planning have made clear that demographers, economists, sociologists as well as planners, failed to predict a growth in population and the evolution of a more affluent, mobile society with changing habits and aspirations. There were obvious implications for the planning of towns, principally in the needs for more space and lower housing densities. The effects on the countryside were less sudden, but no less significant.

Two groups of new demands were placed upon the resources of the countryside: those 'external' pressures associated with changes in urban society, and those arising within the rural environment and economy.[13]

Principal among the 'external' pressures has been the demand for building land. Despite nearly three decades of stringent controls upon development and, until recently, the presumption against building in the open countryside, more than 40,000 acres (15,600 ha) of farmland have been lost annually to urban development.[14] Rural land is lost to inter-urban roads, reservoirs, industry, airports, out-of-town hypermarkets, mineral excavation, public utilities and a host of other activities spawned by the expansion or renewal of urban areas (Table 1). The spread of affluence and personal mobility coupled with the growing preference for suburban and country living has brought new pressures for village development from city commuters and second home users, and also from the retired. In recent years, one of the best documented external pressures on the countryside (though not necessarily the most significant in terms of numbers or area affected) has been recreation activity, a major consequence of increased affluence and mobility. A less tangible 'external' influence upon the rural environment, but one which is already powerful and growing more so, arises from an increasingly articulate amenity lobby supported largely by urban and suburban residents.

All these 'external' pressures have been felt first in the countryside of the city region[15] but also, particularly with increasing recreation activity, in the uplands and remoter rural areas. All have generated greater or lesser degrees of conflict in rural areas: rapid urban expansion has led to insecurity among farmers on the fringe of urban areas, often resulting in

TABLE 1

Land Use Change in England and Wales

	% total area			
	1900	1925	1950	1965
Agriculture	83.6	82.9	80.6	78.6
Forestry	5.1	5.1	6.4	7.5
Urban uses[a]	5.4	6.2	9.7	11.5
Unaccounted for[b]	5.9	5.8	3.3	2.4

Source: Best, R. H. (1965) Recent Changes and Future Prospects of Land Use in England and Wales, *Geographical Journal*, Vol. 13.

[a] Includes land closely built over together with associated 'open' spaces such as gardens, sports grounds and roads, together with roads and railways in the countryside, villages, isolated dwellings, farmsteads, airports and open cast mineral workings.

[b] In 1900 this included many pockets of wasteland now included in the 'agriculture' category; the loss of farmland to urban and forestry use is greater than 5% suggested by these figures.

the under-use and dereliction of good land; communities have been disrupted by the influx of commuters, and the quality of rural services has declined. Recreation activity in some areas has brought problems of trespass, litter and traffic congestion as well as damage to valued ecological environments. The views of city conservationists have sometimes outweighed those of rural communities in the arguments for new sources of employment in rural areas.

Not only have planners and others been unprepared for the rural implications of these changes but they have failed to appreciate the nature and scale of 'internal' change that has taken place in the rural economy, with economic, social and environmental consequences for the countryside. Technical changes in agriculture, especially on land of the highest quality, continue to have the most impact in visual as well as social terms. New patterns of cropping, greater specialisation, mechanisation and the increasing use of chemicals have brought to some areas a monotony of landscape and great poverty of natural species. Some of the conflicts generated by change within the rural environment are obvious: commercial afforestation and mining in National Parks; the flooding of valuable natural habitats to conserve water resources. Others are less obvious, and less often the concern of public opinion: the disappearance of lowland coppice woodland; the drainage of marshes and ponds; the development of industrial farm buildings.

The Complexity of the Rural Environment

In all these changes which affect the countryside, the influence of the statutory land planner has been slight. The influence of resource planners has been strong and single-minded. But it is now becoming clear that for resource planning to operate in the tightly closed boxes of agriculture *or* forestry *or* nature conservation (in the way that immediate post-war and later developments in legislation and organisation have encouraged) is no longer satisfactory. There are three fundamental reasons why this 'pocket planning' in the countryside — compartmentalised policy-making which parallels the notion of single-use zoning in towns — will not work.

First, although rural resources may be directly *used* by only one interest group, in the way that good soils on gently sloping, well-drained land will be intensively farmed; these resources are *valued*, in a less tangible way, by other groups such as ecologists for their wildlife, or tourists for their scenic interest. As in any complex system, the spillover effects of change in its components affect the working of other parts of the system.[16] In the rural environment, the side effects of intensifying a number of activities become increasingly undesirable and begin to frustrate the aims of other activities which directly use or otherwise value rural resources. We discuss some examples of these interactions in subsequent chapters; for example, in Chapter 6 we consider how the wildlife of the countryside is now so influenced by a number of rural activities that it is no longer feasible to imagine that plants and animals can be protected only on a few National Nature Reserves. The viability of most protected species depends upon conservation measures being adopted, to a varying degree, throughout the countryside. Likewise, we discuss, in Chapter 4 the dangers of recreation planning in isolation, divorced from its implications for other rural activities. The pursuit of single-purpose objectives by different resource interests, serves only to curtail the extent to which others may achieve their aims.

Secondly, extra benefits may be derived from co-operation rather than segregation, although these may be indirect. Throughout this book, we try to identify the multiple interests in resource use and management.

Thirdly, pursuing further the analogy with systems theory: the appearance and functioning of the *whole* is as important as the working of its component parts. In rural terms, increasing values are placed upon the total 'fabric' of the countryside as well as upon good food, pure water or clear air. Yet no-one is responsible for this fabric; it is the unplanned consequences of many different activities which, in sum, produce the rural environment we see and feel.[17] The pace of change may be too fast and the use of the countryside too intense for its fabric to survive for long in this incidental way.

A Changing Countryside

Traditional views of the countryside as changeless, are fast being eroded: visual evidence and the increasing pressure of environmental groups see to that. Yet behind all this is still the feeling that somehow the balance will be restored, that the changes are local, that the rural environment and country life will continue to offer, to those who seek it out, the simplicity and permanence which seem to be so absent in the town.

The rest of this book argues that this is not only erroneous but a dangerous notion for it is a recipe for continued piecemeal action and sectoral campaigning. It does nothing to modify what might be fundamental inadequacies in our use and management of rural resources; and it may contribute to our failure to think, in ways which are comparable to visions of urban society, about a countryside of the future. The rural environment is certainly not changeless. Over three decades, rapid developments have taken place in its social and economic character, with significant environmental implications. The changes have equalled, and at times exceeded, the pace and scale of those in urban areas, Moreover, the notion that the countryside we see is somehow the happy 'accident' of an entirely natural, rural way of life is a myth. In reality, the countryside is intensively planned; its activities and resources are subject to a variety of directions and controls even though the ways in which these are applied may be unfamiliar to those more concerned with the urban milieu.

Notes and References

1. The terms: 'planning'; 'land planning' and 'physical planning' in this and subsequent chapters refer to the statutory activity of town and country planning unless otherwise qualified.
2. The idea of rural interest groups is discussed further in:
    Wibberley, G. P. (1971) *Rural Planning in Britain – a Study in Contrast and Conflict*, Inaugural lecture, University of London, May 1971.
    Gripps, J. (1972) *Whose Countryside?* Town and Country Planning Association Conference on Planning and the Countryside, February.
3. For a discussion of prewar planning history see for example:
    Cherry, G. (1974) *The Evolution of British Town Planning*, Leonard Hill Books.
4. A brief account of development control is given in Chapter 3 of:
    Dobry, G. (1974) *Review of the Development Control System*, Interim Report, H.M.S.O.
5. Planning Advisory Group (1965) *The Future of Development Plans*, H.M.S.O.
6. Ministry of Works and Planning (1942) *Report of the Committee on Land Utilisation in Rural Areas* (Scott Report), H.M.S.O., Cmnd. 6378.
7. Under the 1947 (and 1962) Planning system, the presumption was against development on all land classified as 'white' or land where "existing uses should remain for the most part undisturbed".
    A reversal of this policy so that land formerly zoned as 'white' no longer carries an automatic presumption against housing development followed the publication of a White Paper and Circular in 1973:
    Department of the Environment (1973) *Widening the Choice – the Next Steps in Housing*, H.M.S.O., Cmnd. 5280.
    Department of the Environment (1973) *Land Availability for Housing*, H.M.S.O., Circular 122/73.
8. Foster, J. (1973) Planning in the Countryside, *The Planner*, Vol. 59(9), November.
9. Policies on leisure and nature conservation are dealt with in chapters 4 and 6.
10. Green, R. (1971) *Country Planning – the Future of the Rural Regions*, Manchester University Press.
11. Hookway, R. J. S. and Hartley, J. (1968) Resource Planning *Estates Gazette*, July 13.
12. Davidson, J. (1974) A Changing Countryside, in Goldsmith, B. and Warren, A. (eds.) *Conservation in Practice*, Wiley.
13. Committee for Environmental Conservation (1973) *Urban Pressures on the Countryside*, CoEnCo.
14. Best, R. H. (1968) Competition for Land between Rural and Urban Uses, in *Land Use and Resources: Studies in Applied Geography*, Institute of British Geographers Publication No. 1, 93.
15. Smart, A. D. G. (1968) Rural Planning in the Context of the City Region, *Report of Proceedings, Town and Country Planning Summer School, Manchester.*
16. See for example:
    McLoughlin, J. B. (1969) *Urban and Regional Planning – A Systems Approach*, Faber.
17. This notion has been explored, primarily in the context of the urban environment in:
    Solesbury, W. (1968) *The Needs of Environmental Planning*, Unpublished paper delivered to a Symposium on Environmental Planning, organised by the Ministry of Housing and Local Government and the Ministry of Transport.

Part I: Activities: Planning for Development

CHAPTER 2

Agriculture and Rural Land

It is right and proper that early in a book dealing with the rural environment, agriculture should be given priority. It is the dominant rural industry and this dominance extends over most of the areas and problems with which rural planners of today and tomorrow will be concerned.

For centuries, economic and social change within agriculture has influenced the distribution and character of rural — and, until recently, many urban — communities. But in all long-settled rural regions, a great many existing villages and country towns are losing or have lost their original function.[1] They will stagnate and decline unless some new function is found for them. If a modest assumption is made that the average radius served effectively by a market town under present-day conditions of motor transport is double what it was in the days of the horse, this means that approximately three-quarters of existing country towns are no longer needed for their original purpose. The remaining quarter should be sufficient to serve a modern and highly mobile agricultural region in the last decades of the twentieth century.

Yet few of the villages and country towns which are losing their agricultural functions will disappear in the physical sense: the material of which their structures are built is usually much too permanent in character for this to happen. Though some may be by-passed, most will continue to dominate the rural road system. Thus, many of the modern social and economic problems of the countryside derive from the difficulties of matching a settlement pattern, determined by older forms of farming and agricultural service industries, to a very much changed situation of rural employment and the new demands of day and holiday recreation, commuting and retirement.

The major concern of this book, however, is not with the planning of the settled countryside, but with the land and landscape between; it is here that the dominance of agriculture as a rural activity is clear. Heavily populated and long industrialised though Britain is, about 80 per cent of her land surface is farmed and estimates of the likely land use pattern by the end of the century suggest that an agricultural use of some kind will be pre-eminent over at least three-quarters of the country.[2] This means that the majority of land use changes in rural areas will take place within the agricultural industry.

This industry, or rather its farmers and market gardeners, will decide, for example, the crops which are grown from year to year in various fields. They will also decide the numbers and kinds of livestock which will use the land and the extent to which these animals are fed out of doors or in specially arranged buildings. The industry will also decide the types, extent and pattern of its fixed and mobile equipment and, although there may be controls

11

imposed from outside, the types of farm buildings, their size and where they are placed will be largely dictated by pressures and incentives within agriculture. New farming and horticultural methods will determine the size and nature of the field pattern, whether fields will continue to be enclosed with hedges, or whether this form of controlled vegetation is almost completely abandoned, or replaced by barriers and boundaries based upon fenceposts and wire. The agricultural industry will probably be the main arbiter as to whether our unique pattern of isolated trees and copses and the hedgerow hardwood trees will remain or disappear, or be replaced by other forms of planting.[3]

For all these reasons, an understanding of the nature of the agricultural industry and the changes, both technical and economic, which are going on inside it, will be vital for those who wish to control, guide or co-operate with the major agent of land use and landscape change within this country.

Rural and Agricultural Mysticism

The agricultural industry of most long settled countries has been involved in a complex of historical changes and emotional attitudes. This primary industry has been responsible for creating a system of land use and settlements with a definite physical and visual pattern which has changed much more slowly than the technical and social forces within agriculture. Though agriculture is based upon the management of natural fauna and flora, it has been quickly adapted by man into intensive forms of controlled cultivation. Even so, most forms of agriculture and forestry are very much closer to the forces of nature than other industrial processes and the checks and balances imposed by soil type, soil nutrients, water table and microclimate have always been important to all forms of agriculture and forestry, except for certain specialised forms of intensive horticulture and recent types of factory livestock production. It has, therefore, been easy for people to believe that agriculture is a 'natural' industry, that it is dominated by natural forces and that it has a unique importance as a preserver of an Arcadian rural pattern which is significantly different from all other forms of man-made use and exploitation of the environment. Thus, it has been commonly assumed until quite recently (and the Scott Report shows this strongly)[4] that if a rural area is dominated by commercial agricultural production then this will act as an automatic form of conservation of natural fauna and flora and that it will maintain a settlement pattern which will be both effective and picturesque.

This belief in the essential conservationist function of the agricultural industry has been strengthened by the development over the centuries of the personal and group philosophy of 'agricultural fundamentalism'. This is the belief that any person who is actively engaged in performing agricultural processes and who is living and working amongst natural forces and with natural fauna and flora, develops traits of character which are different to those developed by people living in towns. This idea of a marked difference in the character and development of rural as against urban people quickly took on a fundamentalist attitude as urban areas began to grow and to suffer from the early problems of the Industrial Revolution. The rapid degradation of living conditions for human beings that seemed to go along with factory and mining development was contrasted with the slowly changing and evolving pattern of living in rural settlements and in the open countryside.

Although agricultural fundamentalism or 'peasantism', as the French term it, has been strong in parts of the continent and particularly in France, Germany and Austria, it has also been influential in a country like Britain, even though it was not used to stop or even slow down the dramatic changes which occurred in rural Britain throughout the Enclosure movement with its replacement of the communal system of open fields by relatively large scale enclosed and tenanted farms on large estates. The uncritical belief that human character fashioned by rural, and particularly by agricultural, experience was somehow vital to the development of a healthy nation, was fostered in the rapidly growing industrial climate of nineteenth-century Britain. So much of the literature of the time bewails the passing of rural Arcadia and its replacement by the dark satanic mills and hateful conditions of the industrial city. This rural philosophy and mirage is well described by Raymond Williams[5] and, despite objective studies of the realities of rural life and its problems which range from the precise and frightening studies of the Hammonds[6] to the small masterpiece of 'Akenfield'[7] there is still a general British reverence and nostalgia for the 'traditional' rural and agricultural way of life. It has always been hard for the enthusiast of city life to stand up against the many and varied protagonists of real or imaginary country forms of living.

Dynamic Changes Within the Agricultural Industry

Although the agricultural scene has given an appearance of relative permanence in many of its physical characteristics, it is an industry of very real and rapid technical and economic change. In recent years the changes in, for example, the size of fields, the way in which crops are harvested, the size of farm buildings and the materials of which they are made and techniques of livestock production, have been dramatic enough to convince even the layman travelling through the countryside that something dynamic is happening.

This dynamism may be simply expressed in terms of the experience of the writer, involved with agricultural matters for half a century — a short period of time in an industry which is supposed to be concerned with natural factors and the slow tempo of the growth of plants and animals. In reality he is as bewildered as anyone else by the pace of change which he has seen. In his lifetime the draught-horse has given way completely to the large versatile tractor. The hand-milking of dairy cows kept in their tens and twenties has changed to the machine-milking of units of 70 to 100 cows by one man. The small groups of calves, pigs, beef cattle and sheep that used the grass fields of his youth are now to be found in large numbers in intensified livestock units which are organised to give a controlled environment for the animals and high productivity to the few persons employed in looking after them. The hayfork, the wagon, the rick and stack associated in his youth with harvest time are now replaced by the mower and elevator, the bales of hay and straw, the combine-harvester and the grain store and dryer. The long and monotous days of singling, hoeing and harvesting root and green crops, have been replaced by a whole complex of new drilling machines and harvesting techniques which have effectively separated these root crops from direct manual contact. The old barns made of brick, stone or timber with many adaptations from the time of the hand-flail have been followed by simple but large structures of steel, concrete and asbestos which now dominate the countryside and which house silage, hay and intensively managed animals. The quick or blackthorn hedges, where both drudgery and artistry were needed in their laying and cutting, have become scarce and those that remain are trimmed and mutilated by machines. The wire fence will soon reign supreme, for it is more functional, more flexible and easier (though not necessarily cheaper) to maintain.

The power unit of the farm horse has been replaced by the modern tractor run on imported fuel oil and this has become larger and more powerful through the years. The rough grass fields with their pretty but unproductive mixture of grasses and weeds and large areas of wet land have been reduced and changed into vast sweeps of wheat and barley or into new grass leys, productive but limited in their species of grass and clover. Both arable and grassland weeds, previously controlled laboriously through rotational cropping, hand hoeing and cutting, now fall prey to selective weedkillers and systemic fungicides. The slopes and tops of the chalk downlands of England have lost their productively poor but floristically rich old grass turf and are now huge arable tracks with a swirling mass of grain in spring and summer and tongues of flame from straw burning after harvest. The hill country of the West and North, so laboriously farmed and yet giving such low incomes four decades ago are now tidier, better cultivated, more thickly stocked with cattle and sheep, with more machinery and better buildings. The wide sweeps of open moorland and mountain top still dominate the scene but considerably more woodland has appeared.

We are experiencing a revolution in the type of farm buildings being erected, in the materials of which they are made, and in the shortness of life for which they are planned. Field size has become a flexible element in farm planning and more and more field boundaries have been lost or made temporary and movable. The close relationship between grazing and the animal is being broken, with crops grown for harvest and then transported to where the animal can be kept with the maximum of environmental control and the minimum of labour (although effluent control and disposal are made more difficult). Most farms are becoming simplified in their policy and operation with a concentration on just a few products, these being produced in bulk and continuously through the year or at the optimal times. In marketing, the emphasis is increasingly upon production under contract, adapted to the needs of the supermarket chain. No longer is the farm a place where a whole range of food products is grown to satisfy both the farm family and the town dweller. It is becoming a factory: factory-like in its processes and appearance and in the specialised nature of its production.[8]

Changes in Land Tenure

Over the first half of the twentieth-century there was a surprising rigidity in the land tenure situation. For a long time it appeared that there was almost a permanence about the number and size of most farm holdings and whereas there was a slow increase in the number of very large farms, this seemed to be compensated by great variations in the numbers of extremely small farm holdings. The picture in many European countries was similar, although the size distribution was weighted towards small farms rather than the moderate size prevalent in Britain. In many Western countries it appeared as if there was a complex of forces operating which prevented significant changes taking place in the distribution of farm size.

Since about the middle of the 1950's, however, the land tenure situation in most Western industrialised countries has changed dramatically. No longer are very small farms being maintained in large numbers or being created by the sub-division of larger holdings. No longer are farm machines being adapted to the size of small farms and small fields rather than the reverse taking place. No longer is the number of really large farms increasing only very slowly with this increase being restricted by the effects of death and sub-division amongst the members of a farming family. No longer does the farm of between 100-300 acres (40-130 hectares) offer the optimal combination of land, labour and capital, with any necessary increases in output being obtained merely by intensifying the land use.

It is as if Western Europe has suddenly followed North America and some of the newer countries in at last allowing its farm structure and tenure to be decided by changes in agricultural techniques and in the effective use of capital and of labour saving machinery. This has produced a pronounced shift towards a greater scale in all types of farming. There is now a steady decline in the number of all types of farms in Britain of above 2 to 3 per cent per year. Holdings of about 400 acres (160 hectares) in size are increasing but this movement is not sufficient to compensate for the strong reduction in the number of farms of all types which are below this size. For example, during the three years 1968 to 71, the number of farm holdings dropped, on average, by 10 per cent. The biggest reduction was over one quarter of the farms between 5 and 50 acres (2-20 hectares). Even farms previously thought to be of good size (that is 150-200 acres or 60-80 hectares of crops and grass) fell by 6.2 per cent in these years. As a compensation, farms of over 1000 acres (400 hectares) increased by more than a quarter in these three years and those between 500 and 1000 (200-400 hectares) by 12 per cent. The numbers of farms in these large six groups are, of course, relatively small so that their effect on the average figure in rather light. In essence, however, the picture in Britain (and this is duplicated in Western Europe) is that the smaller the size of the farm holding the faster the rate of its disappearance (Table 2).

TABLE 2

Changes in the Size of Agricultural Holdings, 1961-1971

Size in acres	Number of holdings in 1000's	
	1961	1971
Under 5	70.1	23.4
5 and under 15	61.6	32.9
15 and under 20	14.0	10.3
20 and under 30	23.2	16.6
30 and under 50	36.7	25.9
50 and under 100	56.9	44.2
100 and under 150	29.1	24.5
150 and under 300	32.6	29.2
300 and under 500	9.6	10.6
500 and under 700	2.6	3.5
700 and under 1000	1.2	1.9
1000 and over	.7	1.3

In this decade the acreage in holdings over 300 acres (120 hectares) rose from 7 million acres to 9½ million, whilst the acreage in holdings below 300 acres fell from 17 million acres to 14 million.

Source: Institute of Agricultural Economics (1972) *The State of British Agriculture 1971-72*, Oxford.

It might be thought that this relatively sudden increase in the size of farm holdings would be associated with an increase in tenanted land rather than owner-occupied. Although the situation has become confused in the 1970's, the trend since the turn of the century has been in the opposite direction (Tables 3 and 4). The high point of the landlord/tenant system was reached in Britain just before World War I when more than 70 per cent of farms were rented. This has slowly changed to a situation where about 60 per cent of holdings are now in the hands of owner-occupiers and more than one third of the farmed area of England and Wales is in mixed holdings, part owned and part rented.[9] In theory, a strong case can be made out in favour of the landlord/tenant system in that it divides the responsibility for providing different kinds of capital between the landlord and his tenant. The landlord provides the fixed capital on the land, including the permanent buildings, while the tenant provides the working capital of livestock and implements. The system meant that, in practice, much of rural Britain was in the hands of a few large landlords so that, by legislation, custom and

TABLE 3

Change in Agricultural Land Tenure, 1888-1969

	Percentage of the total number of holdings in England and Wales	
	Owned or mainly owned	Rented or mainly rented
1888	15	85
1914	11	89
1925	23	77
1941	35	65
1960	50	50
1969	61	39

Source: Ministry of Agriculture, Fisheries & Food (1970) *The Changing Structure of Agriculture*, H.M.S.O.

TABLE 4

Land Tenure in the United Kingdom, 1969

	% area of land		% number of holdings	
	Owned	Rented or mainly rented	Owned or mainly owned	Rented or mainly rented
England and Wales	53.6	46.4	60.8	39.2
Scotland	58.5	41.5	42.3	57.7
Great Britain	55.4	44.6	57.4	42.6
Northern Ireland	88.0	12.0	100.0	0.0
United Kingdom	57.3	42.7	62.1	37.9

Source: Ministry of Agriculture, Fisheries & Food (1970) *The Changing Structure of Agriculture*, H.M.S.O.

example, certain aspects of rural estate management could be put into practice over large areas of land by the persuasion of relatively small numbers of land owners. The situation in the 1970's is, however, very different. The greater part of rural Britain is now in the hands of people who own and farm their land and this means that only one person or one family has to provide the capital necessary not only for the purchase and maintenance of land and fixed equipment, but also for the mounting costs of livestock and farm machinery. With increasing costs of fixed capital and equipment and of farming practice itself, there are now many more opportunities for farm land to be generally short of capital, a weakness which may underly the recent rise of the mixed tenure holding.

Under the landlord/tenant system, the landlord is concerned with the fixed equipment of the farm: the fabric of the estate (buildings, houses and cottages, roads, woods and copses, the conservation of wildlife and landscape) whilst the tenant is concerned primarily with efficient agricultural production. Under owner-occupation, one person is involved in all decisions: on estate management in the broad sense and on agricultural land use and production. The advantage of all decisions being made by one man must be set against the disadvantages which can arise if this one person is primarily interested in farming techniques and output. The erection and improvement of buildings and the harmony of tree, field and general layout can then be neglected.

Though the market for agricultural land is an unusual one in that it is complicated by so many tax and prestige elements and cannot be easily separated from urban development values, open agricultural land is being used to an increasing degree for investment purposes. Land has been seen partly as a refuge for funds against the effects of inflation, and for the ploughing back of the proceeds of sales for urban development at high figures. Contributory factors have been the uncertainty and variability in the market for stocks and shares. If the purchase of agricultural land for investment purposes, separate from its present or potential agricultural profitability continues, then it is likely that the trend away from tenanted farms to owner-occupation will be reversed and that institutional landlords will become more common. There is a long history in rural Britain of a mixture of private and institutional owners and an increase in institutional landlords will not necessarily produce good or bad results. It could mean, however, that absentee owners with different motives will gain control of considerable areas of the British countryside and their interest may be only slightly concerned with technical and economic problems in food production and with the traditional 'amenity' concern for the estate that formerly prevailed among landlords.

A complicating factor in all long settled countries with a strongly developed industrial and urbanised structure is the rise of part-time farming of various kinds where the owner or occupier is not completely dependent upon the earnings of the farm for his livelihood. There is a wide variation in the types of part-time farmer, ranging from people with large estates who yet have their main income from urban property, commerce or inherited wealth, to the small man with an extra large garden where he produces surplus fruit and vegetables for his own family or for sale. Of some 150,000 farm holdings in Britain which do not appear to generate enough income to cover the needs of a farmer and his family, it is estimated that about half are part-time.[10] Studies at the University of Reading and at Wye College in the University of London suggest that the acreage of land held by part-time farmers is very large around a city such as London where people wish to use the commercial and cultural facilities of a large city but also want to live in open countryside close to the rural activities of food production, nature conservation and the traditional sports of hunting, shooting and fishing.[11]

The presence of those with a part-time interest in agricultural activities may bring new problems for the countryside. It means the rise of a class of people whose land use activities are not strongly influenced by changes in the price of agricultural products because only a small part of their total income arises from the sale of food from their land. These are people who have bought or rented their land and farm houses for a complex of reasons such as prestige, local amenities, the opportunities for their children to have a rural upbringing, tax evasion, the subsidisation of private costs and capital accumulation. Whereas these people may well be more sensitive than full-time commercial farmers about matters such as environmental conservation, they can also be dangerously resistant to change. Because the number of part-time farmers has increased so markedly around the conurbations (especially London), the environment of considerable areas of countryside will be conditioned by a group of people who, basically, wish to maintain the *status quo*.

The Planning of Agriculture

Though the pattern of land uses within British agriculture depends directly upon the decisions and activities of individual British farmers, there is considerable influence exerted by Government policy on price and subsidy incentives. The farming pattern of today arises from the action of these incentives operated under the 1947 Agriculture Act, with a changing emphasis, in recent years, brought about by the introduction of the Common Agricultural Policy of the European Economic Community. In the post-war agricultural legislation of 1947, it was laid down that British agriculture would be encouraged to produce the commodities and the quantities of those commodities considered to be in the national interest; that food producers should receive satisfactory incomes and the owners of agricultural land satisfactory rent levels. The general method adopted was the establishment of minimum national price levels for the main agricultural products (wheat, barley, oats, rye, mixed corn, potatoes, sugar beet, milk, eggs, fat cattle and calves, fat sheep and lambs, fat pigs and wool); prices which were related to the output needed and the costs which efficient farmers incurred in production.

These minimum prices and cost levels were to be examined each year, and changes could be made at the 'Annual Review and Determination of Guarantees' – the well-known February agricultural price review. Throughout the years between 1947 and 1972, the pattern and output of British agriculture were formed by the decisions made at these annual reviews in which different types of agricultural production were encouraged or discouraged by a combination of general exhortation, changes in the minimum prices of the 'review' commodities and by a series of grants and subsidies on specific products as, for example, hill cows and hill sheep. Financial help was given towards certain agricultural inputs like fertilisers, for operations such as the ploughing up of old pasture and for structural improvements as in the hill farm improvement grants. There were grants for drainage, water supply and new farm buildings.

The influence of these various measures was further intensified by the establishment of a national agricultural advisory service which was freely available to farmers and by the continuation of the wartime county agricultural committees as agents for the administration of grants and subsidies. As the years passed this complex system of guidance and stimulation was modified to take into account actual and potential national surpluses of some products: there were, for example, national quotas for wheat, barley and milk and the system of price changes was smoothed so as to give farmers the maximum of forward assurances.

Although this system of planning in agriculture produced farm support prices at levels above those of the world market for individual agricultural products, British consumers were able to buy these products, whether home produced or imported, at the world prices, for the higher prices being paid to British farmers were financed directly by the Treasury from general taxation. The cost of the agricultural support system was, therefore, measurable and the detailed amount involved each year was published.[12]

The farming pattern which emerged under this support system was one with a strong emphasis on arable cultivation and especially on wheat, barley, potato and sugar beet production. A large home milk industry grew under an active marketing board. There were large pig and poultry sectors and hill farming was strongly supported. A reduction in the area of permanent grassland and of badly drained lowland, the enlargement of field size by the removal of hedges, the erection of new farm buildings as additions to the huddle of existing farmsteads or on new sites were all directly stimulated by this system of specific grants and subsidies. In the hills and uplands, the provision and renovation of farm houses as well as farm buildings, the reclamation of unimproved hill land, the improvement of farm roads, the provision of piped water and grid electricity and the increase in hill flocks of sheep and herds of hill cattle also arose directly from the grant aid policies.

In all, the planning of agricultural production in Britain since the end of World War II has been considerable and reasonably effective in terms of bringing forward the amounts and qualities of farm products thought by the Government to be desirable.

The European Economic Community

But in 1972, with the acceptance of British membership of the European Economic Community the system of agricultural planning began to change. The essence of the Common Agricultural Policy is very different from the principles underlying the 1947 Agriculture Act. Within the large protected market of the nine member countries of the Community, all home produced products — agricultural as well as industrial — are freely exchanged, but products imported from outside the Community have to climb over a protective wall of tariffs, often combined with quotas. The tariffs paid on products imported from outside are used to support the price levels decided upon for individual products produced within the Community and it is these tariffs which provide the large agricultural support funds used to pay farmers for their home produced products. Consumers within the Community pay for these protected agricultural prices directly in their food purchases and not through their taxes as was the case with the former British 'deficiency payment' system.

British entry into the Community was a confident one, for our agricultural system seemed to possess some important comparative advantages. True, the people directly involved in farming in this country were only about 3 per cent as against 9 per cent of all civilian employment in the Community as a whole, with 13 per cent in France and Italy. But numbers of farmers in a country does not appear to be directly related to their political bargaining power and the National Farmers' Union had already the confidence of many years of successful and sophisticated bargaining with government and other interests. The pattern of yields for most crops and animal products on British farms were above those of our European partners (with the exception of the Benelux countries). We were a rather more pastoral country than the others, with the exception of Eire, but labour productivity was high and rising. But the most important strength of British agriculture lay in its structure — the size of its farms, the layout of fields and the condition and adequacy of its farm buildings. Even though numbers of farms are falling and their average size increasing in the mainland countries of Europe, the structural advantage of British farming is likely to exist for many years ahead.

The changeover in the system of agricultural support was planned to be slow rather than abrupt with a gradual adjustment over seven years from 1972. It has been accidental to the system that in the early 1970's unusual conditions outside Europe made world agricultural prices higher than those within the Community for many farm products. Britain, however, as the largest importer of agricultural products from non-European sources, has substantial payments to make to general Community funds and it was the size of these which was one of the main elements to be discussed in renegotiations about the conditions of Common Market membership begun by the British Labour Government when it came to power in February, 1974.

Now we are a permanent member of the European Economic Community, the British agricultural industry will gain from its advantages and suffer from its defects. The Common Agricultural Policy is a crude form of agricultural protectionism, over compensating in its price levels the large, well structured European farms on good, easy, low cost land in order that small marginal farms in the uplands should be able to continue. Though farmers' organisations will fight hard to maintain their preferential position, their position is weak in the long term for this kind of protectionism leads to endemic surpluses in the market. In 1975, for example, the Community was dogged with surpluses in beef, fodder cereals, wine and apples, with large stocks of butter remaining from earlier years. Looking ahead one can foresee, from time to time, surpluses arising of products such as liquid milk, potatoes, and even sugar beet.

During these early years of Britain in Europe affairs in the outer world have combined with changes in weather to produce both gaiety and despair amongst individual farmers. Sharp increases in cereal prices because of C.A.P. and a world shortage, with costs rising at a much slower pace, produced boom conditions in the arable farming areas of the east and south of Britain. In contrast, depressed views on the potential surplus of milk products and euphoric views of the buying habits of millions of meat eating Europeans produced a surplus of cattle and a shortage of milk, aggravated by the low yields and bad weather conditions of 1973/74. Regional differences were exacerbated. Straw from rich Eastern farmers was delivered to panic stricken farmers in the west where heavy stocking with cattle and low grazing and hay yields threatened starvation. Farmers' cost increases began to gallop forward in line with generally high rates of price and wage inflation throughout 1974 and 1975 and high priced fuel, fertilisers, chemicals and animal feed cut into farmers' profit margins. Dairy farmers were particularly hard hit in these years and though price rises to the farmer and to the consumer were agreed, these agreements came late and at the expense of an 8 per cent fall in dairy cattle numbers between 1975 and 1976. After a few good years hill farmers have returned to their usual battles against poor quality but high cost feed, small and variable grass and hay crops, and variable prices for their store lambs, ewes and cattle.

The uncertainties of recent years, in both arable and livestock farming, may encourage a return to mixed farming in Britain, but this is unlikely to be of the old kind. Some cereal land will be intensively cropped for grass to be fed to livestock reared indoors throughout the year.

In all, the British agricultural industry moves into the later seventies with confidence dented by the weather and inflation hazards of recent years. Negotiations with London and Brussels combined are more complicated and slower than with London alone. Though the green light is still showing towards greater home self sufficiency in agricultural products, the way ahead seems less assured than the early days of entry into Europe.

Future Agricultural Production in Britain

In a country where, for centuries, the home production of food has been much less than the total food needs of the population, it is to be expected that debate will continue on the linked questions of how much of home food needs could and should be produced from home land resources. This debate has become sharpened at times when total food supplies have been threatened by the physical severance of imported supplies, as in the German submarine activities of two World Wars, or at times of severe balance of payments difficulties. With high fuel costs and rising world prices for foodstuffs, the pressure for import saving in Britain is once again high.

To forecast potential agricultural production is complex. The main parameters which determine the amounts of food needed by a country are the size and distribution of its population, their relative incomes and food consumption patterns, the amount of land available for cultivation and likely changes in this brought about by the competition of other uses, and the yields to be expected from land under different crops and livestock. Even if all of these parameters could be accurately measured and forecast this would give only a picture of what is possible in the future. Whether or not this is realised depends upon other factors: the structure of the agricultural system and whether farmers can be motivated to produce the quantities and qualities of those foods capable of home production. In a capitalist democracy such as Britain this motivation involves a complex and sensitive set of price and profit stimuli to very many individual agricultural entrepreneurs.

An attempt has been made to construct such forecasts through to the end of this century for agricultural production in Great Britain.[13] Although the research for this work was carried out before the political decision was made for Britain to join the European Economic Community and before the sharp increases in world food prices (and relative reductions in world food supplies, especially of key commodities like wheat, maize and soya beans), the picture which emerges as to the potential future of agricultural productivity has not been dramatically changed by the events of the early 1970's.

The study suggested that the population of the United Kingdom would be between 67 and 70 millions by the year 2000. Later estimates made by the Registrar General in the early 1970's suggest that the total population is likely to be at the lower end of these limits. It was forecast that real disposable incomes in Britain (that is, incomes adjusted for changes in the value of money), would increase at an average rate of 2.5 to 3.0 per annum, that is, at least a doubling of the standard of living by the end of this century. This now looks like an over estimate but the scale of this is difficult to judge on recent evidence. It was thought that the total effect of population increases and changes in real incomes would be to produce an overall demand for food in Britain by the year 2000 which would be between 33 and 41 per cent above that of 1965. Here again this, as judged by the experience of the early 1970's, is likely to be an over estimate of our needs at the end of this century. A careful examination of the import substitution possibilities of British agriculture suggested that home production is potentially possible for most imported temperate products, and that we are likely to move into a situation of 70 to 75 per cent self-sufficiency by the end of this century. A look at likely changes in the land use pattern arising from urban development and afforestation suggested that 75 per cent of the British land surface will still be available for agriculture by the end of this century. There is nothing in the events of the early years of this decade to undermine this particular estimate.

One of the most difficult parts of the whole analysis was the study of likely changes in the physical productivity of Britain's land under different kinds of crop and livestock production. There is considerable controversy amongst agricultural scientists and economists as to whether likely future increases in productivity will be linear or exponential in nature. If, in practice, demand for increased home production of food is low because both population and real income per head grow slowly and there is only a 10 per cent loss in potential agricultural production through urban extension and a slow increase in home self-sufficiency in food supplies to 65 per cent of total needs by 2000, then a low exponential yield increase of 1.0 per cent per annum or a linear one of 2.5 per cent will meet this low demand assumption. Looking at the changes which have to be made in these estimates if situations of medium or high demand for home food production in the immediate future are to be met, then the demand for food producing land and the available supply of it are not likely to conflict badly unless agricultural output fails to increase in an exponential manner, albeit at a low rate.

But the study does show the relative importance of each separate parameter in the land budget. Population growth is much more important than personal incomes in determining the demand for food. Population and economic growth markedly affect non-agricultural demands for land. In all, there are a number of alternative courses for British agricultural policy. If Britain can recover her position as a relatively wealthy nation with a secure external trading balance then she will gain the maximum degree of flexibility in relation to land use matters. If, however, her policies are to be dominated by pressures of rising population, high self-sufficiency in food supplies and low levels of increase in agricultural productivity, then the national land budget will become much tighter than it is at present.

The Quality of Agricultural Change

These changes in the British agricultural scene, caused by the interaction of many individual farmers and the push and pull of changing minimum prices for agricultural products and of grants and subsidies for specific foods, farming activities and geographical areas, can be judged both good and bad. Judged by rising self sufficiency in temperate foods, by greater yields per acre of crops and better livestock production, by rising output per man and per £100 capital invested, the period since World War II has been one of achievement. All of these considerations are likely to be stressed in this and the next decade as world food shortages reinforce Britain's desire to cut down the cost of imports, even though many of these come from her neighbours within the European Economic Community.

At the beginning of the 1970's it was thought that one of the major rural problems in Britain, as in Western Europe, was likely to be the retirement of marginal and unwanted land out of commercial agricultural production because of incipient food surpluses and the pressure towards greater agricultural efficiency and higher farmer incomes. But the problem of land retirement, associated so much with Dr. Mansholt, one-time Community commissioner for agriculture in Brussels, has been removed, at least for some years, by movements of the world agricultural terms of trade against Britain and the deepening problem of adverse balance of payments, aided by the rising cost of imported oil. The support of agricultural systems in areas of natural difficulties, such as in the hills and uplands, is likely to be maintained and even extended as a part of European agricultural and regional policy.[14]

It should not be thought that this planning of the agricultural resources of Britain has gone along without difficulties. British farmers have suffered in some years from costs rising faster than market prices and there has been over-expansion in the production of some commodities from time to time: chaos in the prices and supplies of calves and beef cattle in 1974 was a dramatic example. More important and longer term problems have arisen from the post-war system of agricultural planning and these have been of an environmental nature. In general, agricultural changes have been actively breaking down the Enclosure landscape, removing, especially in the east and south, many of the small fields and hedges, isolated trees and small woods. Much of the permanent grassland in the lowlands, handicapped by wetness, has been drained and then ploughed and cropped with cereals. The huddles of old farmsteads have been changed into newly erected, industrial farm buildings, often on new sites. Many of the large livestock buildings have effluent disposal problems of high cost and of potential danger to public health. Natural fauna and flora have been changed by modern farm operations; the number and variety of species have been reduced and their conservation made more difficult. Many rough places, and the paths to them, have disappeared.[15] Finally, a reduction in the numbers of farmers (through the increase in farm size) and of farm workers (through the replacement of men and women by machine and the movement of service personnel out of villages to the market towns and cities) has left the countryside thinly used by its primary population.

Agricultural Britain has ceased to be an area with inbuilt forces acting towards the conservation of natural things. It is becoming more and more an industrial area, with great productivity and great possibilities for environmental change and damage. The planning legislation and administration of this country has left agricultural matters largely outside planning control or advice, with minor exceptions such as tree preservation orders and controls on large new farm buildings.

Yet the myth that the agricultural use of land represents its effective conservation has stayed surprisingly dominant. The agricultural lobby is strong in Britain as it is in many European countries both in national and local government and as a force in the moulding of public opinion. Farming interests have encouraged a belief in agriculture as a constructive factor in rural conservation. On this basis they have obtained, in practical terms, the virtual exclusion of statutory planning from non built-up rural areas and yet have persuaded the Government, public opinion, and planning authorities to protect much agricultural land from non-agricultural development. The belief that urban development is a heavy user of better quality farm land is a strong one. Table 5 shows how the proportion of the land of the United Kingdom in urban use has increased and is expected to change by the end of the century.

TABLE 5

Land Use Change in the United Kingdom, 1950-2000

	Percentage of total area		
	1950	1960	Estimated 2000
Agriculture	84.1	81.5	75.2
Woodland	6.4	7.5	10.9
Urban Development	6.8	7.9	10.9
Unaccounted for	2.7	3.1	3.1
Total land	100.0	100.0	100.0

Source: Best, R. H. and Edwards, A. M. at Wye College, University of London, from Ministry of Agriculture Statistics and Development Plans.

The rate of urbanisation was at its highest point in the 1930's when some 60,000 acres (25,000 hectares) of land was transferred to urban use each year in England and Wales. This had reduced by 1965-70 to just over 40,000 acres (17,000 hectares) and the loss of land to all non-agricultural uses remained steady at just over 50,000 acres (20,000 hectares) each year between 1950 and 1970.[16] It can be said, therefore, that the preservationist approach to agricultural land has reduced the quantity of it moving each year to urban purposes; but has the higher quality farmland been saved?

It has always been assumed that urban growth, if left undirected, would take place on the better cultivated land. Recent work at Wye College refutes the contention that our towns and cities are built predominantly on land of high agricultural quality.[17] They appear to have been constructed mainly on medium and poor land (grades III and IV of the Ministry of Agriculture's 1974 Land Classification). In addition, recent extensions of these towns do *not* appear to have taken more than average amounts of good land. It could, therefore, be hazarded that even in the one part of statutory planning control strongly applied to rural land, that is, the attempt to restrict the urban development of better agricultural land, this concern has been unnecessary. General planning control has, of course, kept down the area of land being taken by urban development out of productive agriculture and this has been more important than the selective use of the poorer land. Even so, the estimates made relating to future land budgets for Britain[18] suggest that urban expansion in the United Kingdom between 1965 and 2000 will require a 10 per cent food replacement because of the loss of productivity from the land which will be permanently urbanised during this time.

The Agricultural Future

Despite the uncertainties induced by world and European influences upon British agricultural policy, it is possible to speculate upon some future trends.

The movement towards larger holdings will probably continue, but at a slower pace. Although land values in rural areas fell back in 1974 from the high levels reached at the end of the rapid rise between 1970 and 1973 (Table 6), they are now (late 1975) rising again.

TABLE 6

Sale Value of Agricultural Land in England and Wales

Year	£ per hectare with vacant possession on all farms
1937-9	62
1940-2	86
1943-5	116
1946-8	170
1950	202
1955	198
1958	210
1960	304
1965	581
1966	597
1967	638
1968	692
1969	739
1970	640
1971	783
1972	1,635
1973	Increase of 40% over 1972 in the first six months of 1973
1974	Decline in values back to 1972 levels

Source: Edwards, A. (1974) Resources in Agriculture — Land, Ch. 5 in Edwards, A. and Rogers, A. (Eds.), *Agricultural Resources*, Faber.

Farmers who cannot extend their holdings and those who have paid dearly for extra land will intensify their farming practices. It is likely that agricultural land will continue to be bought and sold for reasons other than its agricultural productivity and we discuss the problems of speculation in Chapter 8. The growth in farm size will continue, while the tenure pattern of British agriculture is likely to become more and more mixed in the types of occupiers, with a probable increase in part-time holdings of all kinds and in institutional holders of land. There will be more physical restructuring of farm buildings, enlargement of field size, and continued reclamation of rough and ill-drained land.

The pace of change in the application of new technology with its implications for productivity and increasing specialisation is unlikely to slow down (Tables 7, 8 and 9). The

TABLE 7

Increase in Agricultural Productivity, 1966-1972

Year	Net product at constant prices	Labour gross product per person engaged in agriculture
1966-7	100	105
1967-8	107	116
1968-9	100	114
1969-70	105	124
1970-1	111	135
1971-2	116	143
Average of 1964/5 to 1966/7 = 100		

Source: Institute of Agricultural Economics (1972) *The State of British Agriculture*, The Institute, Oxford.

TABLE 8

Concentration in Food Production, 1960-1968

Products	Total number of producers in 1000's for England and Wales	
	1960	1968
Wheat	77.7	50.6
Barley	90.8	92.1
Potatoes	92.3	51.7
Dairying	140.1	96.8
Beef	64.1	55.3
Sheep breeders	87.8	70.8
Pigs	81.8	51.7

Source: *The State of British Agriculture*, op. cit.

world shortage of cereals will continue to strengthen the emphasis on cereal production in Britain. Productivity will increase but it will be affected by the high cost of fertilisers and other heavy energy using inputs such as chemical sprays and dressings. The recycling of organic wastes on farms will only improve if new labour-saving ways of doing this can be developed. The emphasis on livestock farming will be strong in the long term though it may take some time for farmers to recover confidence from the unfortunate combination of poor weather and excessive cattle numbers in 1974. The hills and uplands will continue to receive help to maintain incomes and to increase the breeding of hill cattle and sheep.

TABLE 9

Changes in Crop Yields, 1961-1974

	cwt per acre		
Crops	1961	1971	1974 Estimate
Wheat	28.2	35.0	38
Barley	26.0	29.9	33
Oats	21.1	30.1	32
Potatoes	8.9	11.1	12.6
Sugar beet	14.0	17.0	12.2 (disease and poor growth)

Source: *The State of British Agriculture*, op. cit.

In a perceptive review of British agriculture since the end of World War II, Beresford warns of long term difficulties ahead for the industry in its new European context.[19] One of these is the prolonged reduction in the British hired farm labour force with the added complication of low minimum wages and the vexation of the agricultural tied cottage. This is likely to push farms into even greater mechanisation and rationalisation and into simple, standardised farming systems. These might further reduce the variety of the farmed landscape in this country. Beresford also makes the point that the labour shortage will push farmers themselves into doing the jobs which involve long and awkward hours.

Rearrangements of land and wealth taxation pose new and uncertain problems. Capital Transfer Tax, introduced in March 1975, alters the taxation on property changing hands on the death of an owner.[20] A number of implications could follow. Farms could be broken down into uneconomic units in order to meet the tax, although this might give a few more opportunities for newcomers to enter farming. Exploitive farming may occur so as to minimise increases in the capital value of the farm and some artificially low rents might be arranged for tenant farms. Lastly, planning authorities might be pressed to allow non-agricultural developments on part of a farm so that the owner can build up funds to meet oncoming Capital Transfer Tax on the whole property. Certainly there will be pressure on owners of buildings and land of historical, architectural, scenic or scientific importance to offer them to the nation or to seek exemption for at least a generation from the attentions of this tax. New arrangements have also been introduced for the taxation of land sold for development.[21] The implications of the Community Land Act, by which local authorities will acquire land for development at existing use values, are discussed in Chapter 8. Proposals for a wealth tax are still at the consultative stage.[22] The special position of farmers has already been acknowledged in the suggestion that they might be allowed to defer payment of tax, subject to interest, unless the asset is sold or the owner retires or dies. But about 50,000 farmers could be seriously affected by this tax which, like Capital Transfer Tax, will tend to emphasise the commercial exploitation of agricultural and forest land unless the exemptions, delays to later generations and the increase in public land ownership are extensive. Certainly the dangers of commercial attitudes within agricultural land use are not likely to be reduced by these rearrangements of land taxation.

The emphasis on agricultural self-sufficiency will continue to be strong and it is not fanciful to believe that Britain will become 75 per cent self-sufficient in temperate foods by

TABLE 10
*Contribution of Home Agriculture to Food Supplies
of the United Kingdom*

Products	Home production as % of total supply	
	Average 1960/1 – 1962/3	1970/71
	%	%
Wheat	42	44
Barley	93	90
Oats	98	109
Potatoes – maincrop	97	97
Sugar	30	33
Beef and veal	71	84
Mutton and lamb	42	42
Pork	96	100
Bacon and ham	34	42
Poultry meat	99	99
Butter	12	14
Cheese	46	46
Eggs	94	99

Source: . *The State of British Agriculture*, op. cit.

the end of this century (Table 10). The political pressures towards greater self-sufficiency in food are strong, amongst them being the almost constant problem of a large adverse balance of payments, a European Economic Community rather dominated by agricultural considerations and the pressure of rural and agricultural organisations such as the National Farmers' Union and the County Landowners' Association. The Government White Paper presented to Parliament in April, 1975, is evidence of this.[23] Following discussions with representatives of farmers, workers, landowners and the food and drink industries and looking at European and world trends in supplies and prices, the Government presented the following three conclusions:

"1. the likely levels of World and Community prices for major foodstuffs between now and the early 1980's, and the risks of possible shortage and sharp price fluctuation, justify a policy of expansion of food production in the United Kingdom;
2. the net product of the agricultural industry should be capable of a continuing application of about 2.5 per cent per year on average, and this is the objective at which the Government and industry should aim;
3. within this overall objective most benefit is likely to come from higher output of milk (with its by-product, the beef from the dairy herd) and sugar beet. Cereals and sheepmeat should also make a significant contribution."

The Government recommendations for discussion were only slightly smaller in magnitude than the proposals of the Farmers' Unions, published at the same time. They would give a net increase in agricultural output of about £630 million by 1980 and a net saving on imports of £530 million. Beresford is more sceptical of the potential for expansion.[24] He argues that British agriculture lacks enough capital, skilled men and, most of all, the confidence necessary to respond to a further programme of expansion. Memories of recent losses in the beef and dairy industry, continued inflation and the uncertainties of land taxation may discourage farmers from investment and long term improvement of their enterprises. But if the movement towards greater self-sufficiency continues, several questions remain. The cultivable land of Britain may be unable to continue its upward trend in yields of the main arable crops and in livestock production. Although certain warnings about the effects of 'high' farming on yields and on soil structure have been made in the Strutt Report,[24] it was thought that most of the damaging effects were of a temporary nature and could be rectified by known farming techniques, with the possible exception of heavy compaction by modern farm machinery damaging the structure of certain unstable soils. Shortages and high costs of fuel and fertilisers could provide more serious limits to increases in crop yields. Alternative agricultural futures, less consuming of imported energy and less destructive of the environment, have been suggested and we refer to these in chapter 13. But their realisation seems unlikely at the present time.

Perhaps the continued emphasis on more efficient agricultural production will mean a greater dominance of the farming interest in public and political affairs in this country, and an even more singleminded approach within the Ministry of Agriculture upon technical and economic problems.[25] This may mean even less consideration than so far is paid to environmental matters in the countryside or to the wider problems of rural development. An emphasis upon commercial farming and commercial farmers, concerned only with the problems of industrialised food production and insensitive to the needs for trusteeship of rural land, may mean that it fails to be passed on 'in good heart' as an attractive environment for the future dwellers of both town and country. Some of the pressures upon farmers in the short term may well be eased: with the development of British oil, increasing control over inflation and the reduction of uncertainties in our relations with Europe. But the fabric of the countryside cannot necessarily wait for more generous investment in the long term.

Notes and References

1. The changing functions of rural settlements and the movement of so many of them into the ever widening pattern of urban living are dealt with by a number of authors; see for example:
   Bracey, H. E. (1970) *People and the Countryside*, Routledge & Kegan Paul.
   Best, R. H. and Rogers, A. W. (1973) *The Urban Countryside*, Faber.
   Clout, H. D. (1972) *Rural Geography*, Pergamon.
   Green, R. J. (1971) *Country Planning*, Manchester University Press.
   Wibberley, G. P. (1974) Old Villages and New People, *The Countryman*, Vol. 79, No. 2.
2. Edwards, A. M. and Wibberley, G. P. (1971) *An Agricultural Land Budget for Britain 1965-2000*, Studies in Rural Land Use No. 10, Wye College, University of London.
3. These and other issues are discussed at length in Chapter 7 on landscape conservation.
4. Ministry of Works and Planning (1944) *Report of the Committee on Land Utilisation in Rural Areas* (Scott Report), Cmnd. 6378, H.M.S.O.
5. Williams, R. (1973) *The Country and the City*, Chatto & Windus.
6. Hammond, J. L. and B. (1911) *The Village Labourer*, Vols. I and II, Longmans.
7. Blythe, R. (1972) *Akenfield*, Penguin.
8. This general and rather personal description of agricultural change can be given in statistical terms: see for example Tables 7, 8, 9 and 10 near the end of this chapter.
9. Hill, B. (1974) The Rise of the Mixed-tenure Farm, *Journal of Agricultural Economics*, Vol. XXV, No. 2, May.
10. Britton, D. K. (1974) The Structure of Agriculture, Ch. 2 in Edwards, A. and Rogers, A. (Ed.), *Agricultural Resources*, Faber.
11. Harrison, A. (1965) Some Features of Farm Business Structures, *Journal of Agricultural Economics*, Vol. 16.
    Gasson, R. M. (1966) *The Influence of Urbanisation on Farm Ownership and Practice*, Studies in Rural Land Use No. 7, Wye College, University of London.
12. For example, in the financial year of 1972-3, the total Exchequer support to British agriculture was £390 millions, of which £180 millions were in the form of direct grants or subsidies and the

remainder as price support.

13. Edwards, A. M. and Wibberley, G. P. (1971) *An Agricultural Land Budget for Britain 1965-2000*, Studies in Rural Land Use No. 10, Wye College, University of London.
14. See Chapter 9 on the Uplands for a more detailed discussion of agricultural problems in marginal areas.
15. Chapter 7 on Landscape considers these effects in more detail.,
16. Champion, A. G. (1974) Competition for Agricultural Land, Ch. 10 in Edwards, A. & Rogers, A. (Ed.), *Agricultural Resources*, Faber.
17. Best, R. H. (1974) Building on Farmland, *New Society*, 31st October 1974.
18. Edwards, A. M. and Wibberley, G. P. (1971) *An Agricultural Land Budget for Britain 1965-2000*, op. cit.
19. Tristram Beresford (1975) *We Plough the Fields*, Penguin.
20. The Treasury (1974) *Capital Transfer Tax*, H.M.S.O., Cmnd. 5705. Capital Transfer Tax replaces existing Estate Duty by new taxes which tax at progressive rates the cumulative value of gifts made during a person's lifetime as well as on his or her estate at death. The new tax has a threshold of £15,000 below which no tax is due but above this the rate of tax progresses from 5% to 75%. The exemptions from this tax are important and they cover gift transfers between husband and wife, small gifts to one person, gifts to charities and gifts for national purposes and of importance in the national heritage.

      Prior to this 1975 Act farms were the subject of 45% relief from Estate Duty. The relief to be given under C.T.T. is a special valuation on land farmed by a full-time working farmer, with a limit to the amout of tax being 20 years purchase of the rental value of the farm offered with vacant possession, subject to a limit of £250,000 or 1000 acres, whichever is most favourable to the taxpayer.
21. Department of the Environment (1974) *Land*, H.M.S.O., Cmnd. 5730. Since April 1975, owners of land or property sold for higher value uses will have any difference between the existing use value of the property and the new higher development value taxed as income at normal income tax rates for an individual or at corporation tax rates for a company. Eight years will be allowed in which to pay the tax but allowance will be given for interest paid on original costs, together with a profit margin of 20%. Where the proceeds from the sale of land or property are less than £10,000 or the sales are by owner occupiers, these are exempt from the tax. Arrangements have been made to dovetail this tax into the arrangements for the Capital Gains Tax which operated before April 1975. No tax will be levied on sales of land to local authorities at existing use value under the Community Land Act.
22. *Wealth Tax*, Consultative Paper issued in August 1974, H.M.S.O., Cmnd. 5704. It is proposed that wealth will be taxed in a progressive way as is the case with income. The published 'Green Paper' suggests that most assets will be included for this tax with few exemptions. The illustrations given show an exemption limit of £100,000 with two alternative rates of tax, one with four broad bands leading to a maximum rate of 2½%, the other with five narrower bands leading to a maximum rate of 5%.
23. Ministry of Agriculture, Fisheries & Food (1975) *Food from Our Own Resources*, H.M.S.O., Cmnd. 6020.
24. Beresford, T. (1975) Food from Our Own Resources, *The Countryman*, Winter, 1975/76.
25. Agricultural Advisory Council (1971) *Modern Farming and the Soil* (Report of the Strutt Committee), H.M.S.O.
26. In response to Directive 72/161 from the European Economic Community (which argued that, to improve farm structure, many agricultural workers would have to make a fundamental change in their occupational orientation) the British Ministry of Agriculture appointed nine Socio-Economic Advisers, within the Agricultural Development and Advisory Service. These will help farmers improve the agricultural potential of their holdings and explore the opportunities for additional income from non-agricultural sources, such as recreation and tourism. They will also advise on retraining outside the agricultural industry.

CHAPTER 3

Forest and Woodland Management

Trees play an important role in our lives whether they are individual specimens in a garden, street or park or are grouped in copses, woods and forests. They provide beauty of form, contrast and colour. Wood retains most of its age-old utility for buildings, furniture, log fires, and even boats, whilst the newer uses of papermaking, veneers and fascias make large demands on forests at home and abroad. Whether as part of a combined farm and forest industry or as a separate enterprise, the growing of trees provides both income and employment to people living and working in rural areas, especially if these are remote with few other employment possibilities. Moreover, forestry almost alone among other rural activities, can be successfully integrated with agriculture, with wildlife conservation and water catchment, with the enhancement of landscape variety and beauty and with outdoor recreation.

With all of these advantages, it might be thought that a country like Britain would be using the tree abundantly and skilfully in its environment — in town and suburb as well as in the countryside. But this is not so. The characteristics and needs of trees clash with much of our behaviour. Left to market forces alone and the short term nature of many human desires, trees and woods get felled and very few new trees are planted or retained beyond economic maturity. The roots and branches of mature trees get in the way of building development and commercial arable farming; trees shade crops and keep light out of windows; their leaves clog drains and have to be swept up from lawns and streets. Most land in Britain, except that of the very poorest quality, continues to yield a smaller financial gain under trees than in most other commercial uses such as agriculture or residential development. Moreover, commercial forestry has always suffered from the long interval between investment in planting and early tending and the final return from the sale of mature timber. This has involved years with quick growing conifers, to periods of more than a century with most hardwoods.

Background to Forest Policy

Any discussion of policy relating to the retention of existing trees or woods or the production of new ones in a continent like Europe involves a number of contrasting situations. The position in the mountains and hills is very different from that in the valleys and on the lowlands. Commercial uses only sometimes blend with the growing of trees for amenity purposes; often they are in conflict. Considerations arising from conifer planting are very different from those involved in the growing of hardwoods: in time spans, in the value

31

of timber produced, in the qualities of land needed, and in the effects upon landscape and wildlife. The implications for local employment may vary widely between forest enterprises, just as the effects of public and private agency investment may yield rather different local and national benefits. This chapter reviews some of the changing emphases in the continuing national debate on these issues.

In many countries the area covered by trees, whether planted or natural, is the second largest land use after agriculture. Even in Great Britain, with its chequered history of attention and neglect in relation to woods and forests, tree production is the third largest use of land in terms of area, being exceeded only by agriculture and urban development as separate uses (Tables 1 and 11). Even so, the proportion is small: woodland in Britain

TABLE 11

Areas of Forest Ownership and Use, 1975

	Thousand hectares			
	England	Scotland	Wales	Great Britain
Productive				
Forestry Commission	245	432	132	809
Private	479	297	62	838
Total	724	729	194	1,647
Unproductive				
Forestry Commission	9	11	3	23
Private	174	82	30	286
Total	183	93	33	309

Source: Forestry Commission, 1975.

occupies less than 8 per cent of the land surface. In Europe, only Ireland and the Netherlands have a lower proportion than this; Germany and Austria have more than 30 per cent of their land under forest. One consequence of this low woodland acreage is that more than 90 per cent of British timber requirements have to be imported.

There has been a slow increase in the area under woods and forests during this century but it has not been consistent through the years. Expansions and contractions in the rate of planting reflect both the changing attitudes of people and government towards tree planting on a considerable scale and the pressure of two national war emergencies within a half century. In 1900, about 5 per cent of our land area was covered with woods of different kinds and there was little change until, during World War I, the needs of a beleaguered nation for home produced timber cut into stands of mature trees. These losses emphasised the value of timber reserves within the country during periods of economic and military blockade and out of this concern came the decision to set up the Forestry Commission in 1919. It was charged with the task of encouraging a major increase in home timber supplies by the acquisition and afforestation of suitable open land and by persuading, with advice and grant aid, private land owners to increase plantings and improve the management of their existing woodlands.

Before the next wartime crisis hit Britain in 1939, the Forestry Commission had secured and planted 190,000 hectares of new trees; an additional 81,000 hectares had been planted by private landowners. But the emergency felling of timber which took place during World War II cancelled the effectiveness of this pre-war programme of expansion. A new look at the timber needs of Britain, and a detailed post-war census of existing woodlands in 1947, suggested a total target of 2 million hectares for the country by A.D. 2000, of which 60 per cent would come from the planting of new forests. Although this would result in a commercial woodland area almost twice as large as that of 1900, the proportion — at less than 10 per cent of all land used — would still mean that Britain, as compared with most of her European neighbours, remained a lightly wooded country.

In practice, this programme of expansion has gone ahead, with an annual rate of planting of between 30,000 and 40,000 hectares in the 1960's, of which about three quarters has been on open land and the rest a replanting of existing woodlands. In recent years, the rate of afforestation has been close to the rate of urbanisation although the quality of open land taken for new planting has been very much lower than that consumed by housing, factories, roads and other forms of urban development. The Forestry Commission has only been permitted to purchase land for planting close to the margin of agricultural cultivation so that new plantations have been forced up on to the poor high land of Wales, northern England and Scotland. This has enabled the Commission to provide new jobs in areas suffering from a long history of rural depopulation but it has also forced it into a programme of conifer planting which has exposed the Commission to considerable controversy about the effects of its plantings on the appearance of the countryside.

So the expansion programme has gone on but its objectives, for the public sector, have changed. New policies in 1958 and 1963 emphasised three main goals for the Forestry Commission: to produce more wood for industry as profitably as possible (and encourage private owners to do likewise); to provide employment and foster related industrial and social developments; and to give greater attention to the aesthetic and recreational roles of public forests. All these objectives have been further defined in a 1972 White Paper and in more recent policy statements.[1]

Public and Private Forestry

The British landscape, especially in the uplands, has changed substantially in the extent of its tree cover during this century. At its beginning, nearly all woods and forests were privately owned, but by 1970, about one third of a much larger acreage was in the public sector.

Private owners have been encouraged in various ways to plant and manage trees commercially, both in the lowlands and the uplands. Grant aid has been available to the owners of existing or projected woodlands through the Dedicated and Approved Woodlands Schemes and the Small Woods Planting Grant.[2] Private owners have been further encouraged by the excellent advisory services available from the Forestry Commission and by a favourable tax structure relating to the establishment and exploitation of private woodlands. Provision has been made for setting off woodland expenditure against income under Schedule D of income tax. In addition, a low rate of tax has been payable under Schedule B from the time when the ownership of a wood changes, and relief from Estate Duty was possible in a number of important ways.[3] Capital gains tax is not levied on sales of timber. All these fiscal incentives have made investment in new woodlands very attractive to those with large incomes.

With uncertainties in the equity market, a bad record since the War in the value of gilt edged securities and these special grant and tax advantages, there has been a marked increase in the response of private investors to the financial advantages of forestry. Their interests have been aided by the formation of syndicates, employing specialist agencies such as the Economic Forestry Group and Fountain Forestry, who plant and manage woodlands on behalf of private owners.

It has been estimated that up to the beginning of the rapid rise in land prices of 1972/73, the return received on land under commercial trees was about 3 per cent on the total investment and that the effect of these various grants and tax exemptions was to raise the rate of return to the private investor to about 6 per cent. Under recent policy changes, the special tax advantages to private woodland owners are to continue, although private woodlands will fall under the provisions of capital transfer tax.

Under the old Estate Duty, tax on the value of growing timber was not charged on the death of the owner but deferred until the timber was actually sold. This kind of exemption has been continued under C.T.T. but the tax is now levied in the case of life-time transfer of ownership of the trees and the tax load on death transfers is heavier. Forest owners, and the organisations representing them, believe that C.T.T. will, in general, discourage forestry. Some premature felling may occur in order to raise money to pay the tax if an owner is disinclined to make a dedication agreement with the Forestry Commission. Felling will normally be subject to a replanting requirement, unless conversion to agriculture is intended and this might make the agricultural use of felled and scrub woodland sites more attractive, financially, than forestry. The proposed Wealth Tax may place a further burden upon woodland owners. As a result of both these new tax arrangements, more woodland could be lost, with implications for the landscape and the retention of wildlife, particularly in the lowlands.

Woods in the Lowlands

Most of the recent public and private tree planting has taken place in the hills and uplands, on poor land, where the main competitive alternative uses have been hill sheep and cattle farming. Until the sharp increase in values from 1972 onwards, land in the uplands has been relatively cheap but as most of it has been open and uncultivated its fertility has precluded the planting of timber species other than conifers, which now make up more than 74 per cent of all productive woodland (Table 12).

TABLE 12

Forest Types in Britain, 1975

	Thousand hectares
Broad leaved high forest	390
Coppice (with or without standards)	30
Conifer high forest	1,230
Unproductive woodland	310
Total area under trees	1,960

Source: Forestry Commission, 1975.

Although some restocking of devastated private woods has taken place, there has been almost no new public planting in the lowlands. The Forestry Commission have been unable to bid for land at rapidly rising prices and where they are precluded because of its quality for farming purposes. The Commission do own some lowland woodland estates all of which are exploited commercially, but amenity considerations increasingly dominate woodland management in some areas as, for example, the New Forest and the Wealden woods of Sussex and Kent.

Yet, paradoxically, it is in the lowlands that there has been the greatest wastage of trees (particularly in recent years from Dutch Elm disease) and where, because it is the living environment of most people, the many benefits of trees and woods outlined earlier in this chapter would seem to be especially needed.

Much of the mature woodland of today was originally planted as part of private estate management plans, often to provide timber but mainly for the long term effects of planting on the appearance of the estate and on the improvement and maintenance of game for shooting and hunting. Timber production and profitability were then of lesser importance.

But much of this lowland woodland, especially individual trees in hedgerows, has continued to grow towards maturity, and sometimes beyond it. The rate of felling has exceeded the rate of replanting because of urban development, the value of hardwood timber, the lack of tree planting and maintenance on farm land, and the many technical and economic pressures within agriculture. In the context of hedgerows and copses, the movement of permanent grass fields into arable and cereal production and the mechanical cutting of hedges with its disastrous effect on young tree saplings have all contributed to the losses.[4] Recent research has confirmed that the age structure of trees remaining in the lowlands is such that the rate of decay of the tree cover will increase.[5]

Thus, it is in the lowlands of Britain which are famed for their patchwork quilt of fields, woods, villages and farmsteads, and where the majority of people live, that least is being done to protect maturing trees or to produce new trees and woods for the future.

Review of Policy

Where are we at the present time in the argument about the right place of trees in the landscape and in the economy? Are we content with the area of woodland we have or do we want something different? Is the balance between conifer and hardwood plantations the preferred one? What of the balance between State woodlands and those in private hands? Should there be more or less planting on the hills? What of the lowland with its wooded heritage from past centuries — is the individual tree, copse and small wood to be a continuing part of its matrix?

Without preferential taxation, financial incentives and State participation, it is likely that the felling of trees would greatly exceed their planting. Even so, most modern capitalist communities are not prepared to give the State complete control over the life and death of trees. Rather do we see many variants of a partnership between private holders of land and public ownership and control. The main area of argument lies in the size of the industry wanted, the form, purpose and location of new plantings and the nature and amount of financial stimulus to be given to private individuals to take part in forest development.

In the Government White Paper of June 1972, the use of State funds to stimulate private forestry was queried — not as a principle, but in terms of the objectives served by the 'dedication' of private woodlands. The scheme, it was thought, had outlived its usefulness in relation to the original purpose of rehabilitating the private woodland devastated by war, as the bulk of new tree plantings were now taking place on open land. It was suggested that the important emphases, in both private and State forestry, should now be placed upon planting schemes as providers of more employment and as improvers of the 'natural' (particularly the visual) environment. Greater weight was also to be given to the realisation of recreation opportunities, especially in State forests.

These are not entirely new criteria in the evaluation of forest policy and investment. The argument that afforestation, in certain areas of the hills and uplands, provides more permanent employment than hill farming is an old one and was strongly argued in the 1947 White Paper on Post War Forest Policy. The 1972 White Paper, supported by a Cost Benefit Analysis[6] argues the case rather more moderately: comparative figures are given in Table 13.

TABLE 13

Comparisons of Employment in Agriculture and Forestry

	Regions where new forests are being planted		
	North Wales	South Scotland	North Scotland
Jobs in forestry per 5,000 acres	33.0	14	18.5
Jobs in agriculture per 5,000 acres	13.5	7	1.5
Average cost[a] per job in State forestry	£16,500	£23,000	£17,500
Average cost[a] per job in agriculture	£9,500	£7,500	£8,000

[a] This is the cost to the Exchequer of each job provided or maintained expressed as a capitalised figure by discounting, at a rate of 10 per cent, to a net present value, the stream of cash revenues and expenditures over the rotation period.

Source: H.M. Treasury (1972) *Forestry in Great Britain: An Interdepartmental Cost Benefit Study*, H.M.S.O.

On the basis of these calculations it was concluded that forestry provides and maintains more jobs than agriculture in these areas but at a heavier capital cost. The emphasis on this employment contribution is likely to remain an important factor in the public component of afforestation, although it has been omitted from the more recent statement on support for private forestry.[7]

The second criterion raised by the 1972 White Paper relates to amenity and recreation. Although there has been pressure on the Forestry Commission, particularly since the Countryside Act of 1968 to take these factors into account in the management of its own properties, this White Paper proposed, for the first time that amenity and recreation could be deciding considerations in public planting. Under the new Dedication Scheme for private woodlands, amenity and recreation criteria will also figure in decisions upon their eligibility for grant, formerly based upon simple commercial forestry principles. To be accepted for Dedication, all new plantings or existing woodlands must be managed in a way that is acceptable to the Forestry Commission (and those whom it consults) not only on silvicultural matters, but

> "from the point of view of amenity, agriculture, nature conservation public access and recreation, and general planning considerations".[7]

The overall implications of the White Paper proposals are that the Forestry Commission's estate should continue to expand, but at a declining rate, until early in the next century; and that greater attention should be paid to amenity even if this reduces profitability.

Limitations of the Policies

The specific proposals have met with strong opposition from individuals and organised groups concerned with commercial timber production and with the wider implications of forestry. Concern, for example, was expressed by forestry interests as to the effective standards of management that would be maintained on private estates under the new Dedication Scheme which now receive a once-and-for-all-grant rather than periodic aid throughout management.

But it is the environmental facets of recent policy that have been most seriously criticised, notably by the Countryside Commission, the Ramblers' Association and others who have argued for much more control over the location and form of new public and private planting schemes, particularly in the uplands.[8] The Ramblers argue further that not only should new planting be more stringently controlled, but that there is nothing inherently bad about having a smaller area under trees in Britain than in most other countries. The hills are better used, they argue, for food production and landscape conservation than for growing trees. The phasing out of the Small Woods Planting Grant removes a further incentive to create new tree cover which is so badly needed in some lowland areas.

Dower,[9] Wibberley[10] and others have also criticised the emphasis in recent policy upon the supposed benefits of afforestation to rural employment. The high cost of providing more jobs in tree planting suggests that other forms of long term employment in remote rural areas should also be examined, such as the establishment of small industries, perhaps with the help of the Development Commission, the Council for Small Industries in Rural Areas and other agencies. Neither the cost-benefit analysis nor the White Paper of 1972 compare job opportunities in the whole range of rural industries (of which forestry is only one) nor do they assess the benefits of combined enterprises involving forestry, agriculture, tourism and other industries.

In all, the criticisms of recent policy support what we argue elsewhere in this book: that the forest resource planning system in Britain is too singleminded and blinkered in its purposes for the future. In many ways this single-mindedness is best demonstrated by past and current policy and practice in forest recreation and the conservation of landscape.

Forest Recreation

The recreational element in established and new forests first outlined in a 1963 policy statement, was reaffirmed in the 1972 White Paper and in the supporting cost benefit calculations.

But it is only a relatively recent emphasis in the British argument about trees in the rural environment although in Europe and elsewhere, especially North America, the principle as well as the fact of forest recreational use has been long accepted. Certainly, private woodlands have always been important to the owners of rural land for shooting and hunting but this has involved relatively few people who have been privileged by their family connections, wealth and place of living. Although the Forestry Commission began to open Forest Parks in the thirties, the scale of their use for several decades was insignificant.[11] But by 1970, about 15 million day visits were being made annually to State Forests; more than a million people used the camping and caravan sites.[12]

The recreational benefits of Forestry Commission properties were valued, in 1972, at £1.5 million, and they were expected to reach £6 million within ten years.[13]

In 1970, the Commission established a special Conservation and Recreation Branch to formulate policies; Recreation Officers were subsequently appointed in each Conservancy to implement plans.

Most forest visitors come by car seeking, so the surveys have shown, the simpler pleasures of walking and picnicking.[14] In response to their demands, parts of many forests in the hills and on the lowlands have now been adapted for these activities, with mixtures of deciduous and conifer plantings, forest drives and walks, car parks, information centres and wildlife museums, and overnight stopping places for tents and caravans.

Although more gregarious activities and more intensive facilities have been, at times, suggested for state forests[15] and there are successful examples abroad, the Forestry Commission is committed to the idea of providing only for those activities which seem to depend on a forest setting for the pleasure of their experience. For most Commission holdings, particularly the more remote and those already part of designated conservation areas such as National Parks, this is probably a desirable and practical policy. But there may also be room in the lowlands and close to conurbations, for more experiment — with a greater variety of activities which may benefit no less from forest or woodland surroundings, as we suggest in Chapter 8.

More important is the overall emphasis now accorded to recreation in forest policy. Many improvements have been made in recreation research, planning and provision. But the achievements of the Forestry Commission are still not of the scale, nor everywhere of the quality, which might be expected of an agency which manages such a valuable recreational resource, and one which is the largest single public owner of land. There are anomalies in the present system: in the relative autonomy of the Forestry Commission, and in the proportionately higher rate of government financial support for forest facilities compared with other kinds of informal recreation provision. Individual Forestry Commission Conservancies have been largely responsible for the degree to which the recreational potential of the nation's forest estate has been realised and, as with other areas of provision, there is an uneven geographical spread, nationally and locally. The new Regional Advisory Committees may bring about more provision and more co-ordination between different providers (especially in the public sector) but there is inadequate representation of amenity interests.[16] It is obviously desirable for recreation in forests, along with other kinds of facilities, to be drawn into the ambit of local recreation planning at structure and local plan-making levels, with the possibilities for much more co-operation on the ground.

Access to Private Forests

Many owners are now taking more account of the visual and wildlife implications of their woodland management practices. Some are replanting amenity trees to replace the losses on their estates; others have shown increasing willingness to accept — and encourage — visitors into their woodlands.

But there have been less desirable recreation developments, for example in the Weald. In this extensive area of mixed mainly deciduous woodland of beech and oak, the management of public and private land achieves a fair degree of harmony between commercial and amenity purposes. The system of felling, for example (group or shelter wood), ensures that large bare tracts are avoided, and some areas of coppiced woodland, now of little economic value, have been retained. It is on public access that the differences emerge. Of the 162,000 hectares of woodland in the Weald, about 20,000 are owned by the Forestry Commission, 16,000 hectares are Dedicated Woodlands in private hands and another 12,000 have been managed under the Approved Woodland Scheme. In the Forestry Commission woodlands, picnic sites, car parks and a network of trails are provided. On some private woodlands there is *de facto* access by walkers but many are still fenced off from the casual visitor. A scheme known as the "Countryside Club" offers private gate keys on a selection of these woodlands to visitors paying a £10 annual fee.

It is this kind of very selective development which suggests other flaws in forest policy, and should cause us to question the balance of recreation provision between the public and private sector. The new policy places greater pressure on the Forestry Commission to provide not only access but also facilities. Under the new Dedication Scheme, private woodland owners must demonstrate some, loosely defined, environmental gain, provide "such opportunities for recreation as may be appropriate", and, if and when requested by local planning authorities, at least negotiate on the possibilities of providing access and appropriate facilities. Even so, in a situation where the more accessible woods, in terms of their nearness to population, are mostly in private hands and in the lowlands, the influence upon owners is slender. There is no indication that state subsidies (in grand aid or by fiscal means) will be withheld for those who do not wish to allow people on to their land nor is there much positive incentive for them to do so.[17] The new measures are an improvement on the past, but their effects have not yet been shown in practice. It would be bad policy to channel the bulk of forest recreation into potentially 'second best' locations in the uplands (where most state forests are) because there are no effective means of making more provision in the lowlands.

As the amount of *de facto* access continues to decline in rural areas (in the lowlands, and also in the uplands where rough pasture and moorland are enclosed for farming and commercial afforestation), woodlands must assume a more important role as purveyors of a more 'natural' environment and as destinations for outdoor recreation. It is only fair that private woodland owners, who continue to receive substantial financial concessions from the Exchequer, should share an equal role in this with state forests.

Trees in the Landscape

Although the harsh lines of early plantations still remain in parts of the uplands, the record of the Forestry Commission on sympathetic design and management of its holdings has noticeably improved over the last decade. But problems remain.

The most recent major controversy in forest policy concerns the degree to which afforestation, especially in the uplands, should be controlled. Because of the scale and kind of new planting (much of it by forest management companies acting for absentee investors) in situations where open hillsides have been suddenly enclosed and ploughed and planted mainly with conifers, the pressure has strengthened for afforestation to be brought under planning control.[18]

It is not surprising that foresters, as farmers would, react against a proposal of this kind, for forestry like agriculture has historically been exempt from planning control for various technical and economic reasons. But conditions have changed and the interests and goals of British forestry have widened into areas in which the planning system is more experienced. Foresters cannot expect to change the terms under which they receive encouragement and help from the State without accepting the controls and guidance which the State asks from other interests in a similar position. The provision of new jobs in rural areas is not best decided only by people with forestry experience. The provision of more facilities for outdoor recreation should not be primarily decided by foresters. The effects of planting and felling on the landscape are not matters on which foresters are necessarily the best, or the only, judges.

It is true that land management practice in forestry, as in other activities, can be influenced in ways outside the statutory planning system, and often more effectively as we discuss in Chapter 12. In some National Parks, voluntary agreements on afforestation have operated between forest and amenity interests to try to harmonise their goals but the procedure has not everywhere been successful; nor does it extend outside the park boundaries.[19] The voluntary agreements could perhaps be strengthened in some way, they could be applied over a wider area and other systems of approval at present relating only to public afforestation could be extended to private schemes. But none of these is likely to achieve the level of control needed, particularly in those areas of finest scenery. The case for planning control of the large scale afforestation of bare ground remains.

But such a measure has not so far been included in the latest forest policy; instead, the system of Regional Advisory Committees will act in situations of conflict on planting, management and felling.[20] But their representation is narrow, heavily weighted towards forestry and timber interests and members will be appointed by the Forestry Commission. In cases of dispute, it will be the Forestry Minister (albeit in consultation with his colleagues) rather than the Environment Secretary, who decides.

Aside from the landscape implications of large scale afforestation, there are more local problems of the loss of tree cover, particularly in the lowlands. Even in National Parks, the powers of Park Authorities to acquire amenity woodland have not prevented the loss of small, unprofitable woods.

Various means exist of imposing some control over the felling of trees; there are rather fewer available to ensure replanting where amenity trees are needed. All the measures are recognised to be inadequate as a way of safeguarding the essential elements of valued landscapes and creating new ones. The felling licence system, although recently improved with more local authority involvement in those decisions which affect amenity, still allows a substantial amount of felling to escape any control.[21] Local authorities can impose Tree Preservation Orders on individual trees and woodlands but these are unwieldy to operate and limited in their achievement.[22]

A variety of ways have been tried to persuade public and private agencies to plant more trees, especially in the intensively farmed lowlands, where recent agricultural changes have severely denuded local cover. Grants for tree planting are available to local authorities.[23] A number of agencies such as the Nature Conservancy Council, the Council for the Protection of Rural England and the Farming and Wildlife Advisory Group have also tried to persuade through conferences and advisory pamphlets.[24] Particular schemes of persuasion have involved payment to those who voluntarily plant trees, as on the Crown Estates in Buckinghamshire, and more recently, in the Lake District and Bollin Valley management experiments.[25] But bureaucratic difficulties and lack of widespread support may limit the effectiveness of direct money incentives.[26]

There are some successful local examples of voluntary public and private management arrangements over amenity issues, for example, in the Chilterns, where a long term management strategy has been prepared for the beechwoods by the owners in co-operation with the Forestry Commission, Nature Conservancy, Countryside Commission and local authorities.[27]

All of these approaches are needed, and some, like the wider use of voluntary support, will bring incidental benefits of greater public involvement in environmental issues. The fiscal system must also be used to promote the wider environmental objectives of private tree-planting as well as the commercial ones.[28]

But it is doubtful whether any of these measures can redress the loss of tree cover which has been taking place over much of lowland Britain. Their combined effect is likely to be piecemeal and on far too small a scale to influence the long term improvement of scenic quality. In terms of landscape as well as recreation, there is a case for much more, rather than less, new public planting in the lowlands; it is particularly needed on the urban fringe.

A New Forest Service?

It can be argued that a real opportunity has been missed in the policy review for a more fundamental restructuring of forest agencies to serve local as well as national needs, to pursue, with equal vigour, environmental goals as well as those of raw material production.

If some of the present damaging processes of rural environmental change are to be redressed; if new agricultural landscapes are to be created and more outdoor recreation areas are to be provided, then a substantial amount of new tree planting must take place, especially in the lowlands and on a variety of scales. Much rehabilitation is needed of the neglected and poorly managed but accessible woodland on the edge of towns. At the same time, many of the areas of amenity woodland that remain will need to be managed primarily for their landscape and recreational value, rather than as commercial investments, as the Forestry Commission have acknowledged will be the case in the New Forest. We cannot afford again the devastations of Dutch Elm disease. We must be better warned, better prepared.

Schemes such as 'Plant-a-Tree in '73' are useful reminders of the importance of trees and the need for public pressure and action, but their effect is small. Likewise, local authority tree-planting schemes must be extended, more authorities encouraged to establish forest departments with their own staff and supplied by their own tree banks. The scale of operation so far, even among the more active authorities, has been so small as to effect almost no change in the continuing erosion of woodland.

It seems odd when so much experience, expertise and equipment is at hand in the many regional departments of the Forestry Commission that our forest service cannot act in much greater partnership with local authorities, especially in the lowlands. Regional forest authorities, acting as woodland conservation and planting *agents* of both county and metropolitan authorities, could play a much more active part in landscape reconstruction along the lines already adopted in other countries, notably the Netherlands. Regional authorities of this kind would require many specialists, not only foresters who presently dominate the staff of the Forestry Commission, but landscape and recreation experts and social scientists.

The Future

The June 1972 Government White Paper on Forestry Policy, the Government statement of 24 October 1973 and the new Dedication Scheme of July, 1974 make clear the general direction of policy for the years to come. Though the planting and management of private woodland will be grant aided by the State and helped through preferential tax arrangements, the schemes will be agreed more and more upon grounds of environmental improvement. Landscape and recreation factors, and the creation of rural employment will dominate the planting programmes of the Forestry Commission, mainly in the hills and uplands. But only if this policy can be linked with an effective programme of tree planting and tree retention in the main agricultural areas of the lowlands, can it be said with justification that Britain has at last a comprehensive and forward looking programme for trees, people and the landscape.

Forestry is only one part of a greater whole which includes a progressive and prosperous agriculture, further development of facilities for outdoor recreation, improved water storage and distribution, a richer mix of natural fauna and flora, and thriving rural communities. Forestry development must find its right place in this balance of interests.

Despite the improvements that the recent proposals for change in our national forest policy will bring — principally in a potentially more efficient use of funds to achieve wider social and environmental goals — the policies still fall short of bringing about the fundamental shift of emphasis which may be required to sustain the kind of rural environment and community needed in future. Perhaps the major limitation is one of short-sightedness: a failure to look ahead far enough, in an area where decisions taken now condition the environment of the next century. The measures proposed do not yet allow us, as a nation or as individuals, to realise the full potential of trees in the countryside.

Notes and References

1. Ministry of Agriculture, Fisheries & Food (1972) *Forestry Policy*, H.M.S.O.
     Forestry Commission (1974) *British Forestry*, H.M.S.O.
     Forestry Commission (1975) *The Forestry Commissions Objectives*.
2. Established under 1947 legislation, the *Dedication Scheme* for Woodlands allowed owners to dedicate their land to timber growing under supervision and to receive state grants in return. These grants were provided in two alternative ways: the owner could choose to accept a subsidy of one quarter of approved net expenditure each year until the woodlands became self-supporting or he could accept a combination of planting and management grants on a sliding scale. (This alternative form of payments provided in 1972, for example, £23 per acre for planting and management grants of £1.06 per acre on the first 100 acres, £0.71 on the second hundred and £0.44 on the remainder.)
     The *Approved Woodlands scheme*, introduced in 1951, gave half the planting grant to owners of woodlands who did not wish to 'dedicate' their woodlands but were prepared to manage them under an agreed plan of operations. Grants were also available for small areas, without an agreed management plan, under the Small Woods Planting Grant.
     In 1971/2 the area of woods under the Dedication Scheme had risen to more than a million acres (400,000 ha) but the Approved Woodlands had fallen to 169,000 acres (67,600 ha). Both the Approved Woodlands Scheme and the Small Woods Planting Grant have now been suspended.
3. For a description of the taxation systems see:
     Forestry Commission (1975) *Taxation of Woodlands*, F.C. Leaflet.
     Hart, C. (1975) *Taxation of Woodlands*, available from the author at Cherries, Coleford, Glos.
4. It has been calculated that a timber volume equivalent to over 100,000 hectares of high forests exists in hedgerow, copse and shelterbelt trees. (Forestry Commission, 1974, *British Forestry*, H.M.S.O.)
5. Westmacott, R. and Worthington, T. (1974) *New Agricultural Landscapes*, Countryside Commission. See also Chapter 7.

6. H.M. Treasury (1972) *Forestry in Great Britain: An Interdepartmental Cost Benefit Study*, H.M.S.O.

7. *The New Dedication Scheme* (Basis III), Forestry Commission Leaflet, 1974. Operative: 1 October, 1974.

Under the new system, it is proposed that grants for the planting and maintenance of forests should be on a once and for all basis and that the level of financial assistance will be reviewed every three years. Owners can receive £45 per hectare (£18.21 per acre) for approved planting or replanting, in return for a continuing obligation to manage woodlands within the scheme in accordance with plans of operation designed to secure sound forestry practice, effective integration with agriculture, environmental safeguards, and such opportunities for public recreation as may be appropriate. £125 per hectare (£50.59 per acre) is payable for planting or replanting where a significant proportion of broadleaved trees are involved.

8. Countryside Commission (1972) *Note of the Commission's Views on the Consultative Document on Forest Policy*, published by the Commission.

Ramblers' Association (1972) *The Future of Forestry*.

Committee for Environmental Conservation (1972) *Urban Pressures on the Countryside*.

Department of Environment (1974) *Report of the National Park Policies Review Committee* (Sandford Report), H.M.S.O.

9. Dower, M. (9172) A One-eyed Look at Forestry, *Town and Country Planning*, Vol. 40 (10).

10. Wibberley, G.P. (1974) Land Use and Rural Planning, *Proceedings of the Royal Society meeting on Forests and Forestry in Britain*, London, 6, 7 June.

11. There are now 7 Forest Parks covering 176,000 hectares.

Source: Forestry Commission (1974), *British Forestry*, H.M.S.O.

12. Ministry of Agriculture, Fisheries & Food (1972), *Forestry Policy*, H.M.S.O.

13. *Forestry in Great Britain: An Interdepartmental Cost Benefit Study*, op. cit.

See also: Grayson, A. J., Sidaway, R. M., Thompson, F. P. (1975) Some Aspects of Recreation Planning in the Forestry Commission, in Searle, G. A. C. (ed.), *Recreational Economics and Analysis*, Longman.

14. Mutch, W. E. S. (1968) *Public Recreation in National Forests*, Forestry Commission Booklet No. 21, H.M.S.O.

Colenutt, R. J. (1970) An Investigation into the Factors affecting the Pattern of Trip Generation and Route Choice of Day Visitors to the Countryside, unpublished thesis, University of Bristol.

New Forest Steering Committee (1971) *Conservation of the New Forest*: final recommendations.

Lloyd, R. (1972) The Demand for Forest Recreation, in *Lowland Forestry and Wildlife Conservation*, Proceedings of Monks Wood Symposium, No. 6.

15. Richardson, S. D. (1970) The End of Forestry in Great Britain, *Advancement of Science*, 27.

16. Under the revised forest policy, Regional Advisory Committees, appointed by the Forestry Commission advise Conservancies on strategies for the establishment and maintenance of forests, Dedication Schemes, tree felling, and individual cases of conflict. Of the 6-9 members, 4 represent woodland owners and timber interests; the rest agricultural, local planning and amenity interests.

17. Compared with some other European countries, for example, The Netherlands.

18. The government have rejected the recommendation that forestry in National Parks should be brought within normal planning control arrangements (Jan. 1976).

19. See Sandford Report (1974), op. cit., Chapter 6.

20. See note 16.

21. The Forestry Commission operates a Felling Licence system which usually ensures replanting. Local planning authorities are normally consulted on applications to fell in areas where amenity is considered to be important. However, exemptions allow a considerable volume of timber to be removed (825 cu. ft. in any quarter) which may have a significant landscape effect: see Essex County Council (1972) *The Essex Countryside — A Landscape in Decline*.

The inadequacy of protection for individual trees and small groups has prompted some to argue for all forestry operations to be brought within the ambit of planning control (with the possibility of exemptions). The County Planning Officers' Society, for example, has considered the transfer of felling licence decisions for all non-commercial trees from the Forestry Commission to local planning authorities to be a desirable, if presently impracticable, objective.

22. Chapter 12 which considers the implementation of rural policies, discusses the limitations of Tree Preservation Orders.

23. Under the Local Government Act, 1974. See: Countryside Commission (1973) *Trees in the Landscape*.

24. For example, see: Nature Conservancy Council (1974) *Tree Planting and Wildlife Conservation*.

25. See Chapter 12.

26. See the findings of a survey of farmers' views in Countryside Commission (1974) *New Agricultural Landscapes*.

27. Chilterns Standing Conference (1971) *A Plan for the Chilterns.*
28. Capital Transfer Tax in addition to income and capital gains taxes, offer possible vehicles. See the suggestions made in:
    Countryside Commission (1974) *New Agricultural Landscapes: a discussion paper*, CCP. 76a.

CHAPTER 4

Leisure in the Countryside

The previous chapters of this book have concentrated upon those rural resources and activities over which planners, especially in local government, have had little control or influence — and, until recently — little apparent interest. The exploitation or conservation of these resources and the management of their dependent activities is vested in other public or private hands.

In many ways it was predictable that leisure activity in the countryside,[1] emerging in the 1960's as a consequence of the changing habits and attitudes of urban people, would be assumed as a new job for land use planners, though it is perhaps surprising that so few other professions (education, for example) have yet seen it as a new arena for interest and action. Clearly, many of the characteristics of leisure in the countryside — the need for land and buildings, problems of access and traffic generation — call for traditional kinds of planning decision-making. Moreover, leisure activity is one among a number of social trends, involving the periodic exodus of people from town to country, which (like commuting and second home ownership) must now influence planning thought and practice. So, planners have tackled their new role; central government has encouraged, local government has responded: some willingly, others reluctantly.

Most planners have tried to treat this new field of concern as they have approached leisure in the town: in terms of areas set aside for particular activities. But the growth of leisure activity has a wider significance for the countryside. By its very nature, the use of leisure time implies choice and freedom which may not be constrained by the boundaries of routes or buildings or discrete parcels of land. The activities of people in their leisure time have stimulated — at times demanded — a wider interest in the complexities of the rural environment and in the conflicts that exist there. Moreover, increasing leisure activity has brought people into the countryside not only with demands for new facilities and services, but with a growing awareness of the environment they have sought. Since the interactions between recreation and other rural activities were first debated during the 'Countryside in 1970' conference and subsequently at Strasbourg,[2] some (though by no means all) planners have begun to look further into questions of rural change and conservation. Likewise, the growth and consequences of leisure activity have to some extent prompted a readjustment of the outlook and practices of some national organisations in the public and the private sector. We have already discussed some of the changes that have taken place in the policies and functions of agencies such as the Forestry Commission and the Nature Conservancy Council. The Countryside Commission, created from the National Parks Commission, was specifically established to advise on policies for the enjoyment of, recreation in the countryside.

The whole of the countryside can be considered, in some way, a resource for leisure so that many different rural planning systems are involved. But not all have yet responded to the new demands of leisure. For those organisations whose approach has been wholly dominated by notions of single land uses, and areas designated for particular purposes, the task of planning for leisure requires not only a clearer understanding of how the countryside functions but some adjustment in attitudes towards leisure itself.

Changing Leisure Patterns

Much has been written about changes in the pattern of free time and in the activities, recreational and otherwise, which people choose to do in it.[3] We know that most leisure time is still spent in and around the home and that for away-from-home activities the town is still the main attraction. But it is also true that leisure time is increasingly being used in a space-extensive way; that there is more participation and less passivity. Yet although leisure and recreation are fashionable topics for discussion (and increasingly respectable for

TABLE 14

Indications of Changing Participation[a]

	1960	1965	1970	1972
Number of visitors to:				
DOE Ancient Monuments	6,844,100	8,907,000	12,540,100	15,435,600
National Trust properties	1,021,509	2,311,076[b]	3,107,747	3,912,225
National Trust for Scotland properties	67,901	279,082	379,296	665,070
Number of overnight stays:				
in hostels of Youth Hostels Association	1,096,880	1,239,679	1,453,776	1,649,014
Scottish YHA	456,935	469,483	483,308	529,644
at Forestry Commission camp sites[c]	350,000	517,000	961,000	1,217,000
Membership of:				
Camping Club of GB and Ireland	52,000	91,500	110,000	144,481
Caravan Club	44,000[d]	41,026	84,127	137,923[e]
Ramblers' Association	11,300	13,771	22,178	29,386[f]
County Nature Conservation Trusts	3,006	20,960	57,000	74,815
Number of:				
Fishing licences issued by River Authorities	976,794	1,269,078	1,215,899	1,230,567[g]
Sales of pedal cycles	582,458	727,474	552,127	712,640

a   In the more informal outdoor recreations; figures for other activities are given in the Digest.
b   Figure for 1966.
c   Number of 'camper rights' including New Forest 'open' camping.
d   Figure for 1961.
e   As at June 1973.
f   1973.
g   1971.

Source: Countryside Commission (1975) *Digest of Countryside Recreation Statistics.*

research) we know surprisingly little about behaviour in detail or how it might change in future.

It is clear from the few national and regional surveys so far carried out that, since the mid-sixties, participation has grown in most outdoor activities and that it may now be growing fastest in those informal, unsophisticated pursuits which commonly take place on day and half day trips to the countryside. The location of these informal activities is fairly predictable, appearing to be governed by questions of accessibility, but also by the attractiveness and diversity of the scene. Participation in other activities which take place in rural surroundings beyond the built up area, like water and winter sports, fishing or golf, is also growing rapidly, and although they involve fewer people than the other less organised countryside activities, their specific requirements of land and water and capital resources suggest no easy means of provision.

The growth of leisure time interest in the countryside — active and armchair — can be charted in other ways: in the expanding membership lists of many clubs and associations, in the growing attendance figures for most attractions in the countryside; and by the increasing volumes of leisure traffic on rural roads (Table 14).[4] The present timing and methods of surveying do not allow the leisure component of traffic to be accurately assessed but circumstantial evidence and a few special studies have indicated the scale of recent growth.[5] The increase in numbers of people, vehicles and other equipment in the countryside for leisure purposes has been paralleled by an extension of the time spent there. Day tripping has grown but so also has holiday-making in rural areas, particularly earlier and later in the season, where it is associated with self-catering forms of accommodation, which, like caravans, tents and second homes, themselves become the focus of recreation activity.[6]

Local surveys at sites and localities in the countryside have allowed a finer definition of these different kinds of recreation; because of the plethora of recent studies, the characteristics of weekend tripping seem now to be especially well established.[7] It has been shown to be a habit of suburban car owners, of young and middle aged family groups and of those in professional, managerial and skilled manual occupations (Table 15). We know that

TABLE 15

Social Class of Visitors to Recreation Areas

Social Class[a]	GB population %	GB car owners %	Ragley Hall %	Tatton Park %	Slimbridge %	Forest of Dean %
AB	13	19	30	20	36	28
C1	22	28	34	34	29	37
C2	31	35	27	36	27	25
DE	33	18	9	10	9	10
Total	100	100	100	100	100	100
Sample size	*	*	489	882	1093	995

a Definitions of social class:
  AB   Upper middle: managerial and professional
  C1   Lower middle: supervisory and clerical
  C2   Skilled working: skilled manual
  DE   Working: semi- and unskilled manual, casual workers and pensioners

Source: Colenutt, R. J. and Sidaway, R. M. (1973) *Forest of Dean Day Visitor Survey*, Forestry Commission Bulletin No. 46, H.M.S.O.

people may spend several hours at a pleasant place in the country: often one with views, where there is space to picnic and play games not too far from the car. When they are questioned, these people seem satisfied and undemanding, concerned only with the state of lavatories and refreshments. They like to look at water and animals and at other people and activities; they may even welcome more activity themselves and are responsive to information about the place they have visited. They fear change in that to which they have grown accustomed, although direct experiment with real choices rather than hypothetical questioning may have revealed other reactions. In all, leisure in the countryside seems to have been accepted (perhaps too quickly) as a definable area of social activity, likely to become, in its execution as in the provision made for it, as entrenched, changeless and uncomplicated a feature of public behaviour as walking in an urban park or going to the library. This convenient stereotype of mass rural recreation has allowed countryside planners to compartmentalise yet another rural activity, and to search out those areas where it will be acceptable. Yet, although we may have partly described the nature and scale of leisure in the countryside, our ability to explain the recreation patterns that have emerged, and more important, to forecast how they might change in future, is far less certain.

The reliability of the results of national and local studies and their value for policy-making, rest upon the validity of the assumptions they make about wider aspects of social behaviour. Despite the many studies, we have no clear understanding of the fundamental questions: of why some people go into the countryside in their free time and others do not, what satisfactions are sought and whether or not they are achieved. We know that age, income, car ownership and other attributes of personal and social life appear to be in some way associated with patterns of leisure activity, but we do not yet know the nature nor the durability of the relationships, or the relative significance of the variables; their individual and collective association are certainly more complex than was first thought. Dower has remarked:

> ". . . the question (is) *why* do people fish, or dance, or go on a camping holiday? . . . not because they earn £2,000 a year but . . . because they need to fulfil themselves in some way.[8]

The low level of explanation of leisure activity shows that few of its determinants have yet been identified and of those we presently suspect, the precise nature of their relationship with leisure time decisions has not been well researched. In measuring age and income, we have used only imperfect surrogates to define the much more complex patterns of different styles and cycles of life.[9]

Future Demands

Since we have so little comparable information, and because strategic and management decisions cannot wait for the results of long term sociological and psychological research, it is tempting to argue for bigger and better surveys of present activities and their participants to provide the factual basis for interim policy-making.[10] Undoubtedly more and more rigorous survey and research is needed at all scales; but with the increasing uncertainty of the times there is also room for some speculation — about how the attributes of society will change and what effect these changes may have upon leisure and the countryside recreation component of it. There are several factors which do seem to be associated with leisure patterns, and which we may surmise will have some influence upon their future development.

Leisure time

The amount and distribution of available free time, particularly within whole family units, has already been shown to be important for the generation of away-from-home activities.[11] Certainly, for most working people, the amount of official free time they have will probably continue to rise: 77 per cent of British workers now have an annual paid holiday of three weeks or more,[12] but they still fare badly compared with those in other EEC countries. The number of holidays (and especially of second holidays) taken away from home but in Britain will probably carry on rising and these will undoubtedly extend (in volume and length of season) the recreational use of rural areas — indeed, the Tourist Boards are promoting it. But more holidays are likely to be less significant for the countryside than an increase of free time at weekends, and here the figures do not yet suggest an imminent expansion of activity. More overtime (and more moonlighting) in recent years have ensured that for much of the working population, the weekly amount of leisure has not increased (Table 16). For some, economic circumstances will dictate that it may even decline as these

TABLE 16

Weekly Hours of Work[a]

	1951	1961	1966	1969	1970	1971	1972
Normal basic hours	44.4	42.1	40.2	40.1	40.1	40.0	40.0
Actual hours worked (including overtime)	47.8	47.4	46.0	46.5	45.7	44.7	45.0

[a] For full-time male manual workers in UK manufacturing and certain other industries only.

Source: Central Statistical Office (1973) *Social Trends*, No. 4, H.M.S.O.

people struggle to maintain the real worth of their incomes. Overtime and Saturday working militate against weekend trips to the countryside. The effects of more shift work, which may leave a family with few blocks of communal leisure time, will be equally limiting. A worsening national economic situation could bring more short-time working, but this is not likely to affect trips to the open countryside. It is difficult to see how shorter working days (and developments such as 'flexitime') can have any effect for some considerable time on the pattern of rural recreation.[13]

At present levels of personal free time, population growth, however limited, will mean an absolute increase in leisure. Moreover, societal changes over the longer term — towards earlier childrearing and longer periods of middle age substantially free from family responsibilities, and towards earlier retirement — may bring rather greater opportunities for trip-making away from home. But for the immediate future, the consequences for the countryside of changes in free time look far less exciting (or worrying) than some would like to believe. The prospect of a truly leisured society now seems rather more elusive than it did in the sixties; and with the present social structure dominated by the routines of work, people may view the prospect of increasing leisure as undesirable as it is unobtainable.

Personal income

The changing distribution of income too must now give cause for less optimistic forecasts of future leisure spending; and the more casual forms of rural recreation may be hardest hit by recent economic events. Perry has shown, for example, that differences in leisure spending between different income groups are large, and the differentials show up most clearly in the distribution of spending on goods and services associated with rural recreation.[14] The high income groups are already big leisure spenders; they are the most resistant to inflation so that their spending is unlikely to change. Those with low incomes rarely participate in rural recreation. It is those in the middle income groups, who presently make up the majority of visitors to the countryside, who may, if only temporarily, restrict their activity in response to a period of reduction in their real earnings. The immediate future may also see further changes of emphasis in spending patterns, with proportionately more of the family budget being spent on food and housing, leaving less for leisure. It may even be that, voluntarily, changing social preoccupations will lead to a lesser rather than greater interest in outdoor activity: Young and Willmott have suggested that we are, as a nation, becoming emotionally and financially more home-centred.[15]

Mobility

Increased mobility, one consequence of increased incomes since the war, has certainly contributed substantially to the popularity of rural trips. All recent studies confirm that outdoor recreation in the countryside is mainly an activity of car owners, and car ownership has emerged as the most consistently useful variable for the explanation and prediction of recreation tripmaking. In the short term, higher petrol prices may limit the range of recreation trips, but they are unlikely to depress the overall growth of activity. Even so, the extension of car ownership is no guarantee of a parallel rise in the number of leisure trips: the different habits of new car owners;[16] the effects of congestion rather than of greater accessibility and growing uncertainty about any long term future for the car should make us cautious. More immediately relevant is the fact that slightly under one half of all households have no car and this proportion is higher in some regions. Although a growth in ownership is still forecast, a sizeable minority will still be without the use of a car by the turn of the century: not only among the lower paid, but also those too old, too young or otherwise unable to drive.

Other factors

Perhaps the only factor which we can be reasonably confident will continue to contribute to a growth of leisure activity out of doors is the expansion — through formal and informal education and the mass media — of information about the countryside and the opportunities it offers for enjoyment. But even the significance of the contribution of this factor is based upon circumstantial rather than any more direct evidence. The effects of change in other factors; such as occupational structures and the general distribution of different life styles, are more difficult to quantify and forecast, though they clearly must influence the physical and social patterns of leisure activity. The fact that these attributes of society appear to be changing only slowly may mask rapid contemporary change in the circumstances of particular groups — those on short-time working or facing redundancy — which could have a profound influence upon their expectations and fulfilments in leisure time.

There are clearly other external contributing factors: not least the continuing improvements in 'leisure technology' whereby developments in clothing and other equipment make it possible for those activities normally limited to daylight hours, to a certain season or to a particular place, to be pursued virtually at any time and anywhere. It may be wise to try to anticipate at least some of the ways in which further technological developments could extend the range of leisure activity.

We have, so far, found no way of adequately measuring the influence of supply upon demand. We may suspect, for example, that the decline in cycling over the last three decades has been mainly a function of busier roads, although this does not account for its current popularity. We can speculate that regional, even local, participation differences in many activities derive as much from inequalities in the supply of opportunities as from more basic population differences. But until we have some means of testing these assumptions there can be no clear guidance for policy-making: indeed, simple belief or rejection of the notion that recreation is supply-influenced has led to totally opposed outdoor recreation policies in different areas.[17] Because we know almost nothing of the personal satisfactions gained from leisure, we know nothing about the substitutability of activities or places — whether this be between urban and rural environments; or between leisure itself and other uses of time.

Finally, among all these factors which may influence leisure activity in future, is the question of fashion. It may simply be that the activities of leisure are so very individual or the patterns so subject to volatile changes in fashion that to attempt to forecast at all, on present knowledge, is meaningless.

Implications for the future

What does emerge from speculation of this kind is that the future form of recreation in the countryside seems a good deal less certain than it did a decade ago. Neither the scale, nor the nature of future activity can be well defined. This is not to argue for totally intuitive policy-making: the nature of trip-making (and of trip-makers) must continue to be monitored to achieve better explanations of present activity and more reliable short-term forecasts. But there is also room for much more speculation: for more detailed scenarios of possible 'leisure futures' both in the short and long terms. What, for example, will be the effects of new roads, new forms of personal and mass transport, developments in leisure vehicles? What changes may alter the balance of activity within the total leisure field — what, for example, would happen if there was regular professional sport on Sundays or cassette television? What are the implications of possible developments in patterns of work, marriage, child-rearing and retirement?

In terms of extremes, we can consider at least two alternative leisure futures.[18] An 'expansionist' scenario, resulting from substantially more amounts of personal free time, increased mobility and the capacity to spend more on leisure goods, implies far greater demands upon rural resources when compared with a 'recessionist' future, in which the desire and ability of people to enjoy the countryside could be less. Moreover, the future for leisure in the countryside must be seen in the context of change in other rural activities. Increasing self-sufficiency in agriculture, in mineral supplies, in power generation could bring such acute competition for rural land that none (or none suitable) is left for outdoor recreation which would then need to be accommodated wholly within the urban area. Even without this, a more industrial countryside may force us to seek more highly managed recreation experiences and only in specific reservations, as the Americans have done in their National Parks. Or perhaps, like them, powerful groups will secure a return to wilderness management, a *de-development* of the most attractive countryside which will extinguish opportunities for all but a few and place mass recreation once more in the town. All these futures require different approaches to the planning and management of rural resources and of rural leisure activity. In all, there is sufficient uncertainty about leisure in the future to make us question the purpose and the flexibility of existing policies, or at least redefine the principles upon which these are founded.

Policies in Practice

In the early sixties, the growth of leisure appeared as a sudden and in many ways worrying phenomenon in the countryside. Defineable interactions emerged with established rural activities which have been most often identified and discussed in terms of the social and environmental costs they have generated. Thus the general nature of many conflicts — problems of trespass on farmland, fires in woods, pollution of water supplies; the effects of tourism on the physical and social fabric of rural communities; congestion on roads; wear and tear on habitats — have been well described, and in recent years some attempts have been made to measure their parameters.[19] Economic benefits too have been assessed, but these do not in general apply, nor have they been measured, for informal recreation, but for a fairly limited range of water recreation and tourist activities in specific areas.[20] But other interactions are relevant. The resource demands of informal recreation in the countryside are ill-defined (compared with those of most other rural activities for which land potential has been in some way assessed or classified) yet they clearly range wide. The recreation 'interest' in land extends beyond the area directly visited to include the management of neighbouring and often distant environments and — a notable feature of recreation activity — a great variety of land and water routes.[21] Policy-making has therefore had to react in a variety of ways to this relatively new rural interest: to deal with the demands for more recreation spaces and routes, and accommodate a greater amenity interest in the way rural land is managed. At the same time, policies have sought to minimise or extinguish the undesirable consequences of mass recreation in the countryside.

The response of central government acknowledged the need to provide places in the countryside which would

> "... make it easier for town-dwellers to enjoy their leisure in the open, without travelling too far and adding to congestion on the roads; they would ease the pressure on the more remote and solitary places; and they would reduce the risk of damage to the countryside — aesthetic as well as physical — which often comes about when people simply settle down for an hour or a day where it suits them, somewhere "in the country" — to the inconvenience and indeed expense of the countryman who lives and works there."[22]

Two primary measures were proposed in the Countryside Act of 1968: a range of single-purpose recreation areas (notably country parks and picnic sites) and an extension of the principles of multiple use to state woodlands and to water catchments so that they, in time, could offer more recreation opportunities. Exchequer financial support was available for local authorities to establish recreation areas, and a new organisation — the Countryside Commission — was established to advise upon and administer some of the new policies.

Following the creation of the Sports Council, the restructuring of tourist agencies and the reorganisation of waterways administration to incorporate an amenity element, this legislation culminated a period of substantial government effort towards provision for leisure in the later sixties.

The record of provision for countryside recreation since 1968 is impressive on many counts with some 125 country parks designated, and 155 picnic sites (Fig. 1).[23] Many other public and private agencies have opened land and buildings to the public, which together offer a wide variety of attractions in the countryside, from large and popular stately homes and other historic centres to small areas of land which may be used for picnics or casual camping; water parks, wildlife and farm parks and others. Chapters 3 and 6 discuss the growing contribution to recreation opportunities made by the Forestry Commission and the Nature Conservancy Council. In the field of water and waterside recreation, recent years have seen the development of waterways owned by the British Waterways Board for amenity and recreation and the more positive management of water supply reservoirs as resources for water sports and for more informal leisure activity, although less than half of all reservoirs are available for public use.[24] The employment of special Recreation Officers among the new Regional Water Authorities is one sign that greater emphasis might be placed on this aspect of water management in the future than so far. Meanwhile, the National Trust has expanded its role as provider of recreation space. In those areas where it owns extensive tracts of fine countryside and coast, much has been done to improve their management for visitors. Other local bodies who (like some naturalists' trusts or canal and railway restoration groups) hold land primarily for other purposes, are now also involved as managers of resources for recreation.

It is meaningless, in Britain, to consider acreages of so-called recreation land and water — for much that serves some recreation purpose would not be so classified, while other areas, such as National Parks, are by no means wholly accessible for outdoor recreation. Rather, it is in the number and the diversity of recreation areas and their linkages, provided by so many different agencies that the wealth of opportunity lies. Yet, paradoxically, the total amount of open land with public access has undoubtedly fallen as the ability and the desire to consume recreation has widened. *De facto* access to much agricultural land, formerly available for informal activities, has been reduced by enclosure and ploughing, particularly in the more intensively farmed lowlands. Rights of way have been extinguished or made unusable by neglect. The allocation of legal responsibility for maintenance has proved insufficient in a situation where the alignment of many routes conflicts with the needs of modern farming, and public pressure has been unable to force the hand of local authority departments. Many new recreation opportunities have arisen in an *ad hoc* way and their location does not necessarily relate to the distribution of those who want or need to use them. It is partly because of this imbalance between a growing demand and a falling effective supply, that the countryside legislation of 1968, with its promise of more accessible recreation areas, has seemed so important. Here, for the first time, was some positive directive to the nature and distribution of opportunities.

But as components of a strategy to provide more accessible recreation areas, some Countryside Act policies have flaws in practice. There are imbalances in the number and distribution of grant-aided schemes, and these have come to reflect more closely the enthusiasms of particular local authorities than any theoretical pattern of demand or need. In some areas,[25] existing deficiencies in countryside open space have only been accentuated by new provision. Not all parks are easily accessible by public transport and surprisingly few have been located close to the major urban areas — partly, though not wholly, because of Countryside Commission policy to ensure that parks were set in obvious rural surroundings which excluded most land on the urban fringe. The policy on distribution at national level has now been modified along with a major change in the structure of grant aid. The Commission can now contribute a more variable proportion of the total costs of a greater variety of schemes and they are able to support, in this smaller way, more projects. Priority is being given to schemes in Green Belts and those designed to protect the more vulnerable environments of National Parks and Areas of Outstanding Natural Beauty. But the initiative remains with local authorities and others to suggest the projects; it would be unwise to predict that provision, under this new regime and especially for non or low revenue-earning activities will continue to increase. Those authorities that were reluctant before will not be encouraged by lower grants; equally, the enthusiasm of the previously active may now be dampened.

The prospects for a better distribution of recreation opportunities may thus be improved by the revised policy, but there is no guarantee that the new schemes proposed will allow it to be realised. The increased initiative and expenditure of metropolitan authorities will help, but for this to continue they, and other urban authorities, must be persuaded, if not coerced, as they have been to provide facilities for active sport (for which the numerical scale of demand is much less). A notable feature of Sports Council policy has been the assessment of regional inadequacies in particular sports facilities (such as golf courses and swimming pools) and the setting of numerical standards for provision. Local bodies have been persuaded to work towards these targets through the Regional Sports Councils and under campaigns such as 'Sport for All'. Provision for countryside recreation cannot be easily reduced to such targets, and no satisfactory regional policy-making framework exists; even so there has been little real pressure upon local bodies to make good apparent imbalances in the supply of opportunities.

The *nature* of the countryside recreation experience offered in and outside country parks may also require some change. In the same way that recreation behaviour has been conveniently generalised by the very selective monitoring it has received, so the response, particularly in the public sector, may have become stereotyped. Inadequacies lie at both ends of the scale of available facilities. In the rush to establish prestige country park schemes, the need has been overlooked for more simple roadside stopping places for parking and walking along waymarked routes. In comparison with some European countries Britain has not made the most of her road planning system in recreation terms.

Likewise, there has been almost no investment in larger scale multi-activity parks: accessible, sheltered and exciting to visit. It is true that there are large variations in park environments: forest and woodland, downland, natural and man-made lakes, cliffed and dune coast and much else besides, but the activities they offer are rather less varied. For most semi-natural environments, facilities for driving, walking and picnicking are all that are required or suited, but opportunities may have been lost for people to experiment with other activities in the countryside. The volatility and the uncertainty of outdoor recreation and its relative inaccessibility to many people suggest the need for the kind of diversification which can accommodate changing tastes and attract people again and again.[26] The dominating concern of recreation policies is for resource protection which is justifiable in many parts of the countryside. But it is a view which perhaps too readily assumes that the prime goal of all visitors is to see fine and seemingly 'natural' landscapes,[27] and it diverts attention away from poorer environments (like the urban fringe) where the need for varied recreation opportunities may be much greater.

Multiple use

As well as the need for a greater number of areas in the countryside set aside for recreation, it has been fashionable to argue for more multiple land use to increase the supply of opportunities. But the concept is vague in definition and limited, in reality, to those fairly simple pursuits which may be accommodated within commercially productive forests, or those specialised activities which may use water catchments. It is more fruitful to think instead of a closer linkage of recreation activities with other land uses, although the different activities may be physically quite separate. In this way it is possible to envisage much greater integration of recreation with farming — by the design of self-guided farm trails, periodic farm open days and farm holidays — and with other rural activities, such as mining and quarrying or power generation. But this too will require new planning and new investment: the rationalisation and signposting of footpaths, the conversion of buildings, and development of warden services.[28] It cannot be a policy of 'something for nothing': In times of limited funds, and for those unprofitable recreation activities for which private owners will not be attracted to provide, such developments may be a most effective use of public money in countryside beyond the urban fringe. There is scope for still greater public use of defence lands and water catchments.

Recreation planning

A plethora of national agencies have some advisory or executive interest in outdoor recreation.[29] But because so much of the initiative for provision lies at local level, and because countryside recreation is itself an activity of regional and sub-regional rather than national scale, it is at these levels that the nature of its planning must be assessed.

For most authorities the activity is a new one, demanding action because of the problems it has brought — of congested roads, irate landowners, litter, fires and other disturbances — rather than the opportunities it has presented. Comprehensive planning methodologies have been slow to develop although progress has been made in specific research techniques and the analysis of recreation patterns at particular sites. But at the county scale, recreation has most often been treated intuitively, with enthusiastic authorities acquiring for recreation those areas they could buy cheaply, conveniently and without opposition from more established rural interest groups. In some parts of the country, recreation seems to have been ignored, perhaps in the belief that such a volatile activity can only be temporary; or that the supply of facilities will themselves encourage an escalating threat to rural values.

In practice, recreation policies have been dominated by the question of available land resources. In many instances, demand has rightly been assumed to be substantial enough to justify all schemes. Where demands have been assessed at all, the rigour and the scale of analysis have often been too limited to provide a basis for acquiring new land or managing existing recreation areas. The supply of land is clearly important: the most sophisticated demand studies are wasted if resources cannot be found; but equally, land which is easily available carries no guarantee of the right size, location, or quality to meet recreation requirements. In this situation, it is easy to see why some planners have tried to treat recreation in the countryside, as they have in the town, in terms of discrete parcels of land of a size which will satisfy the hypothesised demands of their catchment population. The belief in, and search for fixed capacities of land for recreation indicates that many would like to see a list of acreage standards for different rural recreation activities to which policies could aspire. The notion of standards is difficult enough to apply in urban areas; in the countryside, where multiple interests and resource quality are important, such rigidity has limited value, certainly at national level.[30] It discourages the expression of goals for recreation provision and thus any real means of gauging the worth and effectiveness of action. Moreover, it encourages a view of recreation as divorced from the other problems and opportunities of rural areas. Indeed, for some planners, the only notable issue in rural planning is the location and management of leisure facilities, despite the obvious interactions of recreation not only with questions of landscape and nature conservation, with the major rural industries, with rural transport, and with local employment, incomes and housing but also with much wider social problems and policies in the town. Moreover, local authorities have been preoccupied with their own powers and financial limitations and too little interested in guiding the investment of private capital.[31]

In all, recreation planning remains intuitive and parochial. There is no formulation of common goals between authorities, no agreement on working objectives which could guide investment, and too little innovative thinking which could lift recreation out of the planning doldrums and away from the 'rural problem' role commonly assigned to it.

More recently, several studies have emerged which not only explore and match, as far as possible, the demand with the supply aspects of outdoor recreation, but also link analysis and policy-making on recreation with other aspects of rural planning. In Sherwood Forest, for example, site-based recreation demand studies have established the present pattern of outdoor recreation and attempted some forecasting of the scale and character of future activity which could be converted to space needs. At the same time, the recreation potential of the whole area in terms of the accessibility, attractiveness and capacity of resources has been assessed and matched with future resource needs. In the South East of England, a joint study of central and local government agencies has involved more sophisticated home interview-based forecasting and assessments of the future imbalances between demand and supply at the regional level.[32] Besides providing guidance for plan-making authorities, these studies have tackled a number of major theoretical and practical problems, involving the modelling of recreation trips and measurement of the attractiveness of the countryside for recreation.[33]

Local Administration

All these studies have proved expensive in time and manpower; they will need to be streamlined before they are realistic models for authorities in which recreation will never be the most important planning task. Moreover, local authorities will need to adopt the necessary skills and internal organisation that makes possible a positive and co-ordinated view: a number now have recreation departments headed by a specialist recreation officer. There must be adequate machinery for drawing into the plan-making process all those regionally and locally concerned with provision, and not only the relevant public bodies, but representatives of landowning and other entrepreneurial interests. The White Paper *Sport and Recreation*, responding to the Lords' Select Committee, proposed that Regional Councils for Sport and Recreation should be established, replacing existing Regional Sports Councils, to co-ordinate the whole range of sport and recreation interests in their region.[34] It may be that such bodies with local authority representation and including the views of the Countryside Commissions, the Regional Councils of the Forestry Commission, the Nature

Conservancy Council, Regional Water Authorities, and the Tourist Boards and with specialist working parties, would provide the right organisation to prepare regional recreation strategies which could be translated to lower level structure and local plans. The present lack of a regional tier of policy-making (aside from the *ad hoc* regional plans) and of a coherent national policy for countryside recreation means that the recreation content of neighbouring structure plans may go unco-ordinated.[35]

In the current financial climate it is not surprising that local authorities have not been given the *duty* of providing adequate facilities for recreation.[36] Nor will agencies such as the Countryside Commission be given powers to initiate where local authorities have failed to provide themselves or persuade others to do so. Nevertheless, the promotion of a more equitable distribution of opportunities than exists now is worth trying at the regional scale, where action could be concentrated on just those locations, like the urban fringe, where present policy-making is so fragmented and the illogical separation of urban and rural recreation interests persists.

There are other advantages to strengthening the regional structure for recreation planning. Resources which are presently used in the gathering of information nationally (in surveys which do not always yield data in sufficient detail for regional policy-making) and those used in time-consuming unco-ordinated local surveys undertaken by many different agencies might be better employed in joint action at regional level. There is scope for greater co-ordination: of information and management as well as research services.

Recreation management

In many ways, the most tangible advances in work on rural recreation have been made in the management of recreation areas and their visitors for by acquiring land, public and private bodies have often been faced with immediate management problems. From their pragmatism, their experience of trial and error, a substantial fund of management information has been collected and augmented by research advice from central government agencies, notably the Countryside Commissions. Some fundamental principles of recreation management seem now to be well established: the advantages of zoning different recreation activities on land and water, of managing recreation traffic in a positive way,[37] of monitoring and repairing areas worn by heavy use,[38] and of training those whose job it is to guide the public.[39] The English Countryside Commission are presently sponsoring experiments employing all these approaches, in three Heritage Coasts where management plans are being prepared.[40]

Recent work has become more analytical, concentrating upon devising integrated solutions to management problems, and attempting to replace the "hit and miss" approach to problem-solving by more sophisticated studies of very local recreation systems. Such work is supported by and provides further material for the more theoretical work on recreation environments, that is on ecological implications and on the meaning and measurement of carrying capacity.[41] Research has also begun on the less tangible aspects of visitor behaviour — on the perception of recreation opportunities and local recreation space. Here, as at the regional and sub-regional planning scale, the complex nature of demand must be better matched with supply so that recreation systems can be more fundamentally understood and predicted, and more effective use made of resources and investment. In economically hard times, with limited prospect for an immediate or substantial increase in recreation space in most areas, better management of existing areas is essential so that the experience of outdoor recreation can be more widely available while the quality of that experience is maintained and improved. This will mean improvements in the administration of recreation management, involving the training of specialist staff, and the organisation of appropriate local arrangements for representation. Development of these aspects has lagged behind technical work.

Conclusions

We have argued early in this chapter that the demand for countryside recreation will grow but perhaps less rapidly, in the short term, than may have been assumed at the start of this decade. But there is real uncertainty about the nature of future demands, and in the whole meaning of recreation. Developments in plan-making and management methods, and in the structure of grants and agencies, should improve the approach to provision for recreation in the countryside, so that expressed demands are better accommodated, investment is more effectively used, and recreation better integrated with other interests in rural land. Yet, on present evidence of implementation, the opportunities for countryside recreation will still be available to a remarkably small proportion of the British populace; and one sharply circumscribed by particular groupings of income and social class (Table 15). If outdoor recreation does offer the kind of medical, social and spiritual benefits which many protagonists have claimed then the present notions of *accessibility* held by planners and providers ought to be questioned.[42]

Consumption of recreation opportunities has become the most easily measurable component of recreation demand. Furthermore it is upon the characteristics of those who presently consume that forecasts are made of future demand levels, and the form and location of new provision is assessed. Despite their variability in detail, numerous surveys have shown that present users are in the middle rather than the lower income groups, that they are car users, and that they live on the edges of cities rather than in their centres; they are also more likely to be aware of the leisure opportunities available to them. The paradox is that those with arguably a greater *need* for some experience of countryside are least able to express it: they have low incomes, low levels of car ownership and a general lack of awareness about the opportunities available. For these people, who are often otherwise disadvantaged by a poor urban environment, opportunities for leisure in the countryside are largely inaccessible.[43] In the search for generalisations in leisure behaviour, and with the prevailing concern to provide for majorities, there are other groups whose specialist needs have been passed over. It is true that some experimental provision has been made for the blind, but there is no attention to the needs of the old, nor often the very young in most provision. There are groups: mothers with young children, teenagers, the retired and others, who in terms of total leisure time available, have far more to spend than does the family unit upon which most rural recreation provision is based. For these, the investment is sorely under-used. Many of these groups receive some special treatment in the town (though probably not enough); there seems as much justification for it outside.

Inaccessibility relates also to the ways in which people may enjoy the open air. It is right that some tracts of countryside, managed primarily to retain their characteristic landscape character, should offer facilities for only those activities which are compatible with the milieu, and we discuss the importance of wilderness and the National Parks in Chapters 7 and 10. In other places, private enterprise will ensure that the latest in leisure gimickry is on offer, at cost, for public consumption. But there is room, between, for experiment and innovation whereby it is possible for consumers and providers alike to explore the nature of the satisfactions leisure and recreation can bring; where it is possible for people to try activities normally prohibited by the costs of their equipment and training, to enjoy activities in new and open surroundings, to see and to experience the countryside in many different ways, or simply to meet or to watch others doing these things. For many, the countryside is neither familiar nor instantly pleasurable. To offer only those activities which require the understanding and acceptance of rural values is to restrict its pleasures to the few, and to deny that the rural environment may be enjoyed in more ways than may yet have been discovered. Simmons argues:

"Looking to the future, growing prosperity in the West would mean the expansion of areas of choice, and the chance to opt for more leisure and different forms of it. This may mean socially that leisure will increasingly have to bear the fulfilment role which work has traditionally provided . . ."[44]

We have not yet begun to probe the kind of satisfactions leisure can bring, how these relate to other facets of living,[45] and the part rurality (real or artificial) can play. We have applied, for too long, too many untested assumptions (perpetuated by misguided survey design) about the place of countryside in people's lives — that it provides the necessary contrast or compensation to urban living and urban jobs; that people want to escape to wild and lonely places; that natural is better than man-made; that crowds impair enjoyment. We may better understand the nature of recreation satisfactions in the countryside and our need of them, not only by social and psychological research but by being more experimental in the provision of opportunities.

The implementation of policies of this kind implies some redirection of national and local attitudes. The government accepts that 'recreation should be regarded as one of the community's everyday needs and that provision for it is part of the general fabric of the social services'.[46] But it is difficult to see how, with reduced rather than expanded budgets for environmental services, local authorities and others can translate the principle into practice. Potentially, the increasing number of people who will want to visit the countryside for casual recreation represent a powerful group, numerically much larger than those with a more specialised interest — in a particular sport or in natural history. Yet there are few advocates for general enjoyment in the countryside, certainly among central government agencies with some recreation responsibilities if the present representation and priorities of commissions and councils are any guide. It is possible to see, in some of the activities of private owners, the National Trust and some local authorities that countryside recreation (and the use of countryside recreation grants) has been the public face for schemes designed principally to serve other purposes, especially the preservation of landscapes and historic buildings. We have argued earlier that although visitors to the countryside may enjoy the fruits of preservation, their specific interests may be otherwise curtailed.

". . . work has been more concerned with the place than with the visitor . . . (with) what we think the land . . . can sustain than on what people want to do or to experience. (We have tended) to assume that what is good for the land is good for man."[47]

The formation of local Recreation Departments with the intention that all leisure policies will be integrated should help. But the structure of responsibility at national level remains

unsatisfactory. All the many government agencies with some responsibility for recreation were established for some other purpose, and for most, recreation is a very secondary concern. Even where specialist watchdog agencies exist (as in the Water Space Amenity Commission which advises Regional Water Authorities on recreation and amenity matters) the potential exists for recreation to be subsumed among other more important duties. New arrangements of national agencies are possible,[48] but probably unnecessary given a better representation of consumer interests in the present system. It would be bureaucratically tidy to argue for a simplification of the national picture and a separate Recreation agency, as exists, for example, in a number of European and North American countries, to press the case for informal recreation, less influenced by questions of resource protection or Olympic sports standards. Even so, economic circumstances will permit no immediate and massive gain in new rural recreation facilities. Nor is the British countryside quite like those of Europe or America; the pattern of land ownership, the conflict between rural interests must remain key components in negotiating new recreation opportunities. But the case for enjoyment can still be strengthened.

In all, many aspects of national policy-making and local implementation reflect the lack of any clear philosophy for leisure in the countryside; they illustrate a confusion of purpose and assumptions. The objectives of the 1968 countryside legislation, for example, seem fairly to reflect the dilemma of a government on the one hand pressed by powerful agricultural and conservationist lobbies (alarmed by increasing pressures) and on the other hand anxious to fulfil a desirable social goal. This initial conflict — between conservation and development — has emerged as the most durable facet of subsequent implementation. The objectives of provision remain implicit: countryside recreation is seen both as the protector and the destroyer of rural life and values, as the salvation of failing rural and farm economies, as a vehicle for the (often paternalistic) education and moral refurbishing of townsmen, as an inevitable evil, or a passing frivolity. All may be valid in particular circumstances but some have been too dominant; the need is to recognise and question the motives of providers, to make more explicit their objectives and fit them better to the legitimate wants and needs of the community as well as into the fabric of the countryside.

Notes and References

1. This chapter concentrates upon informal recreation in the countryside rather than sport or tourism.
2. Hookway, R. J. S. and Davidson, J. (1970) *Leisure: Problems and Prospects for the Environment*, Countryside Commission.
3. See, for example, the comprehensive reviews of:
     Patmore, J. A. (1970) *Land and Leisure*, David & Charles.
     Simmons, I. G. (1975) *Rural Recreation in the Industrial World*, Edward Arnold.
     Lavery, P. (ed.) (1974) *Recreational Geography*, David & Charles.
     Coppock, J. T. and Duffield, B. S. (1975) *Recreation in the Countryside*, Macmillan.
4. Much evidence of the expansion of countryside activity is given in Section 2 of:
     Countryside Commission (1975) *Digest of Countryside Recreation Statistics.*
5. Houghton-Evans, W. and Miles, J. C. (1970) Weekend Recreational Motoring in the Countryside, *Journal of the Town Planning Institute*, Vol. 56 (9).
     Miles, J. C. (1972) *The Goyt Valley Traffic Experiment*, Countryside Commission/Peak Park Planning Board.
6. Countryside Commission (1975) *Digest of Countryside Recreation Statistics.*
7. More recent examples are:
     Patmore, J. A. and Rodgers, H. B. (1972) *Leisure in the North West*, N.W. Sports Council.
     Countryside Commission (1974) *Planning for Recreation at the Local Scale: Sherwood Forest Study*, Countryside Commission.

Elson, M. J. (1973) Some Factors affecting the Incidence and Distribution of Week-end Recreation Motoring Trips, *Oxford Agrarian Studies*, Vol. 11 (2).

Colenutt, R. J. and Sidaway, R. M. (1973) *Forest of Dean Day Visitor Survey*, Forestry Commission Bulletin No. 46.

White, J. and Dunn, M. (1974) *Recreational Use of the Countryside: a Case Study in the West Midlands*, University of Birmingham, Centre for Urban and Regional Studies, Research Memorandum No. 33.

8. Dower, M. and Downing, P. (1973) *Attitudes to Man and the Land*, Paper to 'Work and Leisure' Symposium, University of Salford.

9. The relationship of leisure to whole life development and the hazards of institutionalising and compartmentalising activities are explored in:

Rapoport, R. and Rapoport, R. N. (1975) *Leisure and the Family Life Cycle*, Routledge & Kegan Paul.

10. The present data base, both nationally and especially at regional level, is small and dated, relying upon two national surveys of participation rates (Pilot National Recreation survey, 1967; Planning for Leisure, 1969) and two non-comparable regional studies – Northern (1969) and North West (1972) and a survey in the South East (1973) whose results have yet to be published.

11. Maw, R. (1974) Assessment of Demand for Recreation – a Modelling Approach, in Appleton, I. (ed.), *Leisure Research and Policy*, Scottish Academic Press.

12. Central Statistical Office (1973) *Social Trends*, No. 4, H.M.S.O. Figures for 1973.

13. Select Committee on Sport and Leisure (1973) *Second Report*, H.M.S.O.

See Chapter 1 for a discussion of leisure time patterns. It is estimated here that, in 30 years, one third of the work force may be on shift work.

14. Perry, N. H. (1974) What Price the Good Life? *New Society*, February 28.

15. Young, M. and Willmott, P. (1973) *The Symmetrical Family*, Routledge & Kegan Paul.

16. Rodgers, H. B. (1970) Leisure and Recreation, in Cowan, P. (ed.), *Developing Patterns of Urbanisation*, Oliver & Boyd.

17. The North West Leisure Survey (op. cit. Patmore and Rodgers) found marked differences in the trip-making habits of people living in the Merseywide and SELNEC conurbations (particularly on visits to the coast and local parks) which could be attributed to variations in the availability of local opportunities. But more recent environmental case studies suggest that contrasts exist in the attitudes and habits of people from different towns which are not necessarily determined by the supply of facilities. See:

Hall, J. and Perry, N. (1974) *Aspects of Leisure in Two Industrial Cities: Sunderland and Stoke on Trent*, Occasional Papers in Survey Research 5, Social Science Research Council.

See also:

Rodgers, H. B. (1974) Regional Recreation Contrasts, in Appleton, I. (ed.), *Leisure Research and Policy*, Scottish Academic Press.

18. Law, S. (1974) Leisure and Recreation: Problems and Prospects; *Planning Outlook*, Special Recreation Issue, Summer, 1974.

19. Notably in terms of the ecological effects of recreation:

Speight, M. C. D. (1973) *Ecological Change and Outdoor Recreation*, University College London, Discussion Paper in Conservation, No. 4.

Social effects have been discussed mainly in the context of second home use:

Bielckus, C. L., Rogers, A. W. and Wibberley, G. P. (1972) *Second Homes in England and Wales*, Wye College, University of London, Studies in Rural Land Use, No. 11.

Downing, P. and Dower, M. (1973) *Second Homes in England and Wales*, Countryside Commission, H.M.S.O.

Coppock, J. T. (ed.), (1975) *Second Homes*, Methuen & Co., London.

Jacobs, C. A. J. (1972) *Second Homes in Denbighshire*, Research Report No. 3, Denbigh County Council.

20. See, for example:

Smith, R. J. (1974) The Economics of Outdoor Recreation, in Lavery, P. (ed.), *Recreational Geography*, David & Charles.

Gibson, J. G. (1974) Recreation Cost-Benefit Analysis: a review of English Case Studies, *Planning Outlook*, Special Recreation Issue, Summer 1974.

The estimation of recreation benefits of day visits to Forestry Commission holdings are described in:

Grayson, A. J., Sidaway, R. M. and Thompson, F. P. (1975) Some Aspects of Recreation Planning in the Forestry Commission, in Searle, G. A. (ed.), *Recreational Economics and Analysis*, Longmans.

21. Patmore, J. A. (1974) Routeways and Recreation Patterns, in Lavery, P. (ed.), *Recreational Geography*, David & Charles.

22. Ministry of Land and Natural Resources (1966) *Leisure in the Countryside England and Wales*, H.M.S.O., Cmnd. 2928, para. 18, p. 6.

23. By January 1976 there were 106 local authority country parks, 19 private country parks; 140 local authority picnic sites and 15 private picnic sites.

24. British Waterworks Association (1969) *Amenity Use of Reservoirs Survey.*

25. See, for example:
    Waterhouse, S. (1972) *Country Parks and the West Midlands.* University of Birmingham Centre for Urban and Regional Studies, Research Memorandum, No. 17.
    White, J. and Dunn, M. C. (1975) *Countryside Recreation Planning: Problems and Prospects in the West Midlands*, University of Birmingham Centre for Urban and Regional Studies Occasional Paper No. 33.

26. Chapter 8 suggests that the fringe may be an ideal locale for these experiments, in which, for example, open-air swimming, drama, crafts might be among the activities on offer; where countryside could be seen in less familiar ways: from treewalks, underground routes.

27. The relative unpopularity of wild places, the public enjoyment of coniferous forests (contrasting with pressure group concern) show otherwise.

28. See discussion of The Upland Management Experiment and the Bollin Valley Study in Chapter 12.

29. The main national agencies with some advisory or executive interest in outdoor recreation are: the two Countryside Commissions; Sport Council; Nature Conservancy Council; Forestry Commission; British Tourist Authority and the National Tourist Boards; British Waterways Board; Water Space Amenity Commission. Co-ordination is considerable, particularly on research, and should further improve now that there is a Minister for Sport and Recreation.

30. See the discussion in:
    Lords Select Committee on Sport and Leisure (1973) *Second Report*, H.M.S.O. Paras. 329-332.

31. Long, J. (1974) Public and Private Investment in Non-Urban recreation, in *Planning for Leisure*, Proceedings of Seminar D, Summer Meeting of P.T.R.C., University of Warwick.

32. See discussion of the Sherwood Forest Study in Chapter 11.
    Countryside Commission (1973) *Planning for Informal Recreation at the Local Scale: Sherwood Forest Study.*
    Countryside Commission (1974) *Planning for Informal Recreation at the Sub-Regional Scale*, South Wales Standing Conference Area.
    Palmer, J. E. (1974) Recreation Structure Planning and Provision, *Planning Outlook*, Special Recreation Issue, Summer 1974.
    Davidson, J. M. and Sienkiewicz, J. (1975) Study of Informal Recreation in South East England, in Searle, G. A. (ed.), *Recreational Economics and Analysis*, Longmans.

33. Perry, N. H. and Sienkiewicz, J. (1972) *Recreation Modelling in the Context of London and the S.E. Region*, Unpublished paper, Centre for Environmental Studies Seminar on recreation modelling.
    Zetter, J. A. (1974) Application of Potential Surface Analysis to Rural Planning, *The Planner*, Vol. 60 (2).

34. Lords Select Committee on Sport and Recreation (1973), op. cit.
    Department of the Environment (1975) *Sport and Recreation*, H.M.S.O., Cmnd. 6200.

35. See the critique of recreation planning in the West Midlands:
    White, J. and Dunn, M. C. (1975) op. cit.
    The Countryside Commission, which must vet the recreation and landscape content of structure plans, is hampered in its attempt to co-ordinate policies by the lack of adequate regional representation.

36. Department of the Environment (1975) *Sport and Recreation*, op. cit.

37. Miles, J. C. (1974) Recreation Traffic Management Policies, *Planning Outlook*, Special Recreation Issue, Summer 1974.
    Miles, J. C. (1972) *The Goyt Valley Traffic Experiment*, Countryside Commission and Peak Park Planning Board.
    Peak Park Planning Board (1972) *Routes for People*, Derbyshire County Council and Peak Park Planning Board.

38. Goldsmith, F. B. (1974) Ecological Effects of Visitors in the Countryside, in Warren, A. and Goldsmith, F. B. (eds.), *Conservation in Practice*, John Wiley.

39. Aldridge, D. (1975) *Guide to Countryside Interpretation*, Part I, H.M.S.O.
    Hookway, R. J. S. (1974) *Interpretation of the Countryside*, Proceedings of Annual Conference of National Park Authorities, Great Malvern.

40. Glamorgan, Dorset and Suffolk.

41. The Countryside Commission are sponsoring a series of site management experiments in varied environments in which site damage, rehabilitation and visitor activity are carefully monitored and alternative solutions tried.

See also: Brotherton, D. I. (1973) The concept of carrying capacity of countryside recreation areas, *Recreation News Supplement*, No. 9.

42. Emmett, I. (1971) The Social Filter in the Leisure Field, *Recreation News Supplement*, No. 4.

43. Mercer, D. (1973) The concept of Recreation Need, *Journal of Leisure Research*, Vol. 5 (1).

44. Simmons, I. G. (1975) *Rural Recreation in the Industrial World*, Edward Arnold.

45. Roberts, K. (1974) The Changing Relationship between Work and Leisure, in Appleton, I. (ed.), *Leisure Research and Policy*, Scottish Academic Press.

Smith, M., Parker, S. and Smith, C. (1973) *Leisure and Society in Britain*, Allen Lane, Part 2: Work and Leisure.

46. Department of the Environment (1975) *Sport and Recreation*, op. cit.

47. Dower, M. and Downing, P. (1973) op. cit.

48. Rodgers, H. B. (1974) Some problems of Administration and Policy in Recreation Provision, in *Planning for Leisure*, Proceedings of Seminar D, Summer Meeting P.T.R.C., University of Warwick.

Part II: Resources:
Planning for Protection

CHAPTER 5

Resources and Conservation

At the beginning of this book, we described the 'fabric' of the countryside in terms of the resources it contains and the activities which are dependent upon the manipulation of those resources. We have already discussed some of the most prominent rural activities, which exploit and, in some cases, renew different rural resources. Most of these resources have already been substantially modified by man; some — good soils, certain minerals, particular water catchments — are those which society has valued highly for a long time.

But the notion of what constitutes a resource is clearly not fixed. Not all features of the rural environment are seen as opportunities for social or individual benefit, nor have many of them always been highly valued. The definition of resources at any one time depends upon the attitudes and aspirations of society, its perception and knowledge of what opportunities the environment can offer, and the assemblage of technical and organisational skills so far devised for realising those opportunities.

"As man's appraisal of his environment has altered, so the concept of resources has changed in meaning. Our amazing ingenuity for technological substitution, the tremendous rise in the demand for services as opposed to primary raw materials, the increasing elaboration of commodity processing . . . and the recent upsurge in the public interest in environmental quality, have led to a new and much broader interpretation of resources (which) Perloff has termed 'amenity resources' . . ."[1]

Before we go on to discuss further the amenity resources of the countryside, this chapter takes stock of the rural environment in terms of the way its resources have been viewed and valued. We try to assess the relevance of concepts of resource management and conservation for planning the countryside before applying, in subsequent chapters, some of these ideas to two attributes of the rural environment — wildlife and landscape — only recently perceived as legitimate arenas for resource management.

Management and Resources

The application of principles of general management is a growing aspect of modern planning. Indeed, many would now argue that urban planning is primarily a task of understanding better, and managing more effectively, the physical, financial and human resources of very complex urban systems.[2] But the notion of management, of using various techniques to reach defined objectives, is equally relevant for the countryside, although the components and functioning of the rural system may differ in important ways from those of the city.

Quite obviously, 'resource management' can be applied in a general sense to the whole body of techniques employed by any decision-maker responsible for the allocation of resources of whatever kind: it may be capital, or manpower, or land or energy or any number of a host of other inputs to a particular production process, whether this is designed to build a town, produce a crop of wheat or repair a car. If the decision-maker is concerned with *managing* rather than otherwise manipulating resources, then his allocation decisions will be based upon defined objectives derived from various sources such as national laws and directives; boardroom or council chamber decisions; or a more direct encounter with public opinion.

But resource management in the countryside has commonly, and more specifically, been applied to decisions involving natural and semi-natural resources: it is closely associated, for example, with the task of 'range management' and with those resources, like air and water, which are 'common property' components of the environment. A good deal of theoretical progress has been made by economists, notably in the United States, who have been concerned with the allocation of resources which can, in some way, be priced.[3] But their theories rest upon knowledge and assumptions which may not apply in many fields of resource use, particularly where the emphasis is upon those environmental components like good landscape, or remoteness, for which no price is directly paid (nor can a surrogate price easily be found) and to which individuals apply very different personal values.

Management, of whatever kind, involves the skills and techniques of many disciplines, and economics is bound to figure strongly. However, a basic input to natural resource management is ecology. Before resources can be handled in such a way that desirable objectives are *achieved* the relationships of these resources, one to another and their response to different treatments, must be understood. But —

> "The perspectives of ecology are different from those of economics, for they stress limits rather than continued growth, stability rather than continuous 'development', and they operate on a different timescale . . ."[4]

Some economists have now begun to question traditional economic principles and assumptions,[5] but in practice these distinctions remain.

Earlier and subsequent chapters of this book illustrate some of the objectives and methods employed in a number of different areas of natural resource management, such as farming, forestry and water conservation. But the concepts and practice of management are relevant for other less tangible resources of the countryside, and for the rural fabric itself. Indeed, the unifying philosophical and practical approach which the ecological principles of resource management offer may be just what is needed to encourage a more rational treatment of these other resources of the rural environment. Four ideas emerge as significant.

First, a fundamental concern of natural resource management is with understanding and manipulating complex ecosystems — like the plant-soil-air system, or the water cycle — in which there are many functional interactions between different components. The interactions themselves are complex, often characterised by chain reactions and spillover effects, as shown, for example, by the research done on the environmental effects of the increasing use and diversification of agricultural chemicals.[6] It is the nature of natural systems to be integrative, with all their components playing an essential role in the system.[7]

Plate 1. Lowland countryside: the North Downs in Kent; well farmed and well wooded, but how long will it last? (*photo: John Topham*)

Plate 9. Ripening wheat: beauty in efficiency. The New Agricultural Landscapes study showed that farmers' attitudes to the landscape differ from those of many visitors to the countryside. (*photo: John Topham*)

Plate 10. Beauty in diversity: waste land on farms may be untidy but ecologically rich; new planting could disturb established habitats. (*photo: John Topham*)

Similarly, the *whole* rural environment can be viewed as a complex interacting system of many resources and activities, whose individual and combined functioning must first be understood before problems and opportunities can be identified, and desirable but realistic objectives set.

Secondly, the viability of natural systems is closely linked to their potential for stability; diversity is seen as an essential prerequisite for this. Man's efforts are often to reduce diversity, for example, in the simplification of cropping patterns for food or fibre, which can only be maintained at increasing costs of materials and energy used. The limits to these increases have yet to be explored; but it is likely that reduction of diversity on a larger scale — in the variety of resources and activities of the countryside as a whole — would yield an environment highly vulnerable to relatively minor technical and economic developments, yet unable to adapt easily to changing social needs and aspirations. We consider, in a final chapter, some of the implications of a rural environment which contains only the highly productive and artificial management systems, with few or no areas of semi-natural, relatively 'unproductive' countryside (at least in conventional output terms).[8]

Thirdly, ideas of conflict and competition figure strongly in ecological theory and in the traditional applications of natural resource management. As some chapters have already shown, and later ones will confirm, conflict exists, and is probably increasing, among the interests at stake in the alternative uses of rural resources. Conflict exists in the definition of rural problems and in the solutions that might be applied. There are major and overt conflicts, as between development and protection of resources, which only partly reflect the long standing clash of urban and rural interests. But less obvious conflicts also exist *within* the countryside, between the advocates of long term versus short term decision-making and between public versus private rights and benefits. The predictable alignment of rural interest groups is by no means always assured. Wildlife, landscape and recreation groups are not always in agreement in opposition to industrial developments, road improvements or agricultural change in the countryside. Nor are farming interests always aligned. For example, the long term improvement of an upland area through the development of a multi-purpose reservoir may well conflict with the immediate damage to the land use and economy of individual farms in the valley bottom which will be drowned.

Finally, this notion of competition implies that choices are offered and preferences, trade-offs, must be made in the selection and attainment of objectives. Resources must be evaluated and the interests in them accorded some ranking of priority. For the whole countryside this, too, is relevant; no one resource interest can necessarily claim a monopoly of worth or value.

McLoughlin has drawn many analogies between the processes operating in 'natural' systems and urban activity patterns. He suggests that many of these parameters of ecological analysis are equally relevant to the understanding of city functions. The relevance seems equal if not greater for the rural environment where natural and semi-natural resources make up more substantial components of the system.[9]

But analysis and understanding is not a prescription for action; what principles should guide the manipulation of rural resources? How important is the idea of conservation as a major objective for resource management in the countryside?

Conservation

The idea of conservation is bound up with the principles and practice of rural resource management; some would argue that it is an essential prerequisite objective for the management of natural resources. But like 'environment' or 'countryside' the term often obscures rather than clarifies. It is widely used but there are considerable differences between the various contemporary definitions and connotations. For some, conservation is synonymous with preservation or protection. It is applied on a variety of scales: from the single species; to a tract of countryside;[10] to the management of urban and rural resources generally; to problems of the world resource base and population control. Its relationship to planning remains ill-defined.

In many ways, it is easier to understand the conflicting nature of conservation philosophy and the evolution of the 'cause' than to identify workable principles which might be applied in practice.

Formal expression of a philosophy of resource trusteeship rather than exploitation emerged first in the United States.[11] In Britain, there is long standing evidence of individual concern for the care and continuity of resources epitomised, perhaps, by the visionary investments of eighteenth century landowners. The notion of personal trusteeship has permeated much local conservation action although Britain seems to have lacked, in the past, powerful exponents of the global ethical case for conservation, equivalent to Leopold and Dasmann.[12]

As an element of national and governmental concern, resource conservation is entirely a product of the twentieth century, beginning with and primarily sustained by, the need to maintain strategic reserves — of timber and of food-producing land. Grafted on to this concern, particularly over the last two decades, has been the need to rationalise resource policies (for example those concerned with air, water and energy) so that improved safety and health standards could be met and sudden disasters such as smogs or severe water shortages could be avoided.

In Britain, there is strangely little evidence, despite structural changes in central government, of a real concern for *efficiency* in the management of some national resources, particularly those of the rural environment, although this does seem to have been an important element in the development of the American conservation movement. It is still possible to identify strongly segmented fields of resource policy-making and inter-agency rivalry in the British system. Multipurpose schemes and multi-interest forms of administration — like the Rural Development Boards which we discuss in Chapter 10 — have not been especially common or successful here.

The development of conservation as an area for political debate and the crystallising of public attitudes is a product of the last decade. A 'conservation movement' seems to have evolved, yet there is no real agreement on meaning or practice and many different attitudes and motivations parade under the one banner. The shifting emphasis of past conservation policies is strongly reflected: the ethical case for stewardship is still heard; at government level, individual resource policies are guided, as before, by questions of national security, health and safety. Policies for preservation are often only thinly disguised by new 'conservation' terminology. But the debate is now widened and motivations have been strengthened by fears, not only of a national scarcity of resources, but of their depletion on a world scale.[13] Conservation, it is argued, now becomes a necessity rather than a philanthropist's luxury.

One other ingredient has been added to this contemporary debate: the notion of 'quality of life'. This is an attractive if nebulous concept, in which resource conservation is identified as the major mechanism for achieving greater human satisfaction. It is the dignified rationale for restricting further escalations of wasteful consumerism; for repairing the ravages of more than a century of resource exploitation, for appeasing retribution before it is too late.

Modern conservationists thus appear to argue a united case which seems to be in everyone's long term best interest. But this disguises profound differences of emphasis, reflected most acutely in the growth — anti-growth argument. There may be agreement on the nature of the problems, but the remedies are often sharply opposed: ranging from the technological solution,[14] to the arcadian dream.[15] The more rational compromise view recognises the existence of resource and environmental limits (although it is not yet possible to define them all) but accepts the need for social and political realism in a debate which so easily polarises opinion between the rich (who see conservation as a convenient palliative to excessive growth) and the poor who can neither afford nor immediately benefit from it.[16] It is a polarisation which applies as much within as between nations.

Practical Applications

In many ways, the idea of conservation, despite its present confusion, is easier to accept than to apply. Nevertheless, from the evolution of the idea and from current literature, it is possible to list what seem to be the more important practical components.

Conservation is concerned with *action* rather than no action; in most cases it implies positive resource use rather than sterilisation or preservation in a museum-like way (admitting that for most resources, aside from geological ones, this would, in any case, be impossible). Conservation thus implies a preparedness to accept some, and possibly considerable, change in resources and/or their context. In both these respects, conservation in an urban context differs only marginally from its rural counterpart. It is true that the major objective of an urban conservation area may be to retain a substantially unchanging external appearance. But the resources of such an area must nevertheless be *used*: lack of suitable functions for buildings and routes may be the recipe for failure.[17]

Conservation implies the use of resources in such a way and on such a scale that they are not depleted, but that, if possible, their values are enhanced. Notions of creativity, of living on interest rather than capital, of 'sustained yield', are characteristic.

Conservation is more often concerned with long-term rather than short-term action, and this last reason, among others, will dictate that conservation is likely to demand public action to augment, but in many cases to make good the deficiencies of private action.

Lastly, conservation is concerned with assemblages of resources as well as individual ones. It implies a realisation that the whole may be more than the sum of the parts, and that for the parts to survive, the whole must be viable.

This conception of conservation — wider than the popular but loosely defined 'wise use' — has been applied to the harmonisation of resource interests in various rural planning studies (some of which are reviewed in Chapter 11). In our view, it is the application of conservation principles and resource management on this wider environmental scale which most clearly describes the elusive nature of rural planning.

Wildlife and Landscape

The theory and application of conservation principles is often easier to understand when the context is a specific resource — a single species perhaps, or wildlife as a whole, or the landscape. As resources of the rural environment, these last two have much in common, although they differ in important respects from other countryside resources discussed in this book.

Both are fundamental and ubiquitous components of the 'fabric' of the countryside. Almost alone among resources they must be experienced where they are found. They cannot be (or are not normally) cropped or mined or piped; nor are they, in any simple or direct sense, substitutable in comparison with many other rural products.

While a number of rural resources, including for example, poorer soils and polluted waters, appear to be improving their values as a result of technical advancements, there is general agreement that, in many areas, the qualities of the wildlife stock and of the landscape are declining. These declining qualities involve absolute losses of particular species and features as well as the gradual decay of once flourishing habitats and vistas. Moreover, wildlife and landscape resource values are themselves not easily defined; they appear increasingly to vary substantially among different individuals and groups. There seems to be little agreement, particularly for landscape, on what is better or more valuable and what is poorer and less so. In contrast to quality assessments of soils or minerals or water, the opinion of experts particularly in matters of landscape count for little more than those of amateurs. Partly because of these differences of view, quantification of relative values, particularly in money terms, is proving to be elusive.

In theory, resources of both wildlife and landscape are continuous and renewable. But their renewability is heavily dependent upon the influence of other (less continuous) activities which take place around and within them. Their survival depends very much upon the degree to which they can remain intact, as integral components of a rural *whole*: they may suffer irretrievably from fragmentation and piecemeal action.

As is common with resources which are becoming increasingly scarce and at risk, they are the subjects of growing emotional and political debate. Indeed, wildlife and landscape are good examples of the way in which our concept of resources widens over time. But neither contributes much that is materially useful to man in an economic sense. Any concern is for their protection for aesthetic, spiritual and ethical reasons — causes less likely to stimulate action by governments or individuals than those involving the cost, availability and quality of *products* (like food or water or timber) which in many ways affect the consumer much more directly. For all these reasons: disagreement on values, technical difficulties of comparing these with other more tangible and measurable resource qualities, and the lack of strong political motivation, it is still usual for wildlife and landscape resources to be given a relatively low priority where situations of conflict must be resolved. The following chapters look in turn and more closely at changing attitudes towards the conservation of wildlife and landscape in Britain.

Notes and References

1. O'Riordan, T. (1971) *Perspective on Resource Management*, Pion, p. 15. See Chapter 1 for a longer discussion of the concept of resources.
2. McLoughlin, J. B. (1969) *Urban and Regional Planning: A Systems Approach*, Faber.
   Friend, J. K. and Jessop, W. N. (1969) *Local Government and Strategic Choice: An Operational Research Approach to the Processes of Public Planning*, Tavistock Publications.
   Chadwick, G. (1971) *A Systems View of Planning*, Pergamon.
3. Perloff, H. S. (ed.), (1969) *The Quality of the Urban Environment*, Johns Hopkins University Press, Baltimore.

Kneese, A. V. (1968) *Economics and the Quality of the Environment: Some Empirical Observations*, Resources for the Future, Reprint No. 71.

O'Riordan, T. (1971) op. cit. reviews admirably the development and fundamental principles of resource management from 19th century preoccupation with resource exploitation to the evolution of welfare economics.

4. For a discussion of the meaning of ecology and its relationship with economics, see:
Simmons, I. G. (1974) *The Ecology of Natural Resources*, Edward Arnold, Chapter 2 from which this quote is drawn.

5. Boulding, K. E. (1966) The Economics of the Coming Spaceship Earth, in Jarrett, H. (ed.), *Environmental Quality in a Growing Economy*, Johns Hopkins University Press, Baltimore.
Mishan, E. (1967) *The Costs of Economic Growth*, Staples Press.
Schumacher, E. F. (1974) *Small is Beautiful*, Blond & Briggs.

6. See, for example:
Mellanby, K. (1967) *Pesticides and Pollution*, Collins.

7. Simmons, I. G. (1973) Conservation, in Dawson, J. A. and Doornkamp, J. C. (eds.), *Evaluating the Human Environment*, Edward Arnold.

8. A useful summary of Odum's classification of the major types of ecosystem which contribute to ecological diversity is given in:
Simmons, I. (1974) *The Ecology of Natural Resources*, op. cit., Chapter 13.

9. McLoughlin, J. B. (1969) *Urban and Regional Planning – A Systems Approach*, op. cit., Chapter 1.

10. See, for example, discussion of the East Hampshire Study in Chapter 11.

11. O'Riordan, T. (1971) *Perspectives on Resource Management*, op. cit. Chapter 1 discusses various stages in the development of the American Conservation movement over the last century.

12. Leopold, Aldo (1949) *A Sand County Almanac*, Oxford University Press, New York.
Dasmann, R. F. (1964) *Environmental Conservation*, Wiley, New York.
But a more recent exception is:
Fraser-Darling, F. (1970) *Wilderness and Plenty*, BBC Publications.

13. Meadows, D. L. *et al.* (1973) *The Limits to Growth*, Earth Island Press, London.

14. Beckermann, W. (1973) Growthmania Revisited, *New Statesman* (October 19).
Maddox, J. (1972) *The Doomsday Syndrome*, Macmillan.

15. Goldsmith, E. *et al.* (1972) Blueprint for Survival, *The Ecologist*, Vol. 2 (1).

16. Crosland, C. A. R. (1971) *A Social Democratic Britain*, Fabian Tract 404.
For a useful discussion of the contemporary environmental debate, see the final chapter of Simmons, I. G. (1974), *The Ecology of Natural Resources*, op. cit.

17. For a discussion of the values and desirable principles of conservation in an urban context, see for example:
Cantell, T. (1975) Why Conserve? *The Planner*, Vol. 61 (1).
Dobby, A. (1975) Conservation and Planning, *The Planner*, Vol. 61 (1).

CHAPTER 6

The Conservation of Wildlife

The reasons why we should conserve food producing land, trees, water and many other rural resources are obvious; the values to us of a varied stock of wildlife are less so — indeed it is likely that, as with butterflies, we remain largely unconscious of them until sometime after they have disappeared. Wildlife changes are far less obvious to the casual observer than are the visual effects of rural activities. Moreover, the cause of wildlife conservation has been closely linked to emotionalism about white rhinos and blue whales, which has generated far greater public concern than changes in our native stock of wild animals and plants. The connotation (and perhaps it is the term 'wildlife' at fault here) is of protection for the rare and the beautiful rather than for the ecologically important (if more commonplace) features of our environment. It is nevertheless possible to categorise some of the major values of wildlife which seem to be worth conserving.

Most obviously, a varied stock of fauna and flora contribute to the diversity of the rural (and urban) environments which are seen, heard, smelt and touched. There is evidence enough of less tangible values to artistic inspiration and, quite simply, to a profound sense of personal well-being. These values, like friendship or security, exist even when they are not directly used. Linked to them are the still less tangible values which involve an ethical and moral concern for living things, although there are clearly unworkable extremes of this notion of the sanctity of life.

Wildlife is valued for the scientific record, and for research which may indirectly have enormous repercussions — socially, psychologically and environmentally — on the way we live. An increasing number of species, for example, are becoming directly valuable as sensitive indicators of environmental change and degradation.

Wildlife species remain the only long term stock of potentially useful crops and animals for cultivation and domestication in the service of man. Improvements in plant and animal breeding to produce resistance to disease, harsh climates and difficult terrain often rely upon the use of natural species; and for these reasons species diversity and rarity ought to be conserved. Meanwhile, wildlife is of direct, short term economic value in a number of ways. Even in the developed world, fish (still among our staple foods) are hunted rather than farmed and production is dependent upon conservation of the wildlife stock. Aside from their economic output, sports like fishing and wildfowling rely upon wildlife populations, and upon their conservation management.

Finally, a varied and visible stock of wildlife becomes increasingly valuable for specialist and general education and all levels.[1]

Realisation of the need for positive action to safeguard some of these values came in Britain at the end of the nineteenth century; protection for certain kinds of wildlife was one of the first topics of amenity legislation in Britain. At the same time, a number of societies and trusts, notably the Royal Society for the Protection of Birds and the Botanical Society of the British Isles,[2] were founded, and it was largely by their efforts, voluntarily sustained, that protection of the more obvious components of the British wildlife stock grew during the first half of this century.

The Role of Government

Effective government intervention, in terms of an executive agency for wildlife conservation, rather than legislation alone, did not come until 1949 with the establishment of the Nature Conservancy.[3] The detailed objectives of the Nature Conservancy at its inception (which may be summarised as the setting up and management of National Nature Reserves and the provision of research and advice on conservation matters) and the success of its early work have been well documented elsewhere.[4] But it is useful to reflect upon the ways in which both aims and methods, and indeed the very nature of the organisation, have changed since 1947 in response to changed conditions in the countryside and evolving conservation attitudes.

The Nature Conservancy quickly grew nationally and regionally in staff and prestige until, by the mid-sixties, it had established and equipped over 100 National Nature Reserves (owned, leased or managed by agreement with private landlords) as part of an expanding programme to safeguard a representative spread of the major British habitats and their communities of plants and animals.[5]

While still expanding its stock of designated areas, the Conservancy began to devote more effort to other activities: some within but some only marginal to the terms of its original charter. Research in nature reserves grew and major contributions were made by the specialist research units at Monks Wood, Merlewood and elsewhere. Throughout the sixties and early seventies, the Conservancy played a vital role in alerting government and public attention to, and providing objective evidence on, the ecological consequences of new and expanding industrial activities, such as the increased use of toxic chemicals; the dumping of pollutants in rivers and the sea; the changing management regimes of grasslands, woodland, hedges and verges; and the growth of recreation.[6] Like other national amenity agencies, the Conservancy was involved in arguing the 'wildlife cause' in cases of major conflict such as the Upper Teesdale reservoir.[7]

Since its inception and especially over the last decade, the Conservancy has become increasingly involved, directly and indirectly, in public attitudes to conservation. Although public access to most National Nature Reserves has been severely restricted (because of special lease or management arrangements or because their wildlife content or research potential was considered too vulnerable to withstand public access), 'open' accessible reserves have been acquired in some areas. Here, the Conservancy has had to be concerned with the management of visitors. But public access offered a new opportunity, which has been carried beyond the local scale, for interpretation of wildlife and the work of conservation, and the Conservancy has been increasingly involved in providing information and interpretive services of many kinds for school and public audiences.

In the long term, perhaps the most valuable role of the Nature Conservancy over the last decade has been that of co-ordinator. In 1965 the Conservancy brought together many of the conflicting interests in Broadland.[8] Under its aegis the three 'Countryside in 1970' conferences were held; it played a major part in European Conservation Year activities here and abroad. The Conservancy's initiative in bringing together many rural interests in the mid-sixties has contributed not only to the exposure of some fundamental rural conflicts but has also allowed common aims and opportunities for co-operation to be identified. A good example of the possibilities for co-operative effort which emerged during this period was the creation of a power station field study centre. After negotiations between the Conservancy and the Central Electricity Generating Board, Britain's first industrial nature trail on an operational site was opened at the Drakelow Station in 1967.

Diversification of the Conservancy's interest and efforts into all these fields — research and advice on the wider ecological implications of rural activity rather than on the functions of reserve systems alone; recreation as well as wildlife management; interpretation of the countryside; and the co-ordination of conservation interests — reflects not only the changing nature of rural activity since 1947 but also the widening of the whole conservation concept. The changing emphasis of Conservancy work can be seen as a response to a wider definition of conservation values and to three particular changes.

First, although the 'key area' concept is still valid (and remains the cornerstone of Nature Conservancy Council policy[9]), it is obvious that the conservation of wildlife in reserves depends to an increasing degree upon what happens elsewhere. It is difficult, if not impossible, to maintain wet-land habitats in a National Nature Reserve if the surrounding agricultural land is being drained. Similarly it is not possible to protect rare species of predatory birds on reserves, if their prey, taken outside these reserves, are already polluted by heavy pesticide residues. Many wild animal species cannot be safeguarded in isolation; links between their refuges must be established and sustained, and the retention of these links is heavily dependent upon the activities of other land and water users.

The decay of traditional systems of land and produce management means the further loss of habitats they once sustained, habitats which became increasingly costly to maintain in other ways. It is, for example, difficult to retain rich unploughed chalk grassland in an environment where arable cropping is so much more profitable, and where sheep and cattle for grazing the grassland are not available in the neighbourhood. Coppice woodland — so diverse a habitat for wildlife — depends upon the maintenance of a timber milling system now virtually lost.

In all, the pace and nature of rural change over the last twenty years, especially in agriculture, has meant not only an absolute decline in the numbers of certain species because of direct toxicological effects but a decline in the number and quality of many of the habitats upon which a varied and viable wildlife stock depends. As with other areas of rural resource management, the conservation of wildlife cannot be confined to a single use zonation. The Conservancy and others must be involved in a whole range of environmental influences.

Secondly, since 1947 there has been a change in the relative emphasis of the values attributed to wildlife. When the Conservancy was established, scientific and ethical values seem to have predominated.[10] Now, much greater weight needs to be placed upon wildlife as a ubiquitous component of the whole rural environment, to be enjoyed and understood by many more people in their recreation.

Thirdly, for both of these reasons, it is clear that many more agencies must be involved in the task of conserving wildlife, including those (like farmers) whose practices, undertaken for some other main purpose, influence its viability profoundly; and others, such as planners and educationists, who have some professional or amateur interest in wider environmental issues.

The Voluntary Movement

In practice, the most significant growth of wildlife conservation interest has taken place outside government. The voluntary nature conservation movement surpasses every other individual amenity cause in the size and number of separate organisations involved. Many new clubs, societies and trusts have been founded, while some established bodies, notably the Royal Society for the Protection of Birds with its astute and timely publicity, have enjoyed a phenomenal rise in membership. In a decade, the voluntary movement, helped by the media, has awakened a public interest, and by informing and educating, has motivated people to participate. Predictably, it is the more obvious and the more beautiful elements of the wildlife stock that have aroused the strongest concern. Even wild flowers have received rather less publicity and legislative protection than birds. Much of the interest is 'armchair' but its political weight is considerable, limited though the representation is in the population as a whole.

The contribution of the voluntary movement to *practical* local conservation is also growing as more groups own and manage local nature reserves. Among many, the work of the County Naturalists' Trusts is notable not only in the acquisition of reserves but in the wider educational and promotional work they do, locally and through various national co-ordinating agencies.[11]

The Response at National and Local Level

One consequence of the changes in attitudes and in the nature of rural activity is that the expertise of nature conservationists and ecologists has been sought in a wide range of pollution and planning studies, and in new departments of government, such as the Royal Commission on Pollution. In recent years, the policies of some national resource agencies have been modified to take account of the growing concern for wildlife. We have seen in Chapter 3 that the management objectives of the Forestry Commission, for so long confined to questions of a strategic timber reserve and the need to save on imports, have been widened to include a number of secondary policies for the provision of recreation opportunities, and the conservation of landscape and wildlife. By their activities — in mixed planting and creating new scrub and pond habitats, in culling certain species, and in leasing reserve sites to local naturalist bodies — the wildlife component of some previously open or poorly managed woodland areas has been markedly improved.[12] Moreover, the Forestry Commission, and in a less direct way, the Countryside Commissions, have been involved in the provision of various interpretive services, for example, nature trails and visitor centres, in which wildlife and conservation themes figure strongly.

But there are still some departments and agencies of government (like the Ministry of Agriculture and the Department of Education and Science) with, it might be assumed, considerable interest and certainly much influence on wildlife matters whose role here remains undefined. Nor is it clear how far nature conservation will feature as a practical function of the Regional Water Authorities.[13]

In many ways, the growing concern for wildlife conservation has been better expressed at the local level, although some authorities have seen it more in terms of a further constraint upon their activities, than as an opportunity for positive action. Even so, more planning authorities are now seeking advice from conservationists and ecologists on a widening range of issues such as the ecological implications of particular developments; the management of

Sites of Special Scientific Interest; the setting up and running of local nature reserves and country parks; and on environmental education.[14] Many local education authorities have established field centres. Most counties have now established countryside committees to decide, or advise county councils, upon rural matters. Some counties, and so far one Development Corporation, now employ ecologists as research, conservation or interpretive officers.

A recent development at local level, and in many ways the most positive for rural planning, is the involvement of ecologists and conservationists in the process of plan-making itself. Officers of the Nature Conservancy were part of joint planning teams in East Hampshire, and in subsequent experimental resource planning studies of this kind in Sherwood Forest and the North Pennines.[15] They have also been involved, though less directly, in other scales of planning — in regional and sub-regional studies, and in the preparation of structure plans.

All these changes have meant increasing pressure for ecologists and conservationists to be actively and practically concerned with environmental change outside nature reserves. Moreover, the demand now is not only for a much wider geographical coverage of skills and interest, but for more emphasis upon creativity and compromise rather than rigorous ecological analysis alone. These changes, together with a parallel concern for the efficiency of government-sponsored research[16] have been in part responsible for the reconstitution of the Nature Conservancy, which became the Nature Conservancy Council in 1973 with a wider advisory mandate. The former tasks have been separated: reserve management and conservation advice are now functions of the new Council while scientific and fundamental research remains a role for the Natural Environment Research Council in its new Institute of Terrestrial Ecology.[17]

The Needs of Wildlife Conservation

The practical value of reorganisation is as yet unproven, but in theory the new structure seems to reflect the changing directions of environmental change and attitudes. The new organisations involved and the way in which wildlife conservation activity and research is developing suggest a closer adjustment to the contemporary requirements of practical conservation which were discussed in the last chapter. Britain now has a larger and more representative estate of National Nature Reserves than ever before and a growing number of local ones (see Figure 2). We have a state organisation and local bodies (both public and voluntary) whose concern is rightly wider than this, with increasing interest in the processes and planning of change over the whole countryside. A more informed public should help to ensure that the conservation case can be argued with more foresight, urgency and success than in the past.

Yet problems remain for the conservation of wildlife. They seem to lie not so much in our failure to protect the best or the most rare, as in our failure adequately to predict or alleviate the ecological consequences of unique, major developments, and, more important still, in our unwitting acceptance of the gradual erosion of wildlife values.

It is true that, over the last decade, greater attention has been paid to assessing the potential ecological damage that may result from major developments. The advance research work, if not always the final response, on decisions about the third London airport or the Morecambe Bay Barrage recognised far more of the conservation claims than was the case in

Upper Teesdale or after Torrey Canyon. But more could be done in preparing for decisions and in mitigating the effects of development. Environmental Impact Statements are required for all projects considered by the World Bank and they are prepared in advance of all major developments in a number of countries, notably the United States. They are equally appropriate and necessary here, however speedily certain developments — the exploitation of North Sea Oil for example — must take place.[18]

The threat of sudden and well-publicised developments can produce much that is of local ecological benefit in research and conservation effort. But this does not apply over most of the countryside where wildlife values may be gradually altered in less obvious ways. These are the values which derive from the smaller scale, ubiquitous components of the rural environment which make up its overall diversity, rather than those which attach to the finest or largest or unique habitats and species.

In some areas, these micro habitats: hedgerows and walls; copses and individual trees, scrub and other patches of uncultivated land, small watercourses, ponds, disused canals and other wetlands; road verges and railway embankments, have already been lost. In others, their interference with productive and efficient land management imposes sufficient costs upon other resource interests for their continued existence to be threatened except where conservation groups have fought for change — as local naturalists' trusts have succeeded in modifying the verge management practices of some highway authorities. Some areas have been acquired by local conservation groups and are managed as nature reserve islands in a hostile sea. But most are too numerous, too small and too scattered to be protected by designation as reserves, nor would they necessarily qualify for this kind of protection for they do not often rate highly on the criteria of richness, naturalness and rarity which may be applied to the selection of reserves.

The Hedgerow Example

For many reasons including rising land and labour costs, and the requirements of modern machinery and methods of crop protection, farmers have been removing the hedges on their land, especially those which serve no useful purpose as boundaries to management or ownership.[19] In uncertain times, fixed internal barriers deny farmers the flexibility they need to alter their patterns of cropping and pasturage. In predominantly arable areas, and increasingly where grazing is intensively managed, there is little or no agricultural justification for retaining hedges. They take up valuable land space, and absorb scarce time and money on maintenance. Even their usefulness in preventing wind erosion is now questioned.[20]

But the wildlife values of hedgerows are unique for they are rich and varied habitats in themselves, and provide extensive links between different ecological environments.[21] As more habitats are destroyed and modified by modern land practices, the wildlife values of hedges that remain are increased, particularly where they are older and more diverse. But these values are dependent upon satisfactory management and not just a token retention of stumps damaged by cutting, burning or chemicals, which contribute neither aesthetic nor ecological interest. Moreover, the values of lost hedgerows cannot necessarily be replaced by retaining or creating new cover — in the form of tree clumps — arranged in a continuous, if more convenient, way.

In the case of most hedgerows and individual trees, where there are hardly any reciprocal benefits for farming, the possibilities for compromise and for resolving conflicts in a way that would allow their dependent wildlife to be conserved seem few. Although the hedgerow example may present the extremes of view, the nature of the conflicts is similar for many other micro habitats which no longer serve a useful land management purpose but which are still crucial for the maintenance of overall ecological diversity and the long term conservation of wildlife.

Policies

Drawing upon his experience with pesticides, Moore ,as argued that the best value for money in wildlife conservation will be derived in two main ways:

"1. Acquiring nature reserves representing as wide a range of habitats as possible;
2. Supporting general conservation measures outside nature reserves *which coincide with other interests* (our italics).
... effort should not be wasted on sites and situations where conservation opposes other activities which have greater public support"[22]

For the mid-sixties, the heyday of discussion between rival countryside interests, this seems a somewhat pessimistic view. In the mid-seventies, with increased pressure for self-sufficiency in most rural products and entrenchment of sectional interests, the notion is totally realistic. Indeed, the case for economically productive and intensively used land may now be so strongly argued that Moore's twin policies seem almost too demanding. The acquisition of new reserves will not be easy and the hedgerow example illustrates some of the apparently intractible conflicts that exist between the aims of wildlife conservation and those of other rural resource systems.

In 1947, when the Nature Conservancy was established, the creation of reserves — 'key areas' of conservation interest — was seen as the basic mechanism by which British conservation policies were to be achieved. It has remained a fundamental goal at national level, reiterated in the most recent review of sites of conservation interest.[23] Inevitably, as ecological research and knowledge increase, and as the pressures upon natural and semi-natural areas intensify, more sites are considered eligible for protection, either as National Nature Reserves or as Sites of Special Scientific Interest. Yet nature reserves still occupy only 0.6 per cent of Britain.[24]

It has already been argued that for many habitats and species, reserves alone will not secure their protection, for the reserves would need to be impossibly large or numerous to provide sufficient buffer against the damaging effects of external change. Moreover, any large-scale, single purpose zoning of land in this way runs counter to arguments for the multiple interest in rural resources to be realised. Moreover, it would not only be undesirable, but unrealistic to think in terms of National Nature Reserve status for areas such as the Broads or the New Forest or large parts of some National Parks which, as whole units, have a unique wildlife value.

It may also be unrealistic, at times of high land prices and interest rates, and consequently greater concern for realising the full economic potential of land and equipment, to suppose that any substantial increase in the number or extent of National Nature Reserves is possible. The Nature Conservancy Council already find land owners less willing to enter into management agreements for reserves or on Sites of Special Scientific Interest.[25]

What then is the scope for implementing an effective wildlife conservation policy?

It is tempting to argue that the tide of opinion will change: that agricultural productivity will begin to tail off and even decline; that economic and social conditions will dictate extensive rather than intensive systems of land management which would allow the less productive and more ecologically valuable areas to flourish again; that public opinion, for these and other reasons, will demand that nature conservation aims be given high priority. But although these may be options, they are for the long term. The evidence of the last decade is that habitats and species, on a world scale, face the possibility of extinction at an escalating rate, and one many times greater than would be the case outside the influence of man. For some species, captive breeding provides the only hope for their survival.[26] For the rest of our rural wildlife a failsafe conservation policy is needed now, even if it proves to be only a holding operation.

Some assessment must be made of the real priorities for wildlife conservation. The pace and nature of present rural change suggest that conservation is most urgently needed in two main kinds of area *outside* designated reserves. First, there are those areas where wildlife and their habitats are already so severely depleted that measures are required not only to safeguard the last vestiges of the wildlife stock, but primarily to create new habitats and linkages to other, richer ecological zones; such is the case in the intensively farmed areas of eastern and southern England. Secondly, there are those areas in which substantial future change may be anticipated in resource management practices and where the main task will be to safeguard and repair existing habitats, and perhaps also to create some new ones. Significant here are the pastoral lands of the west, and those marginal farming areas which must respond to changes in national and international economic and social policies.[27]

Within both these general areas, there must be some ranking of conservation effort among the many valuable features, just as the habitats and species of National Nature Reserves have themselves been singled out for special protection. It is likely that the same major criteria will apply: ecological diversity (which often, but not always, implies greater age); rarity; and vulnerability to change. 'Naturalness', if it remains at all, may also be important, but perhaps greater attention than so far ought to be devoted to protecting and enhancing the ecological interest of recently man-made and local landscapes such as arable farmland and areas of substantial dereliction. These, after all, cover a great deal of the countryside and because they are often close to where many people live they may offer as much, if not more, scope for developing the recreational, educational and interpretive aims of wildlife conservation.

Moore suggests it would be sensible — as well as expedient — to concentrate on the possibilities of protecting and creating ecological features which interfere least with the aims and practices of other resource interests. Taking the hedgerow example further, this would suggest that the protection of boundary hedges, which are often the oldest on any holding, should be given priority in some areas.[28] There are other examples of modifications of practice which might be introduced with little or no loss of economic efficiency but considerable ecological benefit, such as the retiming of pesticide and herbicide spraying operations — on farmland, road verges and waterways — to avoid critical stages in the life cycle of particular species.

Yet there may still be some elements of the rural environment whose retention or creation are vital for the wider purposes of wildlife conservation although such measures would be opposed by other rural interests. There will also be certain practices, like field drainage or stubble burning, and activities in mining or in water management which are particularly damaging to wildlife in certain areas but upon which no compromise is possible.

Appeasement of traditionally stronger resource interests is not enough. Special measures of persuasion, and indeed compulsion, are required.[29] We may need more money and more legal powers, although progress could also be made by a more positive use of existing ones: local authorities could, for example, acquire and designate a larger number of Local Nature Reserves where the multiple values of wildlife conservation might be realised. All the measures are more likely to succeed if conservation policies are seen to be selective, and recognise the costs of adaptations in management.

Strategies

Priorities could be spelled out in local and regional conservation strategies which would contribute to the process of structure and local planning.[30] Much basic work for the preparation of these plans has already been done: in, for example, the habitat evaluation studies of the Nature Conservancy and its successor. But conservation plans would offer more than this. They would not simply state ecological values, as some recent rural plans have done, but give a scale of conservation priorities; identify present threats and forecast future ones; and suggest various mechanisms of dealing with these. They would, moreover, suggest and cost alternative ways of making good the wildlife complement in some areas. Westmacott and Worthington,[31] and Hooper,[32] among others, have devised schemes of this kind for planting and wildlife management but their direct and indirect costs have not been assessed. National Nature Reserves, as areas of vital and probably assured protection would be a part of these plans, but only a part, and their role too might be reviewed, so that greater use, for education or for more general public access, could be made of some.

Strategies of this kind, covering all the countryside and which express the requirements of wildlife conservation in a way that is more consistent and more comparable with those of other rural resource interests, would allow the implications of rural change (of whatever scale or kind) to be more easily and more rapidly understood. By being part of a coherent programme, arguments for wildlife conservation, in situations of dispute among interest groups may, in this way, be strengthened rather than rejected as examples of alarmist and piecemeal local resistance. The task of statutory planners would be simplified; the possibilities for viable co-operation between planners and conservationists would be increased — and not just in the few areas so far covered by resource plans.[33] It is no longer sufficient for wildlife conservationists and ecologists to retreat to their reserves, nor to evaluate what exists elsewhere and bemoan the mistakes of environmental decisions. They must be involved in devising and implementing solutions to their problems. Their role in the planning process for rural areas must increase for they have a part to play not only in practical analysis and policy-making on resource problems, but also in a contribution from the philosophy and methods of ecology.

Futures

As part of all these tasks, there is a continuing need for monitoring the ecological effects of rural change, and more important, for some structured forecasting of the ways in which future change could affect wildlife and conservation values. Only the extremes of alternative futures are now presented — of a world in which Nature will, after all, take care of herself or one which, inevitably, will suffer social, economic and environmental collapse.

The protagonists of both viewpoints look to the longer term rather than the immediate future and both are concerned more with the dramatic results of technological change — with new pollutants, new forms of transport, more horrific weapons — than with the more insidious and perhaps, collectively, as damaging consequences of developments in present resource use.

Public acceptance and enthusiasm for conservation has increased since 1965, but Moore may still be right in identifying the crucial problem as one of confused and generally apathetic attitudes:

"... Conservation is thought of as a negative activity concerned with protecting the past, rather than a positive one concerned with providing for the future.

... Conservationists have failed to put over an acceptable philosophy and rationale of conservation that is meaningful in the modern context."[34]

More recently, Tinker has argued that conservationists have unwisely failed to make conservation a political issue, and in so doing have denied their cause the most powerful means of public debate and action.[35] There is little point in believing that wildlife conservation is something so basic and so morally worthwhile that all politicians will inevitably include it in their programmes: it can only be one among many claims upon their resources and interest. What conservationists must do, like some other rural interest groups have very successfully done, is to argue and justify their case in the most effective way. But to do this with credibility they may need to modify their own attitudes. More money is undoubtedly needed, nationally and locally; legislation may need to be improved; and we have implied a need for some further modification of the policies and attitudes of agencies such as the Nature Conservancy Council. Above all, a convincing rationale for conservation must be argued; unless many conservationists *in practice* appear less élitist, less isolationist and less negative, the immediate prospects for protecting and enhancing wildlife over large areas of rural Britain are slim.

Notes and References

1. Ratcliffe, D. A. (1976) Thoughts Towards a Philosophy of Nature Conservation; *Biological Conservation*, Vol. 9, pp. 45-53. Helliwell has tried to quantify some of the qualities of wildlife and assign money values to them see:
     Helliwell, D. (1969) The Valuation of Wildlife Resources; *Regional Studies*, Vol. 3, No. 1, pp. 41-7, Pergamon.
     See also a criticism by:
     Hooper, M. (1970) *Regional Studies*, Vol. 4, No. 1, pp. 127-8, Pergamon.
2. The Royal Society for the Protection of Birds was founded in 1889; the Botanical Society of the British Isles was established (as the Botanical Society of London) in 1836.
3. Two government White Papers — *Conservation of Nature in England and Wales* (Cmnd 7122), and a Scottish equivalent (Cmnd 7235) — both published in 1947 — preceded the foundation of the Nature Conservancy which was given added powers in the *National Parks and Access to the Countryside Act* of 1949 and a Royal Charter in the same year. The Conservancy became part of the Natural Environment Research Council in 1965 and acquired some new powers under the Countryside Act, 1968. Subsequent changes are discussed later in this chapter.
4. See, for example, annual reports of the Nature Conservancy, also:
     Nature Conservancy (1970) *Twenty-one years of Conservation.*
     Kelcey, J. (1973) A Guide to Nature Conservation — Official Organisations, *Built Environment*, November.
     Blackmore, M. (1974) The Nature Conservancy: It's History and Role, in Warren, A. and Goldsmith, F. B. (eds.), *Conservation in Practice*, Wiley.

5. The concept of 'key area' protection through designation as a National Nature Reserve and subsequent control over management is discussed in detail in the White Paper *Conservation of Nature* (Cmnd 7122) and more recently in:

   Nature Conservancy Council, *A Nature Conservation Review*, (To be published, with the Natural Environment Research Council).

   Less important but still valuable sites for conservation have been scheduled as Sites of Special Scientific Interest. Local planning authorities, land owners and managers are notified of these sites; the Conservancy (and its successor the Nature Conservancy Council) must be consulted before permission is given for any development. But this does not include many changes of use in farming or forestry which lie outside planning control, and the Conservancy have powers to control the management of special sites only where a management agreement can be negotiated with an owner under the Countryside Act, 1968. By November 1974, there were 137 National Nature Reserves covering almost 300,000 acres; and 3500 sites of Special Scientific Interest had been notified to local planning authorities.

6. See, for example:

   Duffey, E. (ed.), (1967) *The Biotic Effects of Public Pressures on the Environment*, Proceedings of a Nature Conservancy Symposium, Monks Wood, No. 3.

   Way, J. M. (ed.), (1969) *Road Verges; their Function and Management*, Proceedings of a Nature Conservancy Symposium, Monks Wood. No. 3.

   Hooper, M. D. and Holdgate, M. W. (eds.), (1969) *Hedges and Hedgerow Trees*, Proceedings of Nature Conservancy Symposium, Monks Wood, No. 4.

7. Gregory, R. (1971) *The Price of Amenity: Five Studies in Conservation and Government*, Macmillan, Chapter 4.

8. Nature Conservancy *et al.* (1965) *Report on Broadland.*

9. Nature Conservancy Council (1974) *Statement of Policies*, H.M.S.O., November.

10. *Conservation of Nature in England and Wales* (Cmnd 7122), op. cit.

11. Examples of co-ordinating agencies are: the Society for the Promotion of Nature Reserves, and the Committee for Environmental Conservation, see:

    Kelcey, J. (1973, 1974) A Guide to Nature Conservation – Voluntary Organisations, *Built Environment*, November and January.

12. Steele, R. C. (ed.), (1972) *Lowland Forestry and Wildlife Conservation*, Proceedings of a Nature Conservancy Symposium, Monks Wood.

13. Under Section 22 of the 1973 Water Act, all Regional Water Authorities must have regard to the desirability of conserving wildlife and amenity and take into account the effects of their proposals on these. The Nature Conservancy Council must notify Regional Water Authorities of areas of conservation interest in the ownership or control of the Authorities.

14. Mercer, D. (1974) The Role of Local Government in Rural Conservation, in Warren, A. and Goldsmith, F. B. (eds.), *Conservation in Practice*, Wiley.

15. See Chapter 11.

16. Rothschild, N. (1971) *A Framework for Government Research and Development*, H.M.S.O., Cmd, 4814.

17. The Nature Conservancy Council was established under a special Act in 1973 as an independent statutory body with members appointed by the Secretary of State for the Environment. Its functions are:

    (i)   the establishment, maintenance and management of nature reserves . . . in Great Britain;
    (ii) the provision of advice for the Secretary of State or any other Minister on the development and implementation of policies for or affecting nature conservation in Great Britain;
    (iii) the provision of advice and dissemination of knowledge about nature conservation;
    (iv) the commissioning or support . . . of research which in the opinion of the Council is relevant to the matters mentioned above.

    The Institute of Terrestrial Ecology will be concerned with independent research on ecological change as a basis for management, but will also provide a research service when commissioned by the Council.

18. The Department of Environment have commissioned consultants to review current practice in the measurement of the environmental impact of large scale projects, assess the relevance for Britain and the need for any standardisation of procedures.

19. A national annual loss of hedgerows of rather less than 1% of the total has been agreed between the Nature Conservancy and the Ministry of Agriculture (quoted in Hooper, M. D. and Holdgate, M. W. (eds.), (1969) *Hedges and Hedgerow Trees*, op. cit.). But the rates of removal vary widely between regions and individual farms; see, for example, the findings of Westmacott and Worthington given in Tables 18 and 19 in Chapter 7 of this book.

20. The agricultural disadvantages of hedges are discussed in:

Westmacott, R. and Worthington, T. (1974) *New Agricultural Landscapes*, Countryside Commission.

Pollard, E., Hooper, M. D. and Moore, N. W. (1974) *Hedges*, Collins, Part IV.

Caborn, J. M. (1971) The Agronomic and Biological Significance of Hedgerows, *Outlook on Agriculture*, Vol. 6 (6).

21. See Pollard, E. *et al.* (1974) op. cit. Parts II and III.

22. Moore, N. W. (1968/9) Experience with Pesticides and the Theory of Conservation, *Biological Conservation*, Vol. I, p. 201.

Moore himself reveals that success in controlling persistent organochlorine pesticides came about only because there were other reasons for their suspension.

23. Begun in 1965 and to be reported in Nature Conservancy Council *A Nature Conservation Review*, 1976. This review has graded conservation sites into 7 main ecosystem groups (coasts; woodlands; lowland grasslands, heaths and scrub; open waters; peatlands; uplands and artificial) on a 6-point scale in which grades 1 and 2 are seen as actual, or potential National Nature Reserves and 3 and 4 as Sites of Special Scientific Interest. Grades 5 and 6 cover the remaining areas of little or no conservation interest. The review thus looks primarily at sites with potential for some designation; it does not consider other means of implementing policies for wildlife conservation.

24. Nature Conservancy Council figure, including National Nature Reserves and Local Nature Reserves, as at October 1975.

25. See Chapter 12 which discusses management agreements.

26. But it is not solely for exotic foreign species; captive breeding may provide the only means of retaining British populations of species such as the red squirrel and the otter.

27. See Chapter 8 on the Urban Fringe and Chapters 9 and 10 on the Uplands.

28. Pollard, E., Hooper, M. D. and Moore, N. W. (1974) *Hedges*, Collins.

Westmacott, R. and Worthington, T. (1974) *New Agricultural Landscapes*, Countryside Commission.

29. Chapter 12 discusses the use of various mechanisms for influencing such activities.

30. See Chapter 11 on rural plans.

31. Westmacott, R. and Worthington, T. (1974) *New Agricultural Landscapes*, Countryside Commission.

32. Max Hooper (personal communication) suggests that plantations at intervals in arable land could partly compensate for the loss of hedgerow cover. The plantations could be zoned for use as wildlife reserves, educational reserves and recreation areas, with these uses periodically rotated within the woodland.

33. Resource planning studies which integrated the preparation of wildlife conservation policies with other areas of rural policy-making have taken place in East Hampshire, Sherwood Forest and the Northern Pennines and are discussed in Chapter 11.

34. Moore, N. W. (1968/9) *Experience with Pesticides and the Theory of Conservation*, op. cit.

35. Tinker, J. (1973) Conservation – End of the Love Affair, *New Scientist*, Vol. 60 (876).

CHAPTER 7

The Changing Landscape

For many people the outward appearance of the countryside is the single most obvious and most valued component of its fabric. Changes in the landscape are generally more dramatic and more widely recognised than the fundamental economic, social and ecological changes they may reflect or conceal. It is not surprising, therefore, that much of the present debate about environmental conservation centres upon a concern for the protection of landscape resources. Indeed, landscape issues have figured strongly in a number of recent battles over proposed developments in rural areas: at the Swincombe reservoir site in Dartmoor; on the A66 route improvement in the Lake District; copper mining in Snowdonia; and the one-time proposed third London Airport. Yet, despite the firmness of stands adopted in these individual cases, it is still difficult to define the nature of attitudes towards landscape, and to isolate the general principles on which conservation action is or should be based.

This is partly because landscape commands such an intensely personal allegiance, which is influenced by familiarity and mood, and is strongly resistant to change. Moreover, landscape qualities, in contrast to those of most other rural resources, demand no special understanding to be appreciated. For all these reasons, it is difficult to identify what it is about landscapes that people value and, more especially, how they differ in their taste.[1] Some landscapes appear intrinsically more valuable than others, and this has been the basis for landscape conservation policies in Britain. But, it is increasingly clear that the *same* landscape will be appreciated in many different ways by different groups, depending not only upon their experience and frame of mind, but upon the particular use they make of it.

For any tract of countryside, the values placed upon its landscape may be expected to differ between, for example, those who come simply to look at it (in different ways and for a variety of reasons); those who visit for some specific activity such as climbing or sailing, and those for whom it is their living or working environment. Those who do not visit the countryside frequently, or who may never have done so, will place other values upon it. All these groups will react differently to landscape change; all have very different criteria of evaluation: diversity perhaps, or rarity, or accessibility; qualities of wilderness or naturalness and contrast to the urban environment; the presence of literary, historic, artistic associations; the appearance and existence of functional efficiency whether as a farmed landscape, or, for example, as one which it is challenging (or easy) to climb, or sail, or pursue some other recreation activity. In all, there are likely to be many other and more conflicting criteria than would be used in the valuation of agricultural land or water catchments or even wildlife habitats. Moreover, taste in landscape is also subject, albeit in a less obvious way than other areas of aesthetic pleasure, to the whims of fashion. Despite the complexity of viewpoints, current attitudes are most often seen to be sharply divided between those who want to protect the best of traditional scenes (which are now no longer functional) and those who see beauty only in landscapes which are efficient. But this polarisation of view may well oversimplify the real diversity of attitudes to landscape which may be only indirectly expressed.

It would clearly be difficult, on the basis of these arguments, to arrive at a consensus view of landscape quality — either for the present, or one that is durable over time. How then can we judge the importance of landscape change, assess the degree to which modifications are acceptable or must be checked, and decide upon priorities for conservation?

In practice, only some of those groups with an interest in landscape have been able to influence the way in which particular parts of the countryside have developed. Representatives of amenity pressure groups — the protagonists of protection — are amongst the most vociferous. But it is the landowners who, in practice, largely control the appearance of the countryside, especially those private owners of farm land and forest who hold 87 per cent of the rural environment, and who are substantially free from restrictions upon their operations, almost all of which have some landscape implications. Apart from those who, like their eighteenth and nineteenth century counterparts, have consciously sought to maintain or create a particular landscape along with the other goals of their enterprise, the landscape is entirely a by-product of their actions. Yet they are not insensitive to its appearance; the evidence shows that they appreciate, above all, its expression of functional efficiency.[2] Implicit in the post-war legislation which established the official machinery for landscape 'conservation' in Britain, was the notion that if the major land activities were pursued efficiently, then a pleasant (certainly an unchanging) landscape would result. Special measures, over and above general restrictions on building development, were needed only in what were assumed to be the best, and the most vulnerable scenic areas. So the National Parks and Areas of Outstanding Natural Beauty were established, not on grounds of rarity, nor accessibility to potential visitors, nor the diversity of their landscapes, but on variable and essentially subjective aesthetic criteria which relied heavily upon the personal views of a few people.

Post-war landscape policies

There is nothing very wrong about being subjective. The people of Britain have reason enough to be grateful to the post-war legislators whose policies — though they came late compared with many western countries — have safeguarded extensive tracts of the finest upland and lowland scenery in England and Wales (Fig. 3). The operation of stringent controls over development in National Parks and Areas of Outstanding Natural Beauty, together with some positive landscape measures like tree-planting and eyesore clearance, have allowed some 9 per cent of the landscape of England and Wales to remain, in many ways, unaltered.[3] The areas in which Green Belt policies apply have suffered rather more visual change since the war; even so, much landscape on the edge of towns has been protected by rigid controls over building development. Since 1950, individual counties have operated firmer control policies in 'Great Landscape Value' areas which were considered to be of important sub-regional value and shown on development plans.[4] Since 1967, more effort has been devoted to conservation of the urban fabric of rural towns and villages;[5] the protection of monuments of architectural value in the countryside is now better secured.[6]

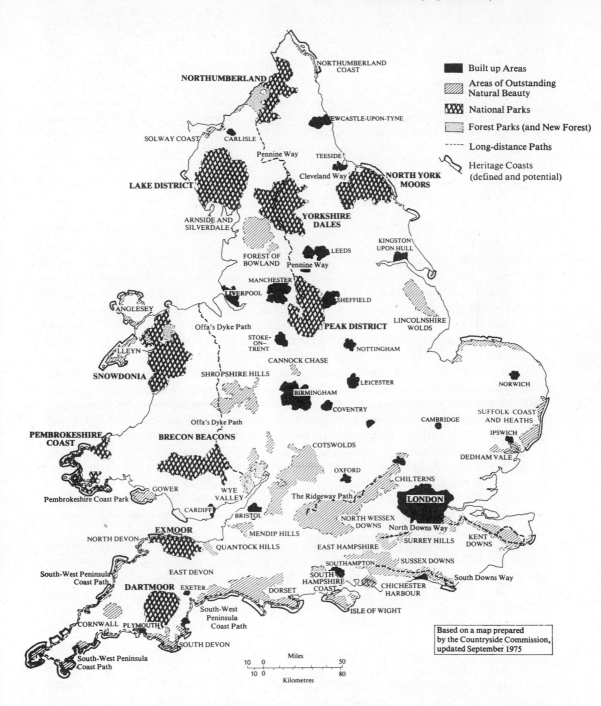

FIG. 3. *Some Protected Areas in England and Wales.*

Add to these measures the work of other public and non-public amenity agencies, like the Ancient Monuments and Historic Buildings Directorate of the Department of Environment; the National Trust; the Crown Estates Commissioners and others, in acquiring and managing land, and a formidable array of policies for landscape protection emerges. The armoury has

TABLE 17

Some Protected Areas in England and Wales[a]

	ml^2	Km^2	% of land area
National Parks[b]	5,258	13,622	9.0
Areas of Outstanding Natural Beauty[b]	5,588	14,473	9.6
National Nature Reserves	136	351	0.3
Green Belts[c]	2,100	5,440	3.6
Proposed Green Belts[c]	3,500	9,067	6.0
	(ml)	(Km)	
Proposed Heritage Coast	729	1,174	

[a] Figures to nearest ml^2 and km^2.
[b] Figures for 1973.
[c] Source: Department of Environment, May 1974.

Source: Countryside Commission (1975), *Digest of Countryside Recreation Statistics.*

now been strengthened by the introduction of measures for the conservation of the undeveloped coast.[7]

In most of the areas covered by some special landscape designation or ownership, the characteristic scenery has been well preserved. In most, the opportunities for this to be enjoyed by many people have grown. There have been unforeseen and undesirable consequences; for example, development of all kinds, often poor in quality, has occurred on the edge of National Parks and Areas of Outstanding Natural Beauty generating extra traffic, trespass and other problems. It can be argued that the landscape advantages within these designated areas have been secured partly at the expense of deterioration outside.[8] Nor have all the groups within them benefited: farmers are notable dissenters from the National Park concept.

But, in all, the experience of the last 25 years is not that we have necessarily failed to protect the best (although there are problems here) but that we may have been too little concerned with the rest. The social and economic changes that have taken place since 1949 dictate some review of the effectiveness of landscape policies and more especially the aims on which they are founded.

Changing needs and attitudes

There seem to be two main reasons for conserving landscapes: to look at and otherwise enjoy them now and in the future; and to retain the body of knowledge which landscapes offer for research and teaching about biological and physical change, and cultural history. The range of present taste, and the volatility of aesthetic judgements over time, suggest that *diversity* ought to be the major criterion on which particular landscapes are singled out for special protection. A secondary factor might be the 'usefulness' of certain landscapes in fulfilling the needs of particular leisure activities: for scenic driving or hiking or skiing or any other pursuit which is dependent upon certain special landscape characteristics, such as abundant shelter, quick-changing views or ruggedness. On this argument, it is clear that landscapes might be protected, indeed some might be created, which are valued for their associations: of wilderness or history rather than for their visual appeal alone.

Despite the difficulties of agreeing upon the values of different landscapes, it is likely that National Parks and some other designated areas would be ranked highly by many sections of the population. These areas contain, albeit in different assemblages, those landscape elements — including strong relative relief, greenness (especially from trees), and water — which appear to be widely appreciated. It is probably right that parts of these areas should be taken into public ownership and management[9] for they are nationally used and valued, and they are worthwhile components of national pride and identity. Present rural change in these areas and the prospect of further pressure upon their resources has led to a reconsideration of their purpose and functions in the report of the National Park Policies Review Committee;[10] the conservation of their landscape has been emphasised as a primary goal in their future planning and management. In all, the National Parks face many internal problems, but their future seems assured. Less certain are the fortunes of other landscapes, especially those which lie outside designated areas, where there has been a less searching analysis of change and where far less effort has been expended on minimising or concealing its impact. If the diversity of the British scene is to be conserved, and in such a way that more people than hitherto can benefit from this conservation action, the balance of effort must be shifted to other landscapes: the most accessible, the most vulnerable, the rare and declining, and the degraded. Four broad landscape types urgently need more attention:

> the urban fringe;
> upland landscapes;
> parkland and other specialised local landscapes;
> lowland agricultural areas — the most productive farming land.

The Urban Fringe

The many problems of this environment, almost all of which carry landscape implications, are discussed in detail in Chapter 8. It is argued there that the edge of most large towns and cities in Britain provides some of the worst examples of visual decay: a no man's land of low density, frequently unimaginative residential development interspersed with the other ugly accoutrements of urban living. Alongside the built up area run open spaces of playing fields and graveyards, farmland, woods and reservoirs; but not all of these are visually pleasing, nor are they generally accessible. In many areas, Green Belt policies have failed as effective tools for landscape conservation; they have placed an assemblage of disparate land uses in an environmental strait-jacket which limits their functional and visual improvement.

But that there should be accessible greenness and scenic diversity on the edge of towns is a desirable aim. Chapter 8 suggests some of the ways in which the broader objectives of green belt policy might be retained although the methods of achieving them must be more sophisticated, more selective and much more creative.

Upland Landscapes

Inside and outside of the National Parks, the uplands offer some of the finest landscape in Britain. Rugged scenery and extensive areas of natural and semi-natural vegetation blends with a unique cultural landscape which is dominated by the practices and buildings of upland farming. Yet here, too, economic uncertainties, the pressure to produce more food and fibre and other raw materials, to increase water supplies and improve communications, bring radical landscape changes which existing conservation measures can neither inhibit nor often modify. Chapters 9 and 10 discuss more fully the nature of these changes, the limitations of piecemeal resource planning and the need for a more integrated approach to upland management.

Local Landscapes

Parkland

Most of the parkland of this country is in private hands: a great deal is well-tended; increasingly so as estates' owners realise the financial benefits to be gained from protecting their amenity assets for public view. But only a few landowners are highly successful here: of the smaller country houses, which still contribute valuable landscapes and have notable collections, very few attracted more than 15,000 visitors in 1972, while, for example, Beaulieu, Blenheim, Longleat (and most certainly Woburn) attracted at least 100,000.[11] Many houses have too few visitors to recoup their outgoings. The parts of these estates which yield little or no return from the traditional activities of agriculture and forestry may be very vulnerable to physical and fiscal pressures.[12] They may be put to more profitable uses within the estate which destroy their landscape; their character and viability may be lost by fragmentation; they may simply decay through lack of management. Since 1945, some 340 notable country houses have been demolished.[13]

One salvation may be the diversification of entire estates, such as is taking place at Beaulieu, Woburn or Goodwood, with the grafting on of new linked uses — field sports, informal recreation, education — which individually may be profitable or unprofitable but which together ensure a diverse and viable enterprise. New uses may be found for limited parts of an estate which may ensure the conservation of traditional buildings and landscapes. In many ways, eighteenth-century parkland is an ideal country park environment, and this too may provide the most valuable new function for the less profitable parts of large estates in the long term. A considerable number of the official country parks so far grant aided under the Countryside Act have been established in parklands, privately owned, or bought and managed by local authorities. Elsewhere, country houses and their grounds have been taken over by institutions of various kinds, to be developed as sanatoria, schools, or research establishments, and these changes may also offer some insurance against landscape decay. The National Trust has played a major role in the conservation of gardens and landscape parks although these were often acquired incidentally to historic houses. Since 1949, the Trust has acquired parks and gardens even where they have been associated with buildings of no particular historic or architectural merit.

There are many more, often small, estates whose contribution to the landscape is significant yet for whom none of these solutions may be immediately appropriate. As the economic climate becomes harsher, more of these estates will be threatened and financial help from the Historic Buildings Council and the Land Fund is unlikely to suffice. If some of these parkland landscapes are to survive, then some means of ensuring positive amenity management must be introduced while new uses are sought. In some cases, management agreements between owners and public agencies may be possible, to safeguard scenic and wildlife values. Perhaps some parklands could be taken into public ownership as local nature reserves or, as in National Parks, under access powers or, if they can be negotiated, new powers for landscape conservation. There are many other local landscapes, like parts of Northumberland, Lakeland and Wessex, which are valued, not only for their intrinsic beauty, but also for their historical, literary or artistic associations. Some areas so valued may have no special visual merit; some, like the remnants of old field systems, may be highly localised, and the case for their permanent protection has been weaker. Many once characteristic landscapes of lowland Britain — chalk downland and the sandy heathlands — are already so fragmented they have become little more than local variations in the agricultural scene. Those areas which lie outside nature reserves will become further fragmented until their viability is lost. The integrity of those that are protected will become more difficult to sustain.[14] Yet all these components are part of the total concept and enjoyment of landscape: failure to recognise and safeguard them only reduces the diversity of environmental interest.

Wilderness

Wilderness is not a British concept; it hardly exists in this country. We have almost no primeval landscapes which have survived human interference; nor is there, as in America, any strong national movement for the retention of untouched ecosystems to which access is severely restricted, and in which almost no concessions, for safety or service, are made to those who visit them.[15] But we do have a brand of all this, in fast-disappearing *remoteness*. Like a sense of history, remoteness is another attribute of landscape although it may carry no peculiarly visual connotations. Relative inaccessibility and low levels of use would seem to be crucial elements of definition,[16] but remoteness may encompass a variety of scenic types which are not necessarily considered beautiful.[17] The whole idea is an arena for rather academic geographical speculation and occasionally, as at Swincombe,[18] for political argument. But the protagonists and beneficiaries, the consumers of remoteness are even less well defined than are those of good landscape — indeed the whole notion of remoteness may be better enjoyed at home. Remoteness is certainly very vulnerable; yet its retention is no one's responsibility.

Definition is difficult; it is even harder to see what policies might be advocated for remote areas. Designation alone is unlikely to work unless this carries with it positive measures to reduce accessibility and the intensification of incompatible activities. It may, moreover, increase the popularity of these areas so that they cease to feel remote. But there can be no rigid exclusion of all economic use: we cannot in present circumstances afford to waste land in this way; more importantly the landscape of these areas would suffer. An unmanaged landscape is probably not what remoteness-seekers have in mind; rather do they want freedom from crowds, from noise and from the obvious signs of human interference. Clearly, all forms of building development would be out of place, afforestation, and any other dramatic change in farm or forest management would need to be controlled; there would be little positive provision for recreation, apart perhaps from wardening and a rescue service. There may ultimately be a need to limit visitor numbers in some way. At the present time, parts of north and west Scotland and smaller areas in upland England and Wales (including the 'heartlands' of some National Parks, discussed in Chapter 10) could fulfil all or most of these requirements of remoteness. The fluctuating fortunes of hill farming may periodically enlarge the area of low economic activity in such marginal zones throughout Europe. But it is unlikely that national economic circumstances will allow extensive tracts of land to remain permanently unprospected or unexploited. The argument is not so much for a new planning concept, a new land zonation (as Tinker[19] and Ballantine[20] suggest) but for remoteness to figure as a legitimate criterion, among many, in the evaluation of environmental decisions for rural areas.

We *may* develop a fundamentally different economy in which remote areas can survive, but in its absence, either we must argue that a small number of remote areas can be retained, to be infrequently used but still enjoyed (from afar) by a growing number of people, or we must prepare for the 'man-made wild'[21] as an acceptable, and the only feasible substitute for true wilderness. It is, moreover, possible to create the illusion of remoteness, albeit relative rather than absolute, within areas generally more frequented than distant National Parks, by the careful zoning of the more and less gregarious activities. The Dutch, among others, have shown that it is possible, even in popular recreation areas, to retain parts substantially unused, by the exclusion of vehicles and all visitor services; Lucas has applied notions of wilderness zoning in North America.[22] Many more people could benefit from a policy which promotes the viewing rather than the visiting of remote areas – from scenic highways (like the Blue Ridge Parkway) or railways or marshland boardwalks.

Lowland Agricultural Areas

Dramatic scenic change is taking place in many ways: by afforestation, by new water catchment schemes, and by piecemeal extensions of mining activity. More localised change – by no means always detrimental – has followed the incursion of urban developments of many kinds into the countryside and some of these are discussed later in this chapter. But it is changes in farming more than in any other single activity, that are bringing about the most widespread modifications of the rural landscape, within and outside designated landscape protection areas, and especially on the best farmland in the lowlands.

Arable areas

Chapter 2 has already discussed some of the landscape implications of recent technical and economic change in British agriculture. In eastern and southern England, these areas which have experienced the arable revolution of the last three decades, the diversity of the landscape, if not always its quality, has been substantially reduced. There is much circumstantial evidence of visual change – in the further loss of downland sheepwalks, the extension of ploughed land and field size, the removal of hedgerows and small woods. The old regimes of mixed farming with crops and livestock have been replaced by arable systems which introduce more uniformity of colour and texture to the rural scene. Those features of the landscape, like hedges, which no longer function in the new farming system, and those areas of scrub, marsh and water which take up productive space, have been cleared. Some features have been damaged by modern mechanical and chemical practices; others have suffered from neglect. Large and standardised buildings, scattered at convenient farm locations, replace the small groups of weathered barns and farmsteads. Many wild flowers have gone from the hedgerows and verges; there are no poppies in the fields.

There has been little objective evidence on the scale of these changes; but the work of Hooper and others on Huntingdonshire hedges[23] and the case studies of Westmacott and Worthington,[24] provide some facts on the nature and degree of landscape change in different areas. The case studies, in particular, shed some interesting and surprising new light upon past speculation. They suggest, as we may have guessed, that the most significant change in the arable landscape has been in the reduction of cover, especially in hedgerows and hedgerow trees (Table 18). The scale of the changes are compared with those of the

TABLE 18

Changes in Hedges and Hedgerow Trees, 1945-1972

	Sample areas		
	Huntingdonshire (specialised cereal production)	Somerset (dairy farming)	Herefordshire (mixed farming)
Average field size (acres) 1945	19	9	11
Average field size (acres) 1972	45	13	16
Length of hedges removed per acre (feet) since 1945	37	20	19
Length of hedges remaining per acre (feet) in 1972	58	125	197
Number of hedgerow trees per 100 acres, 1947	59	50	49
Number of hedgerow trees per 100 acres, 1972	12	15	40

Source: Westmacott, R. and Worthington, T. (1974) *New Agricultural Landscapes*, op. cit.

Enclosure movement. Westmacott and Worthington argue that the present landscape is not, in all arable areas, inferior to the past. Indeed, the clearance of vegetation may accentuate the pleasing landforms of southern and eastern England. In many respects, it is the wildlife complement of these areas that has been more critically affected by agricultural change. But the visual quality of arable landscapes cannot always survive such radical change and it may be that even more drastic measures will be adopted. Larger and more powerful machines (perhaps remote controlled) could bring massive increases in field size and regularity: Weller suggests that units of 100 hectares (250 acres), rather than the present 20 hectares (50 acres) may become the technical ideal.[25]

Under these circumstances, the case is strong in certain areas for trying to arrest the further clearance of trees and shrubs, and curbing other damaging activities such as field drainage. But such restrictions upon farming practice, if they can be negotiated at all, will apply over a limited area. Over most of the farmed lowlands, greenness and variety will need to be created to compensate for the losses. The new landscape will be essentially different from the old, emphasised not by linear features but by large and small scale patches of woodland; in field corner plantings, new shelter belts and coverts for game. Westmacott and Worthington are confident that this new agricultural landscape can be both functional and satisfying; but much less certain is the political, administrative and financial feasibility of all these measures — issues which are discussed later in this chapter and in Chapter 12.

Pasture lands

It is right that we should aim to protect the remaining semi-natural vegetation of arable areas, and create new landscape elements in more functional and visual harmony with modern farming practice. But it may be that conservationists have become dangerously preoccupied with areas where the major change is now substantially complete, while they are ignoring events which may have far more dramatic consequences for landscapes we have come to regard as permanent. It has been common to assume that the grazing lands of the midlands, the borders and the south west will remain largely unaltered, that the farming systems will continue to reproduce (because it is economically desirable to do so) the verderous chequerboard fields, well treed and well hedged between. The implications of Westmacott and Worthington's findings are that if the conservation of these landscapes is to rest on *laissez-faire* policies, they may very well have disappeared while the remaining East Anglian hedges are being counted.

Substantial dietary change to exclude or even markedly reduce the consumption of meat products is unlikely to occur in the short term, and a revolution in grass farming seems inevitable. Improvements in the conversion efficiency of stock farming will entail a number of new developments. In advanced agricultural countries, the permanent housing of livestock has been a consistent trend. In the longer term, we may see in Britain some of the developments already common in America and growing in Europe: beef rearing units for herds of 100,000; large scale dairy units for 1000 head and over, including winter housing. All this will mean much larger industrial farm buildings, new service roads and — unless the many problems are soon solved — more effluent, noise and smell. Optimists might argue that some lowland areas show a welcome return to a form of mixed farming where measures designed to reduce a variety of farm costs will incidentally yield conservation benefits: for example, the use of short-term grass leys to conserve soil nitrogen and the conversion of waste matter to supplement energy sources. But this kind of mixed farming is very different from the old. The land will often be managed as an intensive arable system with the improved grass cropped and fed to livestock indoors. The potential loss of all farm animals from the fields of lowland Britain will reduce substantially the enjoyment of the countryside — certainly for children. Where stock do graze outside, their regime and the whole grazing environment will be rigidly controlled. Intensively managed planted grassland will be severed by temporary electric fencing for paddock grazing, where all internal hedgerows and trees have been removed. If permanent pasture is allowed to remain at all, it will be heavily treated with fertilizers and herbicides.

All these changes on lowland arable and pasture lands are likely to be hastened by the recent political and economic developments which have strengthened the expansionist policy of British agriculture.[26] Even the present crisis over energy supplies may be resolved before any significant brake is applied to the continuing escalation of high energy forms of intensive farming. In all, the rate and scale of landscape change is unlikely to slow down in the next decade and will very probably accelerate.

Landscape decay

Perhaps this is all too pessimistic a view. In predominantly arable and pastoral areas, it is after all only those remaining features of the old landscape which directly impede modern farming operations which are the most vulnerable: in particular, internal hedgerows, small woods and trees, but also areas of scrub and marsh caused by an irregular ground surface which can now be ploughed. Landscape elements which do not obstruct farming operations — those falling on naturally unproductive land which continues to resist cultivation, and those which lie at the boundaries of ownership, beside highways and along other artificially unproductive margins of farmland — are less prone to removal. But although these features do not directly inhibit operations, neither do they necessarily contribute to good agricultural practice, and they may be costly to maintain. They may even, to farming eyes, appear as untidy and anachronistic components of an enterprise which should be — and should be seen to be — wholly functional. Landscape features of this kind may, therefore, be removed; more likely is it that they will simply be neglected. Much of the countryside of lowland Britain is superficially still very beautiful, still flourishing. But much is dying. Trees are dying because they are overmature or diseased or because they can no longer tap a water table severely lowered by drainage schemes; hedgerows have grown so sparse or are managed so poorly that they serve no function for wildlife and are of little value in the landscape. The findings of Westmacott and Worthington (Table 19) reveal not only that the age structure of

TABLE 19

Age Distribution of Hedgerow Trees, 1972

Sample areas	%			
	Mature	Semi-mature	Saplings	Dead
Huntingdonshire	31	31	18	20
Somerset	30	60	9	1
Herefordshire	34	37	27	2

Source: Westmacott, R. and Worthington, T. (1974) *New Agricultural Landscapes*, op. cit.

trees is quite inadequate to replace the stock, but that the major species of the English lowland tree cover (oak, ash and elm) are even less likely to be replaced than the evidence for all species suggests. Saplings, particularly in hedgerows, cannot survive mechanical maintenance. Too few are being planted, and where they are, standards of management have fallen. In the long term, gradual landscape decay is perhaps the most worrying implication of modern land management, for the scale of destruction goes unnoticed, and there is no incentive, indeed no apparent need, for repair or re-creation.

Other Landscape Problems

Degraded landscapes

Land dereliction is primarily an urban problem, stemming from the exploitive activities of industrialists and others since the early nineteenth century. Sadly, it still continues, despite the reclamation programmes, for lack of adequate preventive action and responsibility.

Mining, particularly open cast working, raises the important disparity between private costs and social costs in a capitalistic economy. It is so easy for mining companies to extract minerals at the lowest cost to themselves but leave a plundered landscape which either diminishes the amenities of the area or else imposes costs upon the whole community if land restoration takes place. In many ways, mining in Britain, in contrast with developments in the use of most other rural resources, still retains the guise of a 'robber' economy. The early hill and dale areas of open-cast ironstone working in Northamptonshire and the surface level working of coal in the Forest of Dean are good examples of mineral workings which have been allowed without any restriction on private activity. There are also many examples of the excavation of sand and gravel near large towns where derelict pits and ponds have been left behind unaltered.

It is true that progress has been made in restoration techniques. Examples of compulsory land restoration can be seen in the areas which have been open-cast mined since the end of the Second World War for coal and ironstone. The contribution of particular operators such as the Open Cast Executive of the National Coal Board is notable. But there is less cause for optimism in other areas, where restoration conditions have never been imposed or have not been honoured, and where, as is the case with china clay working, the waste material is highly resistant to revegetation. Moreover we have, as yet, no experience of the restoration problems or costs involved in the exploitation of non-ferrous metals on the scale which threatens some parts of the uplands. Many more safeguards are needed on the way in which operations are carried out and the kind and phasing of restoration. It should be possible for new conditions to be imposed upon existing workings which have so far escaped control. Trust funds should be established by operators in advance of workings to ensure that adequate finance is available for restoration, as in ironstone working.[27]

Dereliction of a less acute kind spills over into the countryside and contributes to the poverty of many rural landscapes — where buildings lie unused and decaying; where rubbish tips are undisguised; where rail routes, canals and roadways have been closed but left unmanaged; where the ravaged landscapes of military training grounds are freely visible. Powers now exist for some of these and many other kinds of dereliction to be removed, screened or converted for a more positive use; but they rely largely upon the remedial action of public authorities whose budgets are already strained, and who operate priorities in rural areas which favour the protection of good landscapes over the improvement of the poor. There are still too few means of preventing despoilation, of enforcing the responsible working of rural resources and of demanding subsequent environmental repair.

Intrusions in the rural landscape

The quality of whole landscapes is clearly dependent upon the nature of their individual components, and particularly upon the success with which more localised land uses and more obviously man-made elements, are integrated with the rural scene. In recent years, increasing attention has been given to the location, scale and design, and the after-management of new forests and new reservoirs; the absorption of new and extended mineral working has been far less satisfactory and major reforms seem to be needed here.

For many reasons, not least the preoccupation of planners with the built environment, it is the introduction of new buildings, routes, power and pipelines that have so far dominated their thinking about the landscape of rural areas. These issues still figure strongly in countryside planning studies and policies. Considerable improvements have been made: an evaluation of the landscape implications, however crude, is now part of the location and design studies for all new trunk routes. Even so, the conclusions of such work do not always influence the final decision, as in the case of the A66 road improvement in the Lake District, and there is a particular need to recast the priorities of road construction in and around areas of the highest scenic quality. General road design has improved; it is possible to argue that some motorway stretches, with their fine bridges and extensive plantings are assets rather than detractors in the landscape. But there is still room for a better approach. Lovejoy argues that landscape works should take at least 1 per cent of the total cost of new road construction (excluding seeding), with shrubs and trees planted not only at the margins but along the central reservation. Service areas could be much improved in design.[28]

But in many ways it is in road management rather than in design or siting where changes are needed. The experience of landscape for many people is dominated by 'the view from the road'.[29] It would be wise, therefore, for improvement of the visual corridor of popular routes to be among the priorities for landscape conservation, and this implies not only the involvement of the owners of land adjoining these routes, but also those whose job it is to manage their immediate margins. Chapter 6 has discussed the increasing wildlife values of road verges; they are also significant in landscape terms. Some highway authorities already manage their verges to a regime which can benefit both interests, by cutting rather than spraying them and doing so in such a way that wild flowers can flourish; by planting, and elsewhere opening up the view; by providing space sufficient to discourage verge parking, and by other measures. Likewise, it is the poor marginal management of other linear routes – rail, river and canal – which traverse the countryside that so often contributes to the poverty of rural landscapes. In comparison with work on roads, the amenity values of railway land have received scant attention. Some water authorities still prohibit all planting within a large distance of any waterway. The recent developments of other public bodies, notably the Central Electricity Generating Board and the Gas Council, show that they have responded rather more satisfactorily to public scrutiny; power stations and processing plants have been better sited and better designed; there is more concern about the routing of power and pipe lines. It is economic nonsense to argue that these can be totally excluded from the rural landscape, but more could be done to define those areas which should take priority in measures to put them underground or otherwise camouflage them, and those where communications of all kinds could be grouped in a single 'working' corridor.[30]

Farm buildings

The problem of new farm buildings has been of continuing concern to planners, for it is the one area of rural change where they have some statutory powers of intervention, although a great deal of agricultural development can still take place without their control.[31] Yet the system, despite its critics, has not worked badly: planners have been relieved of much extra decision-making, farmers have enjoyed the freedom to build how, where and when the demands of good agricultural practice dictate. But certain consequences of the changing structure of agriculture, and especially of livestock farming, suggest that much greater control must be exercised over the nature and location of new farm buildings although this need not necessarily come about through planning legislation. Large scale intensive animal farming means structures of such bulk that their presence, with the associated pollution and the scale of their servicing, will be an unwelcome intrusion in many rural areas unless some means of mitigating their impact can be found. The growing diversification of materials used in the manufacture of farm buildings, many of which are quite out of place among rural colours and textures, can accentuate the presence of new buildings which replace groups linked by a common style. Moreover, the traditional clustering of buildings around the farmstead is giving way to a scattering of new structures located where they are most needed. Many modern farm buildings must be all-purpose and capable of adaptation to rapidly changing technological developments and this will encourage, in some areas, a uniformity in their size and style. Elsewhere, purpose-built structures may become obsolescent, but nevertheless remain, contributing to a new kind of industrial dereliction, while others are built. Old farm buildings which, in an urban context, would be listed, carry no control over their alteration or demolition.

Recent evidence[32] suggests that the total number of farm buildings is not likely to change significantly, but their size, their form and their location almost certainly will. Not all the changes will be detrimental; as with other elements of the rural landscape, we must adapt to a new functional appearance; some modern structures could enliven featureless tracts of countryside. But for much of the rural environment, trends in agricultural building imply a worsening of its qualities, and there is a case, and some considerable scope, for at least three kinds of action.[33]

Very few farm buildings are architect designed. Most farmers are influenced only by the cost and efficiency of structures available from manufacturers and few (outside parts of some National Parks) would agree to spending much more money to improve the appearance of buildings they erect. It would seem sensible, therefore to aim first to influence manufacturers in the designs and costs of buildings on offer, especially as more than half of all new farm building developments are made up from standard 'package' components supplied by manufacturers.[34] Various means of influencing industrial design have been suggested including subsidies for manufacturers, for example, to produce recommended cladding colours of equivalent cost to farmers, and for some national body (such as the Design Council) to vet all new building designs before the manufacturing process is established.

The *siting* of farm buildings (in some contrast to their design) is primarily a farmer's decision, though he may be advised by technical officers from the Ministry of Agriculture. Improvements in information and advice on the implications of location, the possibilities for compromise and for screening, could persuade farmers that it is possible to minimise visual impacts without loss of farming efficiency. Advice will be most effective if it comes not only from pressure groups, but through agencies (like the Ministry of Agriculture) with whom farmers already have frequent contact, and from local authorities who may need to employ specialists for this kind of negotiation. Building upon previous work, the Design Council are proposing to prepare a catalogue of recommended buildings and components chosen for their high design standards which could form a basis for advice and add to the work of the Farm Buildings Centre at Stoneleigh.[35]

Farmers will strongly resist the extension of direct controls on the erection of farm buildings,[36] and planners, so soon after reform, would be hard pressed to find the time and expertise to pass more judgments. Certainly, it seems unlikely, in present economic circumstances, that refusal of farm buildings on amenity grounds could be widely justified, except perhaps in parts of the National Parks. Even so, it can be argued that the present arbitrary size limits which exempt most agricultural buildings from planning control are undesirably high from an amenity viewpoint. Moreover, the assumption that all *small*

Plate 11. Town and country: the environment of the urban fringe in North Kent. (*photo: John Topham*)

Plate 12. The landscape of the fringe: Green Belt land in Hillingdon once worked for gravel, then used for waste tipping, now derelict. (*photo: Joan Davidson*)

Plate 23. A new bridge at Thorneythwaite in Borrowdale. (*photo: Countryside Commission*)

Plate 24. Stile and sign at Scout Crag, Langdale. (*photo: Countryside Commission*)

buildings (which are often quickly, cheaply and badly erected) are of no consequence in the landscape, is clearly mistaken. With more persuasion — of manufacturers and of farmers — to take account of aesthetic considerations in design and location, it may be that problems will diminish, but there are still issues on which only some form of legal control will allow the consistency which is required (in, for example, planting around all large buildings) and guard against the wholesale introduction of new structures with unforeseen environmental consequences. Some extension of the notification system which presently operates in areas covered by the Landscape Special Development Order may be one way of bypassing the lengthy process of normal planning control yet placing the initiative for negotiation and influence in the hands of local planning authorities whose concern is with the rural fabric.[37] If conditions imposed upon farmers bring unacceptable cost increases, then this expenditure ought to be subsidised in some other way, perhaps through the existing system of agricultural grants. Local Planning authorities will themselves need to be better informed and more consistent in their advice on acceptable designs and locations of farm buildings.

Policies: The Arguments for Landscape Planning

Despite the local importance of individual features, it is with whole landscapes that conservation action must be concerned. The approach must be total not piecemeal, and outside as well as within those areas designated for their particular scenic beauty. Two kinds of related policies emerge as offering some solution to present landscape problems outside designated areas. First, there is an obvious need to protect those remaining elements of the rural environment which contribute to its diversity: areas of parkland, heath and down; particular hedgerows and clumps of trees which, for reasons of age, shape or size have a significant landscape value. Features of historical and archaeological importance must be safeguarded. We need to ensure that regional differences in the British scene can be retained just as we are concerned to protect the vernacular in urban environments.[38] Secondly the case is clear for the creation of whole new landscapes which may involve not only tree-planting but earthmoving on a considerable scale.[39] But to protect and to create requires the right mechanisms for implementation, and also the right attitudes. How far do we have those in Britain?

Problems of implementation

In many areas, it is not easy to cost, nor indeed to justify the conservation of landscape. There are no tangible beneficiaries whose gain may be quantified; we lack even qualitative evidence, in any detail, on when and how landscape is enjoyed; its consumption could never be easily charged for. Moreover landscape, good and poor, is largely the by-product of many activities, rather than a conscious creation, so that its supply as well as the demand for it are confused.

Designation of areas within which the landscape is considered to be of conspicuously higher quality than elsewhere, on a national or more local scale, has traditionally offered the way out of this confusion. On paper, at least, the protection and enhancement of National Parks, Areas of Outstanding Natural Beauty, or Green Belts has been assured by the possibilities for greater control over building development, measures such as amenity treeplanting, and (most recently with Heritage Coasts) the intention to manage land and people in a positive way. But with the tools of intervention presently available to local authorities, designation alone can never be the answer to the problem landscapes identified earlier in this chapter (and especially those resulting from recent and extensive agricultural change). The power to make or mar such landscapes rests with farmers and other landowners and managers, and with the Ministry of Agriculture. Control over building development is clearly important; it has retained the rural character of many landscapes, but it has not prevented the decay of some, not the industrialisation of others by commercial farming and forestry operations. Moreover, as we argued earlier, convenient blanket restrictions on development within some designated areas have only exacerbated the problems of sprawl on their periphery.[40] Just as wildlife reserves become increasingly difficult to sustain against outside pressures, so the reservation of particular landscapes, on any scale, seems unlikely to succeed.

Chapter 12 considers in detail some of the main ways in which conservation goals can already, and might in future, be implemented in a variety of rural conflict situations. That chapter looks, for example, at the relative values of statutory control, agreements, various incentives and better information and advisory services. All have their limitations, and for landscape conservation, most of the measures presently available or widely practised are quite insufficient to control either the nature or the scale of change, or to create new and satisfying – if different – landscapes. Perhaps it is because of their impotence in anything much more than cosmetic treatment that most local authorities have found it easier to concentrate, in the years since the Countryside Act, on recreation provision rather than positive landscape conservation on any scale. The Countryside Commission has itself oscillated between its two major interests, and has probably achieved more tangible results on the recreation front than in landscape conservation. More public agency land ownership and management might secure, for example, the protection of valuable parklands, and the improvement of Green Belt landscapes. Even so, public authorities generally have a bad record in landscape management. Improvements must be made in the approach and activities of national land-holding agencies such as the Department of Environment, the Ministry of Defence and the Department of Energy, as well as Regional Water Authorities, and other public bodies. It is possible that some of the problems of particular landscapes will be partially solved by those extensions of control which may be introduced in response to the pressures of various groups, such as the planning control of commercial afforestation, and some modification in farm building regulations. Incentives of different kinds and agreements on management may be valuable means of securing the conservation of particular local landscapes.

But real problems remain in those areas where farming is already highly efficient and improvements in methods of crop and animal husbandry continue to be introduced. Here, farmers do not need, nor are they likely to be tempted by financial incentives (certainly on the levels so far envisaged) to modify their farming practice. Because of uncertainties in the markets for land and capital as well as for farming products, they are also unlikely to enter into binding agreements which limit their flexibility of operation. We have no means of encouraging landscape benefits as part of land consolidation schemes (as, for example, in the Netherlands) for the rationalisation of farm units is now almost complete in lowland Britain. Furthermore, in the present drive for greater self-sufficiency in home produced food, the Ministry of Agriculture as well as the farming unions are not likely to condone measures which restrict increasing operational efficiency, or those which take productive land out of agriculture, to be managed, whether by farmers or others, for amenity purposes. Added to all these impediments is one of organisation. The amenity management of scattered elements and tracts of land within a primarily farmed countryside will not be a simple task for public agencies with their present structure of skills and interests, if private land managers cannot or will not take it on.

The optimists (and Westmacott and Worthington must be so classed) argue that persuasion and bargaining within the present system of grant aid advice on farm improvement can achieve most of what is wanted, certainly in terms of protecting the valuable features of existing landscapes. They argue for priority to be given to the conservation and planting of naturally and artificially unproductive zones within land which may be intensively farmed. But the amount of unused land is already small; it will decline further as agricultural methods develop. With cuts in public expenditure and new measures of capital taxation, little money is available for planting or amenity management. In the face of wider public acceptance that the prime function of land is to produce more food, and an entrenchment of the single-minded approach of the Ministry of Agriculture, it is not easy to see how, in practice, new and satisfying agricultural landscapes can be created unless there is more compulsory public intervention or some other means, more potent than hitherto, of persuading land managers to take account of amenity interests. Perhaps it will become once more fashionable for landowners to invest in planting for aesthetic pleasure. New kinds of enterprise, associated with agriculture — game rearing and various recreation developments — may bring about a greener, richer landscape. A modification of the fiscal system relating to land may help. More likely is the need for a fundamental change in the approach and expertise of the Ministry of Agriculture, perhaps in the whole orientation of British farming.

Landscape plans

Whatever the agents of conservation, new landscapes cannot be reconstructed in an *ad hoc* way, and the notion of a landscape plan, as the framework for protective, remedial and creative action, has been revived. For long considered a panacea,[41] the nature and content of a landscape plan has only recently been discussed in workable terms. Some of the principles and priorities which might govern planning of this kind have been set out, for example, by the Countryside Commission:[42]

1. The maintenance and creation of cover is important;
    i. new cover should be established where it is compatible with farming needs (for example, on unproductive boundary land within or between farms; around buildings; on steep slopes);
    ii. planting should take place on publicly managed land, such as verges and beside railways;
    iii. new cover should not conflict with the maintenance of historic, archaeological, ecological or other valuable landscape features;
    iv. planted species should be those commonly found in the area;
    v. additional purposes should be served where possible, for example, shelter; nature conservation; game rearing; recreation; timber production;
    vi. new cover should be well maintained.
2. Dereliction should be removed; ugly buildings and other unsightly features screened.
3. New farm buildings should be carefully sited and designed.

There are some dangers in this approach, for it does not suggest how regional diversity can be preserved against a new uniformity. The principles will need sympathetic local interpretation.

It would seem logical for landscape plans, like those for wildlife conservation to be prepared as part of the structure and local plans for rural areas, but their preparation must involve not only local authorities but all those with a substantial influence and concern over a particular landscape. Various means and agents of implementation will be needed. It would be reasonable to argue for the costs of plan preparation to be borne by local authorities; but the costs of implementation in those areas where large scale landscape re-creation is required will be large enough to merit additional government assistance, and perhaps some special means of co-ordination. The case becomes increasingly strong for the Ministry of Agriculture to be one, if not a major contributor to schemes for the farmed countryside. Westmacott and Worthington spelt out, in some detail, the possible mechanics of landscape planning, involving, at a very local level, representatives of the relevant national resource planning organisations with local planning, landowning and environmental groups. All sources of advice and practical help must be tapped; the question remains of who takes the initiative.[43]

Priorities

It will be neither possible nor indeed necessary to cover the whole of the country with landscape plans; choices must be made about areas of priority and within these, the landscape measures required, in much the same way as the preparation of wildlife conservation plans was seen to be selective. For many areas, the problems for landscape and wildlife and their solutions, will be similar: for both, the amount and distribution of cover is of prime importance. It may be that composite conservation plans can be prepared and implemented, but the interests will not always coincide, and recent work may have underestimated the differences. The ecological value of residual, unproductive areas of farmland may be destroyed by amenity planting. Linkage of cover may be essential to the retention of some wildlife species, unless sufficiently large and diverse islands of new cover can be created, but this may not yield the most satisfactory landscape. The landscape which best serves the interests of wildlife could be, visually, a very untidy one.

To make choices about landscape priority areas, at least three developments upon present knowledge are probably needed. First, we must find some means of evaluation which implies a fundamental understanding of the ways in which landscape is perceived and the many values placed upon it. This is likely to mean abandoning the search for single, all-purpose landscape evaluations in order to devise methods for many different purposes. Secondly, we need to monitor and analyse landscape change, building upon the work of Westmacott and Worthington and others, so that policies can respond rapidly and effectively to real and not just imagined changes. Finally, the costs and feasibility of implementing landscape conservation measures must be demonstrated in far more detail and with much wider application than so far.[44]

Over a quarter of England and Wales carries some form of national designation for landscape protection. But there is no room for complacency, nor will localised defensive activity, however vigorous, be enough. If the British landscape is to continue to offer inspiration and satisfaction to more people, then perhaps it is our national and individual attitudes which are most in need of modification. We must adjust better to change, accepting for the countryside, as we have done in the town, the challenge it offers to be creative — and in a continuing way rather than every two centuries. We must accommodate to a diversity of landscape tastes and spread greater effort more widely. Most of all we need to accept that good landscapes, like clean air and unpolluted water, cannot be taken for granted.

Notes and References

1. For a philosophical exploration of these issues, see especially:
   Lowenthal, D. and Prince, H. C. (1964) The English Landscape, *Geographical Review*, Vol. LIV (3).
2. Westmacott, R. and Worthington, T. (1974) *New Agricultural Landscapes*, Countryside Commission.
3. Although locally there have been very dramatic changes because of mining, afforestation and other activities; such as the ploughing up of moorland particularly on Exmoor.
4. Under the Town and Country Planning Act, 1947.
5. The Civic Amenities Act, 1967 gave local authorities the power to designate Conservation Areas.
6. Under the Field Monuments Act of 1972.
7. For a discussion of the 'Heritage Coast' policy, see Countryside Commission (1970) *The Planning of the Coastline*, H.M.S.O.
   Countryside Commission (1970) *The Coastal Heritage*, H.M.S.O.
8. Smith, C. W. (1970) Dedham Vale, Summary of a seminar discussion in *Recreation News Supplement*, No. 2, November.
9. See Chapter 10 for a discussion of National Heritage Areas.
10. Department of the Environment (1974) Report of the *National Park Policies Review Committee*, H.M.S.O.
11. Quoted in Cornforth, J. (1974) *Country Houses in Britain — Can They Survive?* Country Life for the British Tourist Authority.
12. The maintenance of country houses has suffered since 1965 from the effects of capital gains tax and rising land values. The revised capital transfer tax and the proposed wealth tax pose new problems (November 1975).
13. Cornforth, J. (1974) *Country Houses in Britain*, op. cit. The figure refers to England, Wales and Scotland.
14. Council for the Protection of Rural England (1975) *Landscape — The Need for a Public Voice*, C.P.R.E.
   Moore, N. W. (1962) The Heaths of Dorset and their Conservation, *Journal of Ecology*, Vol. 50.
15. Simmons, I. (1966) Wilderness in Mid-20th Century U.S.A., *Town Planning Review*, 36.
   Phillips, A. A. C. (1972) *Conservation Planning in North America*, Countryside Commission.
   The 1967 U.S. Wilderness Act allows the National Forest and Parks Services to define wilderness areas over 10,000 acres which (with confirmation by Congress) become almost sacrosanct.
16. Ballantine, G. E. (1971) Planning for Remoteness, *Journal Town Planning Institute*, Vol. 57 (2).
17. Huxley, T. (1974) Wilderness: in Warren, A. and Goldsmith, F. B. (eds.), *Conservation in Practice*, John Wiley.
18. Dower, M. (1971) The Lessons of Swincombe, *Town and Country Planning*, Vol. 39 (9).
19. Tinker, J. (1973) Do We Need Wilderness Areas? *New Scientist*, Vol. 60, 4 October.
20. Ballantine, G. E (1971) Planning for Remoteness, op. cit.
21. Fairbrother, N. (1970) *New Lives, New Landscapes*, Architectural Press, Chapter 14.
22. Lucas, R. C. (1964) *The Recreational Capacity of the Quetico-Superior Area*, U.S. Forest Service Research Paper LS-15.
23. Pollard, E. P., Hooper, M. D. and Moore, N. W. (1974) *Hedges*, Collins,
   See also Chapter 6.
24. Westmacott and Worthington, working as consultants to the Countryside Commission, studied landscape change and farmers' attitudes in seven areas of lowland Britain, representing different farming types. Their findings are reported in: Westmacott, R. and Worthington, T. (1974) *New Agricultural Landscapes*, Countryside Commission.
   Subsequent consultations with interested bodies in regional landscape conferences showed the findings of Westmacott and Worthington to be broadly representative of all lowland Britain.
25. Weller, J. (1973) Land Use and Agricultural Change, Chapter 4 in Lovejoy, D. (ed.), *Land Use and Landscape Planning*, Leonard Hill Books. Weller thinks that internal structural change in agriculture and its distributional network will take place on such a scale that the geographical relationship between population and farming will need to be modified. He argues for a farm-based 'landscape

reconstruction' with new industrial farm processing units, surrounded by breeding and fattening areas, strategically placed on good transport routes to consumer centres.

26. Ministry of Agriculture, Fisheries and Food (1975) *Food From Our Own Resources*, Cmnd. 6020, H.M.S.O.
27. The recommendations of the Stevens' Committee on *Minerals Planning Control*, which exclude any suggestions for a widening of the notion of restoration funds or a tightening of the notion of restoration funds or a tightening of the enforcement of planning conditions, still fall short of what is needed.
28. Lovejoy, D. (1973) Communication Systems in the Landscape, in Lovejoy, D. (ed.), *Land Use and Landscape Planning*, Leonard Hill Books.
    See also: Crowe, S. (1960) *The Landscape of Roads*, Architectural Press.
    Countryside Commission/Lake District Planning Board (1972) *West Cumberland Trunk Road Study*.
29. See for example: Appleyard, D., Lynch, K. and Myer, J. R. (1963) *The View from the Road*, MIT Press.
    Brancher, D. (1968) Traffic in Scenic Areas, *Journal of the Town Planning Institute*, Vol. 54 (6).
30. See for example the proposals in: Coventry City Council *et al.* (1971) *Coventry – Solihull – Warwickshire: A strategy for the Sub-Region*.
31. Present regulations, under the Town and Country Planning (General Development Order) 1973, allow most farmers the freedom to erect new buildings (regardless of siting or design) as long as:
    (i) the ground area of the building does not exceed 465 sq.m.;
    (ii) the height does not exceed 12 m.;
    (iii) no part of the building is within 25 m of the metalled portion of a trunk or classified road.
    These rights can be withdrawn by local Article 4 Directions but the liability for compensation payments restricts their use. The Town and Country Planning (Landscape Areas Special Development) Order 1950 which operates in parts of three National Parks allows for the notification of all farm building intentions; these may be made subject to control on their design.
32. Westmacott, R. and Worthington, T. (1974) *New Agricultural Landscapes*, op. cit. Chapters 4 and 5.
33. The authors are grateful to Richard Lloyd (Countryside Commission, formerly a planning student at University College London) for ideas on this topic.
34. Council for the Protection of Rural England (1974) *Package Buildings*.
35. In association with the Ministry of Agriculture, farming associations and others. See also:
    Ministry of Housing and Local Government/Ministry of Agriculture/Welsh Office/Council for Industrial Design/Countryside Commission (1969) *Farm Buildings and the Countryside*, H.M.S.O.
36. Westmacott, R. and Worthington, T. (1974) *New Agricultural Landscapes*, op. cit.
37. A system of compulsory notification to control farm buildings and to protect many landscape features is proposed in: Council for the Protection of Rural England (1975) *Landscape: the Need for a Public Voice*.
38. It has been argued that the popularity of traditional English landscapes and the need for their protection has been underestimated with the emphasis upon creating new agricultural landscapes. See: C.P.R.E. (1975) op. cit and:
    MacEwen, M. (1975) A New Farming Landscape? *Country Life*, December 25.
39. Nan Fairbrother argues for the creation of new 20th century landscapes on the same scale as in the 18th century. Moreover, landowners and managers should be encouraged to recreate other lost environments such as coppiced and pollarded woodland: Fairbrother, N. (1970) *New Lives, New Landscapes*, Architectural Press.
40. See also the arguments in: Wibberley, G. P. (1974) The Proper Use of Britain's Rural Land, *The Planner*, Vol. 60 (7).
41. Royal Town Planning Institute/Institute of Landscape Architects (1973) *The Future Shape of British Landscape*, Report of a Seminar at West Bridgeford, November.
42. Countryside Commission (1974) *New Agricultural Landscapes: A Discussion Paper*, CCP. 76a, paras. 8 and 9.
43. See the arguments for a new national landscape agency in Tinker, J. (1974) The End of the English Landscape, *New Scientist*, Vol. 64 (926) 5 December; and for a 'landscape planning council' in the *Architects' Journal* (January 21st 1976) Rural settlement and landscape, Part 3; Recommendations.
44. In the Countryside Commission's 'Demonstration Farms Project' multi-purpose management plans will be prepared and implemented for ten commercial farms. The project should demonstrate the costs and feasibility of combining environmental conservation measures with commercial farming.

Part III: Problem Rural Areas

CHAPTER 8

The Urban Fringe

Earlier chapters of this book have tried to show how the rural environment is changing in ways which may not be as immediately obvious as the results of new urbanisation or road building, but which come about as the unplanned by-product of many independent actions. We have discussed the environmental implications of a number of major rural activities and the conflicts of interest that exist between different areas of rural policymaking.

In some parts of the countryside, there is such a multiplicity of interests, it is difficult to envisage ways in which environmental values might be safeguarded or restored. There are two areas — the urban fringe and the uplands — which illustrate well these problems of resource management in a situation of conflict. Both are environments in which many values are at stake and where there is existing or potentially rapid change. In some ways, more so visually than in social terms, they lie at the extremes of the rural milieu and their activities are in many respects marginal. But there is also evidence of wasted opportunities, and of inefficiency in the ways in which resources are used and activities practiced. In neither case is there any unity of administration. Not only is much of the land managed in smaller parcels than elsewhere, but, because of the physical configuration of the uplands (whose watersheds often act as political and administrative boundaries), and the transitory nature of the edge of urban areas, the patterns of local government have been, and are still, complex and fragmented. Both environments figure strongly in political debate and in much emotional argument.

For these reasons, the urban fringe and the uplands provide good examples of the kind of rural problems with which this book is primarily concerned. To a degree they also show the neglect and failure of planning efforts to solve these problems. Yet applied to both environments are planning designations (Green Belts and National Parks) which, perhaps more so than any others, have won popular support. This and the following two chapters will explore some of the problems generated by change in these two areas, and look at various approaches to their solution. Our discussion of the urban fringe and of the uplands in greater depth than other rural regions provides a focus for many of the arguments we make in earlier chapters.

The Urban Fringe Concept

The fringe is not an easily defined geographical area that begins and ends at a certain distance from a city centre; it is rather an area characterised by functional and visual

109

uncertainty about its dominant use. It contains substantial, if discontinuous, areas of urban development mixed with stretches of more extensive and traditionally rural uses like agriculture and forestry. These uses are strongly affected (beneficially as well as to their detriment) by the presence of urban activity. There are other characteristics of the fringe: notably, that it contains an assortment of urban uses which are not wanted in, or cannot afford, the city and are inappropriate for the open countryside, but which nevertheless require a location near to the population which they serve. Thus the fringe contains hospitals and sanatoria, prisons, airfields, slaughterhouses, sewage works, sports grounds and other leisure areas, hypermarkets, offices, mineral workings of different kinds, water works, reservoirs, tips and dumps. This is a vague definition, but the point is that urban fringe does not, for example, extend over the whole of south east England, nor does the fringe of London include the whole of the Metropolitan Green Belt. Rather, it is the inner edge, where rurality and urbanity are truly mixed.

In social terms too, the fringe is an area of transition which is neither town nor country: a desirable living environment for many whose economic and social lives are firmly linked to the town; a less desirable one for those dependent upon local employment, and without the affluence and mobility to enjoy the dispersed pattern of city regional living. Pahl and others have described the social polarisation to be found in some metropolitan villages, and other less attractive features of fringe living, although their findings encompass a wider area, stretching beyond the limits of the fringe as we have defined it.[1]

Perhaps the most important feature of the fringe for many towns is that it is still a transitory environment which will sooner or later be absorbed within a new urban area. Some theoretical analysis and most of the discussion in planning documents seems to ignore this. Fringe problems, if they are identified at all, are seen in isolation, neither linked outwards to the activities and resources of the countryside, nor inwards to the demands and needs of the town. Rarely is the planning of the urban fringe seen as the first stage in planning areas of new development, or as an integral component of an expanding city region. Even so, the fringe is more than this. Although it is transitional in space and time, many analysts argue that it is not simply an intermediate environment which exhibits, with less intensity, some urban problems and some rural ones; at any one time, the fringe is a particular and unique environment with its own unique set of problems.

Many theorists, mainly geographers, have described the assemblage of land uses and activities at the edge of towns.[2] There has been much discussion, particularly in America, of the processes by which urban fringes take shape but not all the conclusions are relevant to Britain where very different systems of public control have operated. It is possible, however, to distil from these and other discussions, a number of points by which to describe the present state of various fringe activities and the way in which they are changing in response to developments in urban areas and also to those in the deeper countryside. As elsewhere in this book, emphasis is placed upon the two activities of agriculture and recreation.

Agriculture and the Urban Fringe

Most of the land which surrounds the built-up area of towns and cities in Britain is still in agricultural use, but in a number of ways, fringe farming and fringe farmers differ from their more rural counterparts. Higbee[3] suggests that there are four categories of fringe farmer:

1. the truly commercial, who aims to sell and relocate a larger enterprise on the proceeds of

the sale;[4]

2. the under-capitalised and uneconomic farmer who is a prey to all the problems of an urban fringe location and who may attempt many changes of enterprise to achieve some success; these are insecure farmers whose turnover may be intermittently quite high but who fail to re-invest in their farm or adequately maintain it;
3. the 'hobby' farmer who is involved for tax purposes or to enjoy a pleasant 'rural' home or for some other non-agricultural reason;[5]
4. lastly, there are the land speculators for whom farming is a temporary, incidental activity, often pursued in an inefficient way.

This categorisation is probably an oversimplification, but nevertheless it is a useful one for analysing the changing nature of fringe agriculture and the kinds of environmental and social problems that are taking place.

Changes in fringe farming

Although little research has been done so far on the changing land uses of the urban fringe, a number of studies suggest that the acreage of land in commercial agriculture has fallen, especially over the last decade.[6] Some urban fringe land is extremely fertile and most of that in Grades I and II (Ministry of Agriculture Land Classification) is assured of continued farming use. But elsewhere there have been substantial losses, although the degree of change has varied with different farming activities. Some kinds of arable cropping seem to have suffered more than pastoral farming: on the western fringe of London, for example, Grade I land under vegetables and other horticultural crops has decreased steadily since 1963.[7] A survey of fringe farming near Slough suggested that severe competition for farm labour from nearby factories had increased the problems of arable cropping so that farmers who could were forced to invest in intensive livestock units.[8] Over the survey period (1968-71) there was a 36 per cent increase in poultry stock. Higbee's own conclusion that the transition is from crop rearing to intensive livestock production – first in the open air, but increasingly in buildings – is borne out by these findings. Extensive pastoral farming, particularly sheep rearing and fattening, has declined in areas close in to urban developments, where trespass, dog worrying and rustling are problems.[8]

The early years of the development of the new city of Milton Keynes, being built on a large site between London and Birmingham, have been monitored in relation to the changes occurring in the immediate farming scene.[9] Attempts were made to secure an orderly transition of agricultural land into urban development.[10] Early purchase by the Milton Keynes Development Corporation was encouraged, with lease back of land to the original owners for short term tenancies, a policy which has helped to maximise land use during the development period. Between 1967 and 1971 the arable acreage increased by 10 per cent, ley farming declined, the number of dairy cows diminished sharply, the number of regular farm workers fell by 30 per cent and the uncertainty made tenant farmers leave more quickly than owner-occupiers.

A further feature of agricultural change on the fringe is the decline of large farm units. Some large farms remain, but many have been severed by various developments and otherwise reduced to scattered holdings. The opportunity for amalgamation of neighbouring units to create a viable enterprise does not often occur. Some farmers have found it increasingly difficult to make a living and have sold out, others have had attractive offers from mineral companies, developers, speculators or part-time hobby farmers. Those farms which remain intact, but are of insufficient size and capital for a commercially successful operation, are likely to have diversified by grafting on non-farming activities such as the stabling and pasturage of horses. Riding schools, kennels and golf courses are increasingly common components of fringe farms.

Some small farms may be acquired by part-time hobby farmers for whom profitability is relatively less important, for their alternative and major source of income can buttress them against financial losses. They can anyway often afford to modify their enterprise in ways which make it more resistant to the problems of fringe farming: by, for example, providing adequate fencing and proper gate maintenance.[11] In environmental terms, an increase in this form of land management may be more beneficial than other likely changes; there is some circumstantial evidence to suggest that these farmers, because they seek a pleasant living environment, may create a well-managed landscape which is not generally characteristic of small farm enterprises on the fringe.

Land speculation

Over the countryside as a whole, there has been increasing evidence of land acquisition as a hedge against inflation; more agricultural land is being managed by tenants for large holding companies. Clearly the most desirable land for this purpose is to be found on the edges of existing cities; and although green belt controls operate over much of this land, the recent escalation of land and house prices has ensured that such controls have been no deterrent to speculation.[12]

Once land is acquired for speculative purposes, there is little incentive to farm it well − if at all − for the prevailing view has been that derelict farmland is likely to be released more quickly for development than land which is better farmed (even though, officially, such a view has been condemned).[13] Conscious 'farming to quit', like the unintended failures of marginal fringe farmers, produces an unkempt, neglected landscape of overgrown fields, unmanaged hedges and woodland, and deteriorating farm equipment.

In many ways, therefore, agricultural changes on the edge of towns contribute to a declining quality of environment, visually and otherwise. There is considerable neglect of farmland which assumes an untended, overgrown appearance. There is an increase in large industrial farm buildings and in the volume and toxicity of waste products from the animal feeding systems they house. In some localities there is a proliferation of the ugly and untidy structures which accompany kennels and riding schools.

The problems of fringe farming

These changes in fringe farming are often attributed solely to the intense pressures for land to be developed on the edge of existing towns. It is true that, despite new town policies and other proposals for large scale urbanisation outside existing urban regions, continued growth is likely to occur around the major cities. Pressures will continue for land to be released for housing and other activities which cannot be accommodated within the urban area, or which, like mineral working and certain types of residential development, are based upon the resources and environment of the fringe. Pressures will continue for farmers, especially those whose profitability is insecure, to take advantage of the high and increasing values of their land — at least until plans for the public ownership of development land are realised.

But in some areas, the decline in farm acreage is proceeding more rapidly than the increase in new development which is still fairly rigidly contained by Green Belt policies, and other factors must be responsible for continuing changes in the agricultural pattern, not least the effects of urban intrusion.[14]

It is common to associate fringe farming with a fairly high level of trespass from neighbouring urban areas. There is considerable speculation about the extent and causes of this, but little hard evidence exists. Despite the opportunities for some biassed reporting, a Ministry of Agriculture survey provides the only indication we have of the scale of trespass problems. Between 1968 and 1971, about 100 farms in an area of good agricultural land in the Thames Valley near Slough were sampled on questions of trespass, labour availability and produce sales.[15] Two thirds of these farms had been troubled by some form of trespass over the three years before they were surveyed; Table 20 lists the kind of damage suffered. The decline in intensive cropping, already noted, is partially a consequence of this degree of urban intrusion. Horticultural produce, it seems, is especially easy to steal although the decline in market gardening, which is so demanding of labour, is also a consequence of the attractions of nearby industry, offering higher wages and often more regular employment. The farm labour force of the Slough holdings shrank by 14 per cent over the survey period — a greater rate than was common for England and Wales as a whole.

For many fringe farmers, the most direct and costly outcome of this form of urban intrusion is the necessity for extra fencing of farm boundaries and footpaths. In some areas, farmers use electronic detection devices, but unsightly barbed wire barricades and a proliferation of ugly signs are more common. There are the added costs, in terms of lost time, of clearing rubbish or arranging for its removal. The damage to plant and livestock and the erection of elaborate defences all imply considerable economic losses which are rarely recoverable, for it is difficult, if not impossible, for farmers to bring an action for trespass, especially against children. Added to the direct financial costs, therefore, are the burdens of frustration and uncertainty which go with farming under these conditions.

It is often difficult to attribute cause and effect to features of fringe farming. Many of the adjustments made to enterprises — the reduction in farm size, the move towards intensive livestock production — result from a combination of circumstances and cannot all be laid at the door of conscious or unwitting trespassers.[16] Low has listed some other forms of urban intrusion which can influence the viability of fringe farms and the types of enterprise which result. Some of these, like the change of drainage and provision of sewerage services, which may permanently damage surfaces and soil structures, or the compulsory purchase of farmland by local authorities, which may divide holdings into uneconomic units, are necessary and legitimate activities of the urban hinterland.[17] But there are also the indirect consequences of urban activity which are not found to the same degree in more rural areas but which impose further costs upon fringe farmers: the extra risks and delays involved in the transfer of livestock along busy roads; pollution from mineral workings, industry and airports.

The adjustments made to farm enterprises, for whatever reason, may lead to the loss of other benefits as, for example, when farmers are no longer able to co-operate with their neighbours for livestock rearing or machinery use. In addition, fringe farmers may suffer from restrictions imposed upon their practices from the pressures of local residents, amenity and conservation groups who may be offended by the sights and smells of farming. Not only

TABLE 20

Trespass Damage Near Slough

	% of holdings affected
Crops damaged/stolen	35
Rubbish left ⟩	32
Damage to fences/gates	25
Damage to fixed equipment	15
Livestock worrying	10

Source: Ministry of Agriculture (1974), *Agriculture and the Urban Fringe.*

do farmers have to suffer the normal restrictions of Green Belt policies (which may prevent them from realising the hope value of their land or engaging in potentially profitable activities which will be classed as non-conforming uses) but in the urban fringe, greater use may be made of Tree Preservation Orders and other planning restrictions.[18]

Benefits of fringe farming

It is easy to dwell, as many representatives of farming interests do, upon the problems of this location. But there are some benefits to be gained from farming on the edge of a town, although these may not all be acknowledged and the value of some is probably declining.

Proximity to urban areas provides opportunities for door-to-door sales of farm produce such as eggs and potatoes, although the value of farm gate sales may be greater. About half of the farmers in the Slough survey sold produce locally, but less than a third of all sales were worth more than £500 a year. Munton suggests that few fringe farmers have restructured their businesses sufficiently to realise these retailing opportunities.[19]

Nearby towns may supply extra sources of casual labour for seasonal activities such as potato-lifting, fruit and vegetable harvesting and the grading and packing of farm products. Farmers may benefit from the nearness of food processing factories: farming under contract with canning and freezing firms can enormously simplify the technical and managerial decision-making for individual farmers.

Proximity to centres of demand means that some farmers can diversify their enterprise by stabling horses and running riding establishments. Revenue is derived principally from riding fees, but may also come from livery and schooling, stable management courses or the sale of manure. Even so, the returns are generally poor. In a sample study of nine riding establishments, Burton found that in only five cases were the net returns in excess of £250 a year, and in only three cases were they more than £500, which represented a low return on capital.[20] The range of possible sizes of establishment and of combinations with a farming enterprise, however, precluded any general conclusions about the extra values of grafting on this recreational use.

More recent evidence suggests that it is possible for fringe farmers to benefit financially from an involvement in the provision of a wide range of recreation facilities. There are already examples of lucrative golf courses and driving ranges on farms, of shooting and fishing enterprises and of the value of letting land for intermittent events like caravan rallies, motorcycling and autocross.

The future of fringe agriculture

The agricultural economy of the urban fringe is thus changing in a number of ways in response to the uncertainty of future land use and values and to a variety of types of urban interference. Some landowners and tenants farming near the economic margin may have little means or incentive to improve the efficiency or appearance of their enterprise. Their personal loss is also a loss in terms of national and local resource use. It is not so much the case that proximity to large urban centres is necessarily a deterrent to good farming, but that some farmers are forced to introduce more robust land use systems — like intensive livestock production — which may be agriculturally efficient and profitable, but which have a number of undesirable environmental consequences.

In future, if present trends continue, we can reasonably expect continued change of two kinds. There is likely to be a further reduction in the number of bona fide farmers and perhaps an increase in land holding as a hedge against inflation. This may bring some decay in the quality of the fringe landscape with the loss of some attributes valued by townsmen including the prospect of a varied and well tended 'working' landscape with animals and crops in evidence. Similar results may be expected on land which continues to be farmed commercially but with no change in the farming system, so that profitability and efficiency decline. There could be a large scale increase in the number of industrial farm buildings.

There are, however, counter arguments for arresting these trends towards a fringe which is becoming increasingly 'urbanised' not only by developments from the town but also from within agriculture. First, much land is of good agricultural quality and this should be reserved for food production for it offers greater flexibility of operation than poorer land. But favourable conditions will have to be created whereby farmers can farm it efficiently; they will require freedom from uncertainty; protection from interference; perhaps some extra financial compensation or encouragement to take advantage of the fringe location but without detriment to the many interests at stake. Secondly, for various reasons, it is desirable that some fringe land (probably in increasing amounts) should remain open and well tended in order to reap short term recreation benefits and also to ensure, for the long term, a pleasant urban environment as some cities expand. Finally, it is desirable that other resources of the fringe — wildlife or minerals, for example should be safeguarded, and this will have implications for agricultural land management.

To meet these objectives, some adjustments to present strategic policy-making will be required, together with much more direct and powerful public intervention in the way fringe land is used and managed. But before these ideas are discussed, a further use of the fringe is considered.

Recreation on the Fringe

There is almost no information by which to assess the scale of recreational use taking place on the fringes of most cities. The location is assumed by many commentators to be either too near urban areas to offer any real focus of attraction for recreation trips or, conversely, to be an ideal location for an activity for which quite inadequate provision is made.

It is true that for those who live in suburban locations — and these make up most of the people who presently engage in outdoor recreation — the fringe may be too close and too familiar to be attractive for a day out; most of these people have cars which allow them to travel further afield. Moreover, the evidence of recreation surveys can be interpreted in various ways. Many popular sites do lie *outside* city fringes, even if these are defined fairly liberally: most day trippers appear to want to travel rather more than ten miles. But what is not clear is how much this distribution of recreation activity reflects not only the location of surveys but also the distribution of recreation opportunities. The figures could equally well imply a resistance to long journeys and a willingness to stop wherever suitable facilities are provided.[21] Increasing fuel costs should produce an even stronger incentive to reduce the distance travelled to a destination.

No firm conclusions about the extent of fringe recreation activity can be drawn until there is more, and more sophisticated data on trip-making between town and country at the regional level, with surveys at origin points as well as destinations. Even so, there is circumstantial evidence to suggest that there is considerable, if dispersed, recreation on the fringe which may take a number of forms, including short trips from neighbouring residential areas; visits by school parties; regular trips to sports grounds by clubs; and the recreation of holiday visitors and second home owners as well as the informal recreation trips of families living outside the city centre.

Yet the amount of land devoted to public and private recreational use on the edge of towns is less than might be expected: for London's Green Belt, Thomas has shown that only 6 per cent is recreation land; less than 4 per cent is in open space to which the public has general access.[22]

Surprisingly few new country parks have been created since the passing of the Countryside Act in an environment potentially so suitable for them.[23] There are many reasons for this situation, not least the attitudes of local residents and planning agencies in the fringe; Gregory, for example, has shown that in the West Midlands Green Belt, many applications to develop recreation facilities are strongly resisted by local residents.[24] The effects of local government reform which leave the fringes of most conurbations under divided administration, the difficulties of special purpose recreation agencies (like the Lee Valley Regional Park Authority) and the present system of government grants, which differentiates between urban and rural parks, all discourage effective recreation provision on the fringe.

Yet, potentially, the environment remains one of the best for recreation development.[25]

Problems and potential of the fringe for recreation

Information on the interaction between recreation and other fringe activities, like the scale of the activity itself, is sparse, although there are many untested assumptions. Casual recreation is generally, and probably rightly, thought to be responsible for most of the trespass experienced by farmers and others and the damage that results from this. In addition, as in the open countryside, recreation can cause congestion on roads and inhibit the passage of local traffic. Recreation pressures can physically damage sites and tracts of country often with consequent damage to ecological and aesthetic values. There is little evidence to suggest that recreation, especially day recreation, brings any tangible benefits to local communities at the destination of this activity.

The problems of outdoor recreation on the fringe, therefore, though not well researched, clearly exist. But there is also the question of *opportunities*, which may have been overlooked in the enthusiasm for studying and providing for recreation further from the town, in environments which are unequivocally rural.

Elsewhere, we have suggested at least four reasons why the urban fringe should be considered an important and unique locale for recreation.[25] It is near to the obvious centres of demand in urban areas, and especially to those people who, because of their financial or family circumstances, have little chance of access to the deeper countryside. Recreation developments can provide the *raison d'être* for many land uses of the fringe like farming and speculative land holding, which face an uncertain future. Moreover, imaginative recreation schemes can transform the ugly unkempt landscapes of past mineral working or old airfields and soften the impact of new intrusions such as reservoirs. Some of the countries of Western Europe, perhaps especially the Netherlands, have many examples of visionary recreation development on the edge of old and new urban and industrial complexes, including the Amserdamse Bos, Delftsehout and the Briellse Maas.

A further reason why the urban fringe may be considered to offer substantial scope for recreation has already been raised in Chapter 4. It concerns the traditional and continuing separation of urban from rural environments in planning for leisure, and a persistence of the notion that what can be enjoyed in the town has little place in the country. But it has already been argued that many features of current recreation behaviour argue for some blending of the urban and rural experience.

> "The fringe can offer this combination. Instead of treating it as a rather undesirable no-man's land, perhaps we should exploit the characteristics of this transitional zone . . .
>
> . . . This could be more imaginative and more feasible than trying to establish a form of second rate rurality, or assigning to the fringe truly urban facilities which cannot afford space or are not wanted in the city."[26]

We have suggested in detail elsewhere that at least three kinds of recreation provision seem most suited to, and most needed in, a fringe environment. These include more single purpose country parks (although their nature would be more diverse than now, and their accessibility much improved); the linkage of recreation with other fringe uses, particularly farming; and the creation of multi-attraction leisure parks set in new urban fringe landscapes.[26]

The implementation of these ideas will not be easy. Effective administrative structures, adequate powers and enough money probably do not yet exist. But the fundamental need is for new attitudes towards a wasted environment.

Other Fringe Activities

Although we have concentrated upon farming and the provision of open space, the edges of most towns and cities are characterised by a multitude of different land uses which themselves pose special problems for the planning and management of these areas.

Mineral working, particularly for sand and gravel, has been and is still an extensive, if fragmented, activity of many fringes. Some past workings have been successfully reclaimed for agriculture, housing or other uses, but many remain derelict, with neither their excavations, nor their plant or machinery removed. Some land has been partially reclaimed, but remains inadequate for farming and now contributes to the growing pool of vacant land. Current workings, like other incursions — electricity substations, water and sewage works, airfields — add to the general air of industrial and commercial use which pervades much of the fringe of built up areas.

In the Colne Valley an attempt is being made to plan some integrated after-use of mineral workings, with lakes zoned for different activities and a new footpath network. But there are few schemes in Britain in which the shape and extent of current and future excavations will be strongly influenced by the needs of subsequent land activity; whereby the creation of functional but attractive new landscapes could be phased with the destruction of the old.[27] Moreover, despite growing interest in outdoor education and environmental interpretation, the notion of exploiting such opportunities as are offered by mineral working, along with a number of other urban services which are located in the fringe, remains undeveloped. Yet farming is not the only activity which townspeople might enjoy learning more about.

Much fringe land is already severed by transport corridors; it is inevitable that most new road (and in some cases rail) routes planned or under construction, fall within the fringes of conurbations. But there is evidence of wasted assets. Few other European capitals with the exception of London, offer such a limited and dismal prospect of the rivers on which they lie. Likewise, roads, motorways and railways, and, most of all, canals, provide few other benefits than accessibility. They certainly do little to reduce the incentive to make rapidly for a definite destination on a leisure trip, for they are unattractive as pleasure routes in themselves.[28]

Urban Fringe Policies

In many respects, policy-making for the urban fringe has failed not only to tackle a number of land management problems, but also to realise many of the opportunities of a unique location.

Green Belts

Green Belt policies, which cover 5,800 square miles of England and Wales,[29] are not the only ones applied to the edge of towns; but in one form or another they dominate present thinking about urban fringe planning (Fig. 4). The idea, with various interpretations by protagonists such as Howard, Unwin and Abercrombie, is of long standing.[30] Two distinct views of its basic purposes — one negative, one positive — have emerged over the last three decades and both can be found in current expressions of the policy.

On the negative side, a reservation of land outside the urban area, protected from certain activities (notably building development) is seen as vital to the containment of a town in danger of becoming 'too big', necessary also to retain its special character and to separate it from neighbouring towns. Such a view was adopted early on by Ebenezer Howard.[31] It has been expressed more recently and in modified form in the circular of 1955,[32] which urged provincial cities to follow the example of London (for which Green Belt policies have applied since 1938), and in the subsequent official policy document.[33]

The more positive approach argues for land outside the town to provide recreational opportunities and to be protected for agricultural use. This was the view of Unwin who built upon Howard's ideas in his 1933 Regional Plan for London. It was also the view of Abercrombie, although he chose to emphasise the role of agricultural protection in his Greater London Plan of 1944.[34] Indeed, until recently, a recreational purpose for fringe land has not been stressed. It remains a secondary reason for Green Belt controls in official

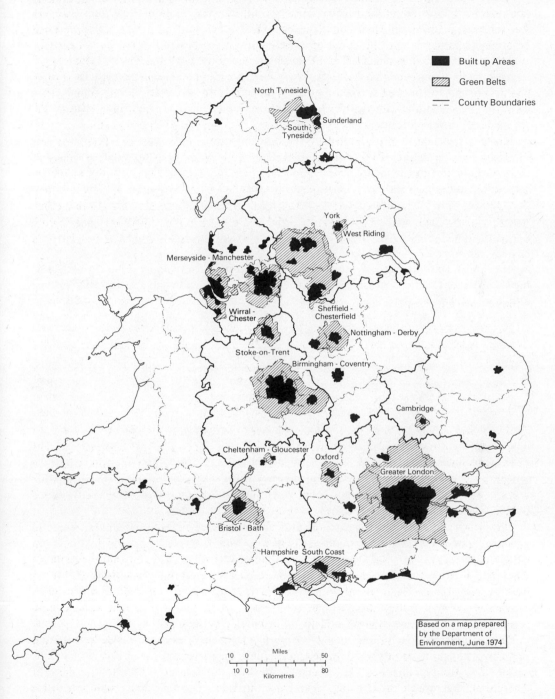

Built up Areas
Green Belts
County Boundaries

North Tyneside
South Tyneside
Sunderland
York
West Riding
Merseyside - Manchester
Wirral - Chester
Sheffield - Chesterfield
Nottingham - Derby
Stoke-on-Trent
Birmingham - Coventry
Cambridge
Cheltenham - Gloucester
Oxford
Greater London
Bristol - Bath
Hampshire South Coast

Based on a map prepared
by the Department of
Environment, June 1974

Miles
10 0   50
10 0   80
Kilometres

FIG. 4. *Green Belts and Urban Areas*

policy, but is increasingly used as a rationale in current planning studies.[35]

The Green Belt policy was thus defined and gathered strength partly upon utopian notions of low densities, garden cities, and a belief in the existence of a maximum desirable size for cities, which would in any case cease to grow when some of their population could be decanted to the superior environment of New Towns. Thomas, in the preface to his study of London's Green Belt, argues that the concept has grown out of and is sustained by an increasing 'emotional attachment to the open countryside' on the part of city as well as country dwellers.[36] But the notion of 'countryside' on which this attachment is founded is a partial myth which does not recognise the existence or speed of environmental change, nor the inequities involved in access to rural amenities.

In the first half of the twentieth-century, these objectives for Green Belts may have been the right ones, even though they did not necessarily grow from a correct analysis of the social, economic and environmental problems of towns and their hinterlands. Even so, little attention was devoted to the method or efficiency of their implementation. Certainly, Green Belt policies have physically contained the areal size of many cities; they have been partly successful in retaining the character of some towns, especially historic centres like Cambridge, York and Chester. Without them, much agricultural land would have disappeared beneath suburbia.

But Green Belts have clearly not stopped urban growth. Development has 'leapfrogged' the protected girdle of most large towns so that their influence is felt considerably further into the countryside than might otherwise have been the case. In fact, some would argue that the economic, physical and psychological problems that fringe farmers face now apply to a much wider area than would be the case without Green Belts.

Green Belts have also failed to meet other objectives. Publicly accessible recreation land makes up a relatively small proportion of the Green Belts of London and the West Midlands. Various reasons can be advanced to explain this, not least the resistance of semi-rural authorities (in whose areas the bulk of Green Belts still lie) to the idea of providing for urban visitors. Nor are Green Belts everywhere green. Reliance upon development control (applied with variable stringency) as the major mechanism of implementation has meant that landscape changes, engendered by many activities over which there are no planning controls, have gone unchecked. Allowance of other 'conforming' activities such as hospitals, cemeteries and sewage works, has introduced many urbanised and often environmentally intrusive elements. 'Non-conforming' uses which pre-date Green Belt designation remain.[37] Often, Green Belt policies have been used as a convenient political tool for restricting change. For some areas, their 'blanket' application has precluded the development of a more positive, more comprehensive approach to rural planning on the edge of towns. These policies still feature strongly in planning studies, often scarcely mentioned in major reappraisals of regional development, although they have been more sceptically treated at the subregional level.[38] It is true that many academic criticisms both of the objectives and of the failures in implementation have found some practical expression in current plans — there is a general call for 'more positive policies' to be applied between and on the edge of towns. But rarely are such policies spelt out; the concept of Green Belts *may* be seen as outdated and unworkable, but inertia and lack of time to develop a new approach have continued to ensure that no radical changes are proposed for most urban fringes.

Some studies do recognise many urban fringe problems, but see the need only for new recreation provision rather than for a revised approach to the planning of all fringe resources.

The predominant analysis is that the fringe is the main arena for a clash of urban and rural interests, in which the latter are more severely disadvantaged. The solutions therefore seek to re-establish 'rurality' in the form of greater protection from obvious urban incursions, particularly of building development. There has been no consideration of the changes that take place *within* the protected zone, especially in those parts nearest the urban area. Among recent work, only the structure plan for South Hampshire appears to look more closely at the specific nature of the fringe, and its place in the process of city regional development.[39] Here, the Green Belt idea is abandoned.

Towards A New Approach

It is generally, and not unreasonably, felt that the notion of Green Belts is too firmly fixed in the public and planning mind to remove, short of a total upheaval of the political and administrative system. Moreover, the relative failure of Green Belts to deal with problems of the urban countryside adjacent to the built up area, does not invalidate their usefulness in areas further from the town. The need is not so much to devise a new or dramatic planning zonation, but rather to develop a relevant and realistic set of objectives for the urban fringe and workable means of achieving them. It seems to us that policies need to be clarified in three ways: at the strategic level, where the nature and purpose of the activities and environment of the fringe can be specified; but more importantly, at the level of local management (whereby strategic policies can be implemented), and in terms of the means of implementation.

Strategic objectives and policies

Among the many objectives which policies might work towards, we have identified at least three groups as important in dealing with the environmental problems and opportunities presented by the urban fringe. In a number of ways, the activities of the fringe could be better arranged so that conflicts of interest could be avoided and the possibilities for mutual benefit realised.

We have argued that, in some areas, certain activities ought to be protected so that they may flourish. For example, land of high agricultural value (Grades I and II) should be reserved for farming while the distribution of holdings may need to be regrouped to provide larger, more economic units, or to allow co-operation between neighbouring farmers or extensions to farms.

Conflicting fringe activities should be separated spatially or protected by buffer zones. In this way, the more sensitive farming systems could be separated from those activities which are likely to interfere with the normal workings of a commercial enterprise, unless some positive integration of activities is planned. This could mean, for example, that arable and some livestock farms do not abut residential or leisure developments, or popular recreation routes with stopping points. Farmland of this type could be buffered from interference by other developments such as public and private woodland, or industry. When these do not already exist, new buffer zones can be created. Activities could be spatially linked when some mutual benefits may accrue from integration, as might be the case with certain types of farming and informal recreation. A fringe location seems to be ideal for certain developments such as demonstration farms, farm centres and markets, which require land, but also good access for farmers and lay visitors from urban centres.

On a larger scale, the more intrusive activities could be grouped so that although an open belt around the built up area may no longer exist, substantial tracts of land remain undeveloped, yet still well managed. These open tracts should be evenly distributed round a town or city and easily accessible from its centre by public and private transport. It seems not unwise to resurrect some of the ideas of the strategy prepared for the South East in 1967, with its proposals for the clustering of urban activities within growth corridors separated by green wedges, but (which the strategy did not suggest) to apply them further into the edge of the town, within the Green Belt.[40]

The present degraded state of most fringe land suggests that the *creation* of new accessible landscapes of woodland, lakes and parkland should be a major component of fringe policy. Nan Fairbrother has advocated the planting of trees on a massive scale to create new 'green-urban' landscapes on the edge of towns to serve as barriers protecting farmland beyond and also as informal recreation areas.[41] In many ways it is sad that Britain has taken so little care and interest in the approach to, and exit from, her major cities. They lack any visionary metropolitan park systems of the kind which already exist or are planned for several conurbations in Europe: the Ruhr in West Germany for example, with its extensive network of fringe woodlands and free-time parks, or the cities of Randstad Holland, surrounded by green girdles of man-made forests and lakes.

In all, the strategic planning of this transitional zone calls for policies which aim to link it in two directions — inwards to the urban area, and outwards to the deeper countryside. Recreation provides a good example of the ways in which urban and rural activities can be linked. The fringe offers a transitional environment appropriate for the development of facilities which may fill the gap between those that are intensive, user-oriented and urban, and the more extensive, informal and resource-based rural facilities. Several schemes of this kind have been proposed or are in progress on the fringes of British cities — the Lee and Colne Valley parks are notable examples for London. Other plans draw attention to the need for radial routes, such as canals, rivers and minor roads, to be used imaginatively for leisure purposes and for new ones to be created.[42]

The successful implementation of these locational policies — and this is the neglected field of action — depends upon the development and operation of more detailed management policies concerned not simply with the broad nature and distribution of activities in a tract of fringe land but with their daily operation and interaction.

Local environmental management

The allocation of land to certain broad categories of desirable uses, even with protection from most kinds of building development (which the Green Belt implies) is no guarantee either of their continued viability, or of the retention of the wider environmental values of fringe land. Strategic policies are not enough. Not only, for example, must some land be *reserved* for agriculture or mining or other uses, but it must be *managed* in ways which ensure the success of these activities. Similarly, we have argued that the enhancement of fringe landscapes and the creation of more recreation areas does not necessarily mean that these are enjoyed by more people: access to them, and information about them, must be substantially improved. In theory so good, in practice the accessibility of open land on the edge of towns is poor and declining for many city-dwellers as the costs and inconvenience of travel increase.[43] Developmental and management action is required to improve physical access to and within the fringe: with the rationalisation of footpath systems, the construction of scenic routes which allow various – and innovative – modes of travel (by road, rail and water) to and between open areas. All this must be supported by policies which improve the availability of public information about the opportunities for access to fringe land.

Hookway and others have argued for as much, if not more, attention to be given to the management of Green Belts (including urban fringes) as is now the case for National Parks.[44] He has suggested that, in the same way, management plans should be prepared and special means of implementation should be established to carry them out. The calls for more positive use of fringe and Green Belt land in a number of recent plans also imply the need for management rather than simply (and solely in the past) generation of the 'grand design'. Not all of these spell out the means of implementation, although some experimental studies – in the Bollin Valley south of Manchester and more recently North West of London – are now suggesting some of the practical and local management issues involved. In a joint project sponsored by the Countryside Commission, Greater London Council, Hertfordshire County Council and the London Borough of Barnet, a variety of means of environmental improvement are being tried over 210 sq. km. of the Metropolitan Green Belt between Mill Hill and St. Albans. Building upon the experience of earlier practical management exercises in the uplands and the Bollin Valley, the project leader is involving landowners and farmers in measures such as treeplanting, signposting, and public education.[45]

It is not possible to prescribe all the elements that might form the basis of a fringe management policy, for the emphasis placed upon different aims and means of achieving them will vary according to the nature and scale of fringe problems and the size of the parent town.

A major requirement is for the reduction of uncertainty about the future, so that land managers can plan ahead. It will be necessary for planners to help here by producing phased long-term policies: Low suggests that farmers, for example, would be helped by 'at least ten years advance warning of changes in land use (including road schemes) proposed by local authorities'.[46] On land for future development and where interference from neighbouring residential or leisure areas is especially severe, efficient farming is unlikely to succeed unless strongly supported by public action. To prevent 'farming to quit' and encourage the best, albeit temporary, use of such land, some transitional management arrangements could be introduced whereby risks to commercial farmers are reduced. One solution is the public acquisition of agricultural land within the designated area which is then leased back, for variable periods, to tenants who farm it according to an agreed management plan which is phased with development. Elsewhere, where conditions will not permit good farming even when uncertainty is reduced, further measures can be tried. Low suggests that part-time farmers, research or educational farms should be encouraged in such areas. Alternatively, it may be possible to graft on subsidiary enterprises to buttress the low returns from farming. In some circumstances, the land may be better employed in some other use, which (as in various recreation schemes) would maintain its open character, but not preclude subsequent development or a return to agricultural use.

The creation and enhancement of good fringe landscapes implies greater attention to siting, design, screening and landscaping of all public and private developments, not only by restrictions imposed upon developments already controlled under the planning system, but also upon those activities which do not require planning permission. But the need may be even greater for creative landscape policies including tree planting and the construction of new lakes and scenic roads, as well as continuous management operations such as bulky rubbish and litter removal. All these tasks may require special administrative and financial arrangements. Better fringe landscapes will mean much more effort devoted to the rehabilitation of derelict land, particularly old mineral workings and transport routes but also degraded farmland. Many old excavations and areas of disturbed ground could be restored for new uses by public, private or voluntary action; indeed some areas are almost ready-made for activities like adventure playing. Existing means of ensuring proper restoration *during* and *after* use must be fully employed, but new legal powers may be needed before the necessary stringent controls can be applied — and enforced. Certainly, it is desirable that all possible measures of securing rehabilitation are explored, such as the wider use of levies upon mineral operators to finance funds for restoration; and perhaps the rating of fringe agricultural land which remains unused.

Implications for implementation

All these strategic and management policies for the land and activities of the urban fringe require many different means of implementation, some of which we explore in Chapter 12. A number of the improvements we have discussed — like the development of profitable recreation enterprises — are already taking place; others can be achieved by the more stringent measures of planning control which can be applied to fringe land where this is zoned as Green Belt, or as an Area of Outstanding Natural Beauty or of Great Landscape Value. The nature and arrangement of new development can obviously be influenced in this way. The imposition of detailed planning conditions can probably achieve more in the way of rehabilitation and new landscaping. There has, for example, been some improvement in the after-use of mineral workings in recent years; but there are still problems of enforcing the planning conditions associated with current workings, and large areas of dereliction remain from past excavations which carried no conditions of restoration. In all, the achievement of fringe goals through the mechanisms of planning control will be limited by the problems of enforcement and by the counter economic arguments of developers, especially on appeal.

More persuasive mechanisms might have greater effect in some areas and over the long term. It may be possible, for example, by providing detailed advice, together with financial and other incentives such as voluntary labour, to persuade more fringe farmers to modify their practices to accommodate certain kinds of recreational and educational activity. Such an approach has worked well in the programmes of farm open days organised by the Countryside Commission.[47] Further work on farm interpretation is now in progress which might lead to more permanent facilities such as purpose-built farm trails and exhibitions. Management agreements between land owners and public agencies provide another means of achieving desirable objectives in fringe areas. This and other less formal ways of influencing the nature and use of fringe land have been tried in the Bollin Valley Experiment.

But for various reasons, persuasive efforts too will be limited. Despite proposals for the public ownership of development land, some landowners may continue to be preoccupied with the future value of their land, at the expense of any real interest in its present use or appearance. National as well as local budgets are strained and not all the land needed for development will be soon acquired; interest in acquiring and hoarding land for investment and speculation may not diminish greatly at a time of economic and political uncertainty.

Where there is a good chance that the hope value of fringe land can be realised at some future time, owners will not be encouraged to introduce uses which might prejudice these prospects; nor will they want to be involved in equally limiting and binding agreements on management. Some landowners, now denied the opportunity for development gains, may try to introduce other profitable enterprises, in commercial recreation or in farming, which may not all be beneficial.

We have argued elsewhere that a much greater degree of public intervention, including public land ownership and management, will be needed in some areas to achieve the necessary control over social and environmental change, and the desirable scale of rehabilitation and creation of new landscapes. The fringe, with its complexity of interests and activities and its still fragmented administration is such an area. Public monies and management (albeit perhaps in association with private enterprise) will be needed to develop schemes where the social benefits will considerably outweigh commercial ones, especially in the early stages. Certainly, public initiative will be vital in developing fringe schemes which have regional and sub-regional identity and which are closely linked to other public policies within the parent town and its rural hinterland. In this way, for example, it is possible to envisage that substantial tracts of the fringe might be acquired, and farmed or afforested or designed as city regional parkland, laid out with a wide variety of leisure facilities to which special access would be made, and on which special information and publicity programmes would be based. In Chapter 3 we argued for a much greater involvement of the Forestry Commission in the creation of new landscapes on the urban fringe, but other agencies, and especially metropolitan local authorities have a part to play.

In theory, the current proposals for public ownership of fringe land for development provide unique opportunities for better planning.[48] The basis for land speculation is removed together with the incentive to hold land which may have no positive use. Local authorities should now have the time and the powers to plan a better mix and phasing of fringe land uses and an improved local environment which can be created alongside new developments. Developers are placed in a position whereby they may be more easily influenced on environmental issues.

But the new measures could also delay improvement of the function and appearance of fringe land. The rapid acquisition of land for development may well mean that no money remains for other areas of public provision — for the 'luxury' of open space. If certain land purchases are ill-judged and fail to be developed for some time, a new type of 'blighted' land will lie vacant for lack of funds and expertise to organise some form of positive interim management.

Implications for local government

The reform of local government administration and the introduction of leisure and recreation departments in many more authorities should mean that greater attention will now be paid to the accessibility and environment of the urban fringe, and its potential for overcoming the traditional barriers between urban and rural activity. Many urban authorities with executive responsibility for their fringes may now be persuaded to act by the more flexible system of grants under the Countryside Act (which acknowledges the urban fringe on a priority for recreation and landscape schemes). But there are problems in practice. Few of the new urban authorities have much expertise on the management of open land.

Moreover, the fringe is most extensive, and the problems are most acute, at the margins of conurbations where local government boundaries have been tightly drawn, so that no one authority can assume responsibility for fringe planning. Many planning policies are divided among both tiers of government within these metropolitan areas, while their margins will be influenced by the decisions of rural counties and county districts.

Faced with these inadequacies of a disparate administrative structure, a number of developments would seem to be essential if urban fringe problems are to be tackled and the potential of this environment is to be realised. Close collaboration between structure plan authorities is clearly vital to ensure that the fringe — which may lie at the margins of interest as well as of different administrations — suffers neither neglect nor imbalanced treatment. What is presently lacking (with few exceptions) is the strategic vision which must come primarily from the centre. The understandable preoccupation of urban strategic plans with more urgent issues of the inner city has been, in part, responsible for the piecemeal approach adopted towards the urban fringe. Policies have been decided and executed by local authorities outside the built up area concerned to protect their particular *status quo* and often to frustrate the wider goals of an urban authority. Despite fears that the Green Belt will be eroded, the current debate on using fringe land for housing — in London, at least — might provide one stimulus for a more integrated approach: forcing urban authorities to think about the values of nearby open land to city dwellers, and forcing those authorities that administer this land to consider the criteria on which land should go for housing, and advance much more positive alternative policies for keeping it open elsewhere.[49]

But even if structure plan policies are positive — perhaps visionary — this is no guarantee of effective implementation. The local management of much fringe land is now a task for the district authorities who will have small planning staffs and limited budgets. Moreover, they will be strongly influenced by parochial thinking which may lead to effective protection from development, but this is not enough to safeguard and enhance the values of fringe land.

Britain has no tradition of strong executive regional planning authorities with environmental planning and management powers.[50] It is tempting to argue for new and specialist structures to implement particular schemes on, for example, the model of the Huron Clinton Authority in Detroit, or the Lee Valley Regional Park Authority. Here, in retrospect, the creation of a separate, statutory park authority with powers to precept on 'the budgets' of all constituent authorities seems to have been an administrative mistake; it has suffered as have other *ad hoc* agencies, from inadequate local support, and from a lack of powers to influence relevant aspects of policy outside its scope. The need for action on the fringe is urgent and policies must treat fringe land in an integrated way. Neither condition is served by an arrangement which requires lengthy legal definition and is subsequently constrained in scope and flexibility. The Colne Valley Park, with its loose association of participants may gain on all these counts, but problems of insufficient co-ordination and stimulus, and too few staff resources may impede progress, just as other proposed schemes like London's M4 Linear Park, show no immediate prospect of implementation.

All this suggests that much stronger action is needed by metropolitan authorities, in execution as well as in strategic planning. For the larger schemes of fringe management — regional parks, extensive planting of new landscapes, rehabilitation and after-use of degraded land — the initiative and finance for implementation must come from the metropolitan authority, working together with the District Authorities, agencies of central government and other organisations. The Tame Valley linear park in Greater Manchester is a good example of such multi-agency co-operation.[51]

Implications for central government

Many of these suggestions imply a much stronger recognition, at national level, of the problems and opportunities of the urban fringe. Perhaps some general powers are needed for authorities to establish regional parks to which the Exchequer would contribute funds. Certainly the present imbalance of financial support for urban and rural parks must be rectified, in such a way that the fringe ceases to become a 'no man's land' of leisure and environmental policy-making and instead receives priority treatment as it now does, under the revised system of grants for recreation schemes under the Countryside Act. But there is room for more co-ordination of the policies and financial support of a number of different public agencies – including the Sports Council, Countryside Commission, Forestry Commission and others. The White Paper 'Sport and Recreation' makes important recommendations for much greater emphasis upon the urban fringe.[52]

The scope of central government agencies may need to be widened. The most recent review of forestry policy places a welcome emphasis upon afforestation for amenity purposes, but no special attention has been accorded (in, for example, the structure of grants or the activities of the Forestry Commission) to the fringes of towns where the need as well as the opportunity for amenity planting would seem to be considerable. Countryside Commission grants for tree planting do acknowledge the importance of the urban fringe, yet it is unlikely that local authorities who are having to expand their expertise in many new fields, will acquire soon the resources needed for extensive plantation work on city fringes. The policies of other public bodies, such as the Nature Conservancy Council in its administration of reserves, or the Ministry of Agriculture in its provision of guidance and grants to farmers, need also to recognise the special nature of the fringe.

Conclusions

Planning strategies and management policies are required on the fringes of towns as much as in the open countryside – perhaps more urgently – because of the rate at which opportunities for a better environment are being lost. In planning terms, the fringe environment is a severely neglected one. But the complexity of activities and interests at stake, and of the administrative structure, suggest that the task of fringe planning may be more difficult than elsewhere. The theory, the strategy, of what might be done is fairly clear. The need is for a more flexible approach to the use of land which reflects the form and growth of city regions; an approach which allows for a wider variety of developments within the fringe but one which, at the same time, makes more beneficial use of open land that remains.

Yet the achievement of these goals for most city fringes may be impossible unless the basic dilemma of Green Belt policy can be resolved and in a way that the planning system has so far failed to do. How is it possible to be less rigidly protective, and accommodate the changing demands of a city, but at the same time prevent the misuse and neglect of land in the face of the uncertainty which may follow such a policy? Even if land speculation can be controlled by legislation on the ownership of land for housing development, there is still a special case, on the urban fringe, for extensive public acquisition of open land which is managed in a positive and dynamic way for local and regional benefit.

Notes and References

1. Pahl, R. E. (1965) *Urbs in Rure: the Metropolitan Fringe in Hertfordshire*, London School of Economics Geographical Paper No. 2.
2. See for example:
   Thomas, D. (1970) *London's Green Belt*, Faber.
   Thomas, D. (1974) The Urban Fringe: Approaches and Attitudes, in Johnson, J. H. (ed.), *Suburban Growth*, John Wiley, and other chapters in this book.
3. Higbee, E. (1967) Agricultural Land and the Urban Fringe, in Gottman, J. and Harper, R. A. (eds.) *Metropolis on the Move*, John Wiley.
4. In Britain, farmers who can sell fringe land at higher prices for development have been encouraged to reinvest elsewhere in agricultural land by the 'roll-over' tax concession which allows capital gains tax on sale to be avoided if reinvestment in land occurs within three years.
5. For a discussion of hobby farming and its distinction from part-time farming, see:
   Munton, R. J. C. (1974) Farming on the Urban Fringe, in Johnson, J. H. (ed.), *Suburban Growth*, op. cit.
6. Gasson, R. M. (1966) *The Influence of Urbanisation on Farm Ownership and Practice*, Wye College Studies in Rural Land Use, No. 7.
   Low, N. (1973) Farming and the Inner Green Belt, *Town Planning Review*, Quarterly Vol. 44 (2), April.
   London Borough of Hillingdon (1973) *Open Land and the Green Belt: An Interim Policy*, Planning Department.
   Ministry of Agriculture (1974) *Agriculture in the Urban Fringe*, Agricultural Development and Advisory Service, Technical Report No. 30.
7. Low, N. (1973) Farming and the Inner Green Belt, op. cit.
8. Ministry of Agriculture (1974) *Agriculture in the Urban Fringe*, op. cit.
   Trespass in the form of dogs not properly controlled may account for the drastic reduction in sheep numbers in the Slough area — 59% between 1961 and 1971 — and their replacement by rough grazing and poultry keeping.
9. University of Reading, Department of Agricultural Economics and Management
   Milton Keynes 1967: An Agricultural Inventory;
   Milton Keynes Revisited 1971;
   Milton Keynes 1973.
10. Llewelyn-Davies, Weeks, Forester-Walker and Bor (1970) *The Plan for Milton Keynes.* See also: Technical Supplement No. 9.
11. Gasson, R. M. (1966) *The Influence of Urbanisation on Farm Ownership and Practice*, op. cit.
12. In 1973 and 1974 there were proposals for a substantial release of Metropolitan Green Belt land for Building:
    Panel of Inquiry into the Greater London Development Plan (1973) *Report* (The Layfield Report), H.M.S.O.
    Department of Environment (1973) *Widening the Choice: The Next Steps in Housing*, H.M.S.O.
    It remains to be seen how far the public ownership of development land on the edge of towns will stem speculation (Community Land Act, 1975). If landholders are convinced of an early reversal of policy with a change of government, speculation will continue.
13. '. . . temporary dereliction does not justify omitting land from the Green Belt . . .' Greater London Development Plan and Inquiry E.14/1, October, 1970.
14. Wibberley, G. P. (1959) *Agriculture and Urban Growth*, Michael Joseph.
    Low, N. (1973) Farming and the Inner Green Belt, op. cit.
    Hellard, D. (1975) Farmers and Landowners — Allies or Antagonists? in Proceedings of the C.R.R.A.G. Conference on *The Recreational Future of the Countryside near Towns and Cities* (to be published by the Countryside Commission).
15. Ministry of Agriculture (1974) *Agriculture in the Urban Fringe*, op. cit.
    The sample of 100 farms represented 60% of the total in 13 parishes. 25% of the sample area was Grade I agricultural land quality (average for England and Wales is 3-4%).
16. In the Slough area, many farms are less than 5 acres, often sufficient land only for an intensive livestock unit and space for its waste disposal.
17. Low, N. (1973) Farming and the Inner Green Belt, op. cit.
    Not all these activities are damaging to the farming interest; for some farmers in the Slough area, the benefits of motorway development in terms of compensation and reduction of trespass outweigh the problems of severance.
18. Mentioned in the discussion notes of Group 7 — *Farming in the Urban Fringe*, in Report of the Conference on Agriculture and the Countryside, organised by the Royal Agricultural Society for

England, in July, 1970.

19. Munton, R. J. C. (1974) Farming on the Urban Fringe, op. cit.
20. In 6 cases, the return was less than the 15% margin considered necessary to cover depreciation and interest charges.
    Burton, T. L. (1967) *Outdoor Recreation Enterprises in Problem Rural Areas*, Wye College Studies in Rural Land Use No. 9. See also:
    Bull, C. & Wibberley, G. P. (1977) *Farm-based Recreation in S.E. England*, Wye College Studies in Rural Land Use, No. 12.
21. A conclusion borne out by findings in: North West Sports Council (1972) *Leisure in the North West*, Department of Environment and N.W. Sports Council.
22. Thomas, D. (1970) *London's Green Belt*, op. cit.
23. Hall, P. (1973) Anatomy of the Green Belt, *New Society*, 4 January.
24. Gregory, D. G. (1970) *Green Belts and Development Control: a Case Study in the West Midlands*, Occasional Paper No. 12, University of Birmingham, Centre for Urban and Regional Studies.
25. The potential of the urban fringe for recreation, and some of the reasons why there is so little visionary recreation development on the edge of towns and cities in Britain are discussed in:
    Davidson, J. (1974) Recreation and the Urban Fringe, *The Planner*, Vol. 60 (9), November.
26. Davidson, J. (1974) Recreation and the Urban Fringe, op. cit.
    See also the suggestions for large-scale, substantially man-made 'green-urban' landscapes on the edge of towns in:
    Fairbrother, N. (1970) *New Lives, New Landscapes*, Architectural Press.
27. It is proposed that this shall be done in the plans for Milton Keynes.
28. Cracknell has suggested that a 'living space' of radius 95 Km is needed around London to contain a rural road network adequate for leisure driving:
    Cracknell, B. (1967) Accessibility to the Countryside as a Factor in Planning for Leisure, *Regional Studies* No. 1.
29. Acreage of Green Belts approved or under consideration as at December 1974. (Source: Department of the Environment).
30. Thomas, D. (1970) *London's Green Belt*, Faber, Chapter 3 traces the development of the idea of Green Belts.
31. Howard, E. (1946) *Garden Cities of Tomorrow*, Faber.
32. Ministry of Housing and Local Government (1955) *Green Belts*, Circular No. 42/55, H.M.S.O.
    Three reasons were listed for the establishment of a Green Belt:
    1. to check the growth of a large built up area;
    2. to prevent neighbouring towns from merging into one another; or
    3. to preserve the special character of a town.
33. Ministry of Housing and Local Government (1962) *The Green Belts*, H.M.S.O.
    The primary purpose of Green Belts was seen as preventing sprawl; the secondary purpose was to 'provide the townsman with the opportunity to escape from the noise, congestion and stress of city life and seek recreation in the countryside'.
34. Abercrombie, P. (1945) *Greater London Plan* 1944, H.M.S.O.
35. See for example:
    Greater London Council (1969) *Greater London Development Plan: Report of Studies and Statement*, Department of Planning and Transportation.
    London Borough of Hillingdon (1973) *Open Land and the Green Belt; an Interim Policy*; Planning Department.
36. Thomas, D. (1970) *London's Green Belt*, op. cit.
37. 'Conforming' uses, which do not require substantial buildings or in which these cover only a small proportion of the total area occupied, include: agriculture, woodland, recreation land, schools, hospitals, water works, cemeteries and unused land.
    'Non-conforming' uses include residential, commercial and industrial development; extractive industry, land used for transport and public services.
    Chapters 6 and 7 of Thomas' book on *London's Green Belt* (op. cit.) discuss these categories of use in detail.
38. The Metropolitan Green Belt remains largely unquestioned in:
    South East Joint Planning Team (1970) *A Strategic Plan for the South East*, H.M.S.O.
    But see the review of sub-regional planning studies in:
    Jackson, J. N. (1972) *The Urban Future*, Allen & Unwin; University of Birmingham Urban and Regional Studies No. 3.
39. South Hampshire Plan Advisory Committee (1972) *South Hampshire Structure Plan*, Hampshire County Council.
40. South East Economic Planning Council (1967) *A Strategy for the South East*, H.M.S.O.

41. Fairbrother, N. (1970) *New Lives, New Landscapes*, Architectural Press.
42. See for example the proposals for 'Greenways' outlined in the Nottinghamshire/Derby Sub-Regional Study.
43. For London, such open space as exists on the fringe of the built up area is virtually inaccessible to the residents of the inner city; the use of public transport at weekends involves prohibitively long travel times and high money costs:
    Law, S. and Perry, N. H. (1971) Countryside Recreation for Londoners — a Preliminary Research Approach, *Greater London Council Quarterly Bulletin of the Research and Intelligence Unit*, No. 4.
44. Hookway, R. J. S., Director of the Countryside Commission, at a meeting of the Regional Studies Association on Green Belts, March 1973.
45. Aldous, A. (1976) Experiment on the Urban Fringe, *New Scientist*, Vol. 69 (983), Jan. 15th.
    Hall, A. (1973) The Bollin Valley Project, *Recreation News Supplement* No. 9.
    Hall, A. (1976) Management in the Urban Fringe, *Countryside Recreation Review*, Vol. 1.
    London Borough of Hillingdon (1973) *Open Land and the Green Belt: An Interim Policy*, Planning Department.
    See also Chapter 12 of this book.
46. Low, N. (1973) Farming and the Inner Green Belt, *Town Planning Review*, Quarterly Vol. 44 (2), April.
47. Dartington Amenity Research Trust (1974) *Farm Open Days*, Countryside Commission.
48. Community Land Act, 1975.
49. See, for example, the detailed analysis and comprehensive policy-making in:
    London Borough of Hillingdon (1973) *Open Land and the Green Belt: An Interim Policy*, op. cit.
    But the response among other London authorities has been far less encouraging, often only a reiteration of the intention to retain a rigidly defensive Green Belt policy.
50. Such as, for example, exists in the Siedlungsverband Ruhrkohlenbezirk (S.V.R.), the regional planning agency of the Ruhr, whose remit includes extensive involvement in the planning and management of land and water at the margins of the Ruhr conurbation.
51. The Tame Valley Improvement Scheme, where derelict land is being converted to a co-ordinated network of open spaces and footpaths, has involved representatives of ten District Councils, three County Councils and the Civic Trust for the North West.
52. Department of the Environment (1975) *Sport and Recreation*, Cmnd 6200, H.M.S.O.

CHAPTER 9

Upland Problems

Like the urban fringe, the uplands are in many ways a marginal planning environment. They are more and more affected not only by the changes in surrounding city regions, but by the progressive spread of other urbanising influences in communications and technology. Yet, like the fringe, they retain a unique character, although this is derived from a different set of circumstances.

The most important differentiating factors about the uplands are the harsh physical conditions and the relative — at times absolute — isolation. But despite (indeed, partly because of) the harshness of the physical environment, the uplands offer an extraordinary richness of resources: meat and wool, water, minerals, space, and great physical beauty. Thus the uplands are an environment of complex and conflicting demands. Like the fringe, they illustrate the difficulties of resolving — administratively and technically — the problems of an area where there are multiple resource interests. Here too, though in a rather different sense, there is a constantly shifting emphasis on conservation or development. The two are often seen to be at odds; the right balance, regionally and locally, has yet to be found.

Implications of the Physical Environment

The uplands have lower temperatures at all seasons of the year compared with the lowlands, with a relatively higher rainfall and more periods of frost and snow. The effect is, therefore, to restrict the range of plants and animals which will grow well in such areas. Although the mountains of Britain can be considered as ecological and geological outliers of the mountain systems of central and northern Europe, they are more exposed to oceanic effects; climatic and vegetational change with altitude is sharper. Much upland topography is very varied, with steep slopes and rapid changes in land level which make the cultivation of crop land physically difficult and costly if not impossible. Underlying and reinforcing these difficulties are the effects of geological structure. Old, hard and acidic rocks give poor, thin soils which, except on the valley floors, have been leached of all the main nutrients for plant growth.

Because of the difficulties of routing and making roads and railways through upland areas, the relative costs of accessibility are increased and many services, including the medical and educational ones which cover large catchment areas containing few people, must suffer. Likewise, public services such as electricity, telephone and piped water are more costly to provide and to maintain. For the upland farmer, remoteness imposes extra costs upon all farming processes, not only those of production but also of storage, processing and marketing.

All of these factors combine to give a generally poor natural resource base (though it may be locally particularly rich in minerals), and a climate and terrain which severely limit the attractiveness of uplands as living environments for man.

> "People living in the hills have become aware of the greater opportunities and amenities offered in the lowlands and have decided to take advantage of them. This drift of population has made life harder for those remaining. It is more difficult in economic terms to provide the basic services and it becomes more difficult to develop agriculture or alternatives to agriculture.'[1]

These areas have interlocking vicious circles of natural, economic and social difficulties which act and interact upon each other in ways which are hard to change with any degree of permanence. Figure 5 shows diagrammatically the interaction of these factors. The low productivity and high cost of most systems of hill farming intensify the difficulties of human settlement in such areas. Usually an area of this nature is fighting the problems which come from the interaction of three situations of marginality. There is the physical margin, that is, the presence of land where certain crops fail to grow or where topography and soils make cultivation impossible. There is also the economic margin: that is, the point at which a system of production fails to pay its way and where marginal returns fall below the extra costs of getting additional output. The economic margin is, of course, present in all business enterprises whether they are situated in the favourable conditions of the lowlands or in the more difficult parts of the uplands but the economic margin is reached quickly on many hill farms as it coincides with severe restrictions in physical possibilities, a rigid land tenure system and shortages of both fixed and working capital. Lastly there is the social margin, that is, the conditions in which human beings and their families refuse to live permanently. Those who live habitually in the hills, through all seasons, have a much more unpleasant set of experiences than the pleasure which many urban people receive from spending a few summer weeks and weekends in the uplands, usually when their children are on holiday and when a certain amount of 'rough living' is looked upon as a challenging contrast to their normal, sophisticated living pattern. The farmer and writer, Tristam Beresford, emphasises the social problem in hill areas by saying that many of them are not 'woman worthy'.[2] By this he means that women are not prepared to accept all the difficulties of living and bringing up a family in such areas, even though their menfolk, finding them easier or more exciting, may value the privilege of upland living.[3]

Improvements must, therefore, be made in the physical and social fabric of hill areas if they are to provide a viable living and working environment albeit for a minority of those who cannot or do not want to live in the city region, or who society wishes to retain as managers of upland resources. But any improvements must be maintained permanently, and without too extravagant a use of social capital, at a number of points along the cycle of upland problems illustrated in Figure 5. The improvements must reinforce each other. Where only one, or a few, isolated problems in this cycle are resolved, the final result may be poor because isolated improvements often ignore the basic interdependence of both problem and remedy in such areas.

The Significance of Hill Farming

The area coming under the definition of hills, uplands and mountains depends upon the

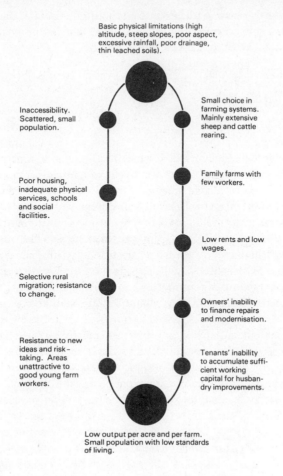

Basic physical limitations (high altitude, steep slopes, poor aspect, excessive rainfall, poor drainage, thin leached soils).

Inaccessibility. Scattered, small population.

Small choice in farming systems. Mainly extensive sheep and cattle rearing.

Poor housing, inadequate physical services, schools and social facilities.

Family farms with few workers.

Low rents and low wages.

Selective rural migration; resistance to change.

Owners' inability to finance repairs and modernisation.

Resistance to new ideas and risk-taking. Areas unattractive to good young farm workers.

Tenants' inability to accumulate sufficient working capital for husbandry improvements.

Low output per acre and per farm. Small population with low standards of living.

FIG. 5. *Interaction of Environmental and Social Factors in many Upland Areas.*

criteria chosen as defining land of this character. In many hill areas there is a sharp line between land which has been enclosed, by hedge or stone wall, and higher land which has been left unenclosed, but this line shifts up and down from area to area according to local differences in climate, so that a simple definition based upon altitude is of little use to distinguish between hill and lowland.

In Britain, because improvements to the hill country began first in agriculture, the definition of hill land used for most purposes is still an agricultural one. It is defined as land of such a nature that it is suited only to the rearing of livestock and not to their fattening. In practice, the altitude to which this restricted type of land use applies varies considerably according to its position and exposure to the prevailing winds. For example, there are parts of the Welsh hills close to the Irish Sea where the altitude limit on livestock rearing land comes as low as 200-300 feet above sea level, and in areas such as the Shetlands, hill farming conditions apply right down to sea level. In other parts of the hills and uplands which are more protected from the prevailing winds and where slopes lie open to the sun, arable cropping and livestock fattening can be found as high as 1,000 feet above sea level. In practice, therefore, the Ministry of Agriculture, Fisheries and Food and the Scottish Department of Agriculture have carefully classified all hill areas in detail for the administration of hill grants and subsidies.[4]

In the late 1950's, a study at Wye College attempted to measure the agricultural contribution of the hills and uplands throughout Great Britain.[5] Using the definition of hill land as that suitable only for the rearing of livestock, it was estimated that the hills and uplands cover roughly 14,000,000 acres (8 mill hect.). This is a quarter of Britain's land surface though it is a rather higher proportion (31%) of all the land in agricultural use in the country. At that time this large land area was farmed in roughly 40,000 separate holdings and these represented more than 1 in 10 of all farms of above one acre in size in the country.

As might be expected the overall agricultural output of hill country is relatively low. Although a quarter of the total land surface, it provided, at that time, only 4 per cent of the agricultural output of the nation. Even its contribution to livestock output, measured as a proportion of all fatstock slaughtered in Britain, was only between 5 and 7 per cent of the total. This relatively low livestock contribution resulted from the large contribution to sheep numbers being compensated by the very low contribution the hills make to total British supplies of cattle, calves and pigs.

The study did point out the major contribution made by hill sheep and wool to national home supplies of these products. The hill breeding flock of about 4.5 million head provided its own ewe replacement and, in addition, exported some 2.5 million sheep to the lowlands. These 'exports' made up between one-third and one-half of the total sheep slaughtered in one year in the country, but the monetary value received by the hill farmers was only about a quarter of the total because of the small physical size of hill sheep and the large proportion of store animals in the total contribution. Again, the hills and uplands were responsible for about one-third of the annual value of the national home produced wool clip.

Research workers have tried to assess the magnitude of the contribution of hill sheep to national supplies by assessing the probable effect of a complete cessation of hill and upland sheep farming. It seemed to them that it would force the total sheep population down to about half its existing level and that, even if sheep become a much more important part of lowland farming, the national sheep flock would not be able to rise above two-thirds of the total sheep flock if the hills and uplands ceased.

In contrast, the hill country produces only between 5 and 7 per cent of the United Kingdom production of cattle for slaughter and, in terms of money value, this was thought to be only about 4 per cent of the national figure. Again, although milk production has crept up into the hills and uplands, it still represents only about 3 per cent of national annual milk sales. But its product is important to many small upland farms for it represents a regular cheque coming in each month; its cessation would take away about one-fifth of the total agricultural income of all the farms concerned and this is the most dependable part.

The particular study on which this discussion is based has not been updated but more recent estimates made by the Ministry of Agriculture and the Economic Development Committee for Agriculture support its general conclusions.[7] But in 1972 the same overall area of hill land supported only 26,000 full time farming units, with a further 35,000 part time units (many of these being in Northern Ireland). The proportion of total British agricultural output produced in the hills and uplands was calculated to be 7 per cent (as against 4 per cent in the Wye study in the 1950's) with livestock production at 10 per cent (as compared with 5 to 7 per cent) and nearly 50 per cent of British sheep and wool output (the same as the Wye 1950's estimate). The NEDO report shows the strengthening, in output terms, of the agricultural contribution of the hills and uplands since the 1950's, although the nature of the contribution has stayed the same.

Support for the Hills and Uplands

Though there were various forms of Government assistance to agriculture in the 1930's, it was not until 1943 that a universal subsidy on hill cattle was introduced. Wartime Committees of Inquiry for both Scotland and England and Waies (the Balfour and Earl de la Warr committees) into hill sheep farming problems proposed the subsidisation of capital improvements on hill farms and gave rise to the comprehensive proposals of the 1946 Hill Farming Act. But this referred only to the improvement of the higher mountain and hill land. The lower farms with similar economic and social problems were debarred from these improvement grants. This omission was rectified in 1951 when, under the Livestock Rearing Act, the Government extended the area of land which qualified for grants towards capital improvement, and increased the fund available. This has continued as the pattern of Government help to hill and upland agriculture. The problem remains of whether or not to subsidise in this long term way the hopelessly small and marginal hill farm or to concentrate financial help on potentially viable farming units, with assistance towards the amalgamation of holdings.

On balance this selective help has maintained the viability of the larger hill farm businesses but the smaller ones, especially in the higher uplands, have not succeeded in gaining incomes commensurate with their fellow farmers on the lowlands or in non-agricultural businesses. Much of the subsidisation has, therefore, proved to be merely a holding operation and a slowing down of trends towards part and spare time farming.

But it must not be thought that the subsidisation of farming in the hills and uplands of Britain has been exorbitant as compared with its productivity. The study made by Davidson and Wibberley did suggest, quite firmly, that although upland farmers were accepting a lower standard of living than British farmers in general, there was no evidence to suggest that the rest of the nation was paying more in the way of subsidies to support agriculture in the hills and uplands than was being paid to support lowland agriculture. In fact, at that time, hill farmers were getting a lower sum of Government assistance than their counterparts in the lowlands, with the suggestion that the system of agricultural guarantees and subsidies was, in practice, widening the gap in incomes between hill and lowland farmers rather than closing it. Other writers have been less certain of the relative nature of subsidisation of hill and lowland agriculture. Some have argued that hill farming produces only 7-8 per cent of the gross agricultural output but absorbs steadily more government support, so that in some upland areas grants exceed farm incomes by substantial margins.[8]

Hill farming is likely to continue to receive subsidised help from the rest of the European Economic Community in the form of special grants to hill farms and through contributions from the European Fund for Regional Development. But hill and mountainous areas form a significant part of the land surface of other members of the E.E.C. and Britain will have to bring the preferential help to her own hill areas into line with that agreed for the mountain areas of the mainland of Western Europe. In a recent E.E.C. directive, the Council of Ministers agreed upon the broad lines of European policy for the less favoured agricultural areas, including hills and mountains where continuation of farming was thought to be a necessary pre-requisite for the conservation of the social and environmental fabric of the countryside, especially in terms of reducing the scale of depopulation.

To qualify for special aid, the average incomes of farmers in these areas would have to be less than two-thirds of the national farm income. In addition, farmers would have to face operating difficulties brought about by steep slopes, unfavourable climates (with a restricted growing season of less than six months) and poor soils incapable of supporting crops, and suitable only for extensive livestock production.

The arrangements proposed by the E.E.C. are broadly in line with the kinds of help already being given to hill farmers in Britain, though in some ways the definition of hill areas is more elastic and includes dairy farms at higher elevations. Negotiations are still proceeding on the detail of the general directive, with particular emphasis on the actual areas in Britain which will be included.[9]

Prospects for Hill Farming

The economic fortunes of hill farmers will probably continue to oscillate, as in the past, with the local climate and with changing world food prices. Conditions favourable because of the world-wide shortage of meat and other livestock products. But the long term uncertainty remains.

Other forms of income have gone into the hill country through such developments as farm-based recreation, the development of second homes and the general growth of tourism. There have been improvements in rural industrialisation and a steady increase in the afforestation of poor hill land. But the situation is not simple: upland farmers suffer not only from the constraints of their physical surroundings and the uncertainties of home and international food markets but sometimes also from these newer and potentially beneficial resource uses. Private afforestation schemes have taken good land out of agriculture and away from farmers in some areas; new reservoirs have flooded valley floors in situations where the regime of upland farming is dependent upon a symbiosis between rough moorland pasture and valley 'in-bye' land; the growth of recreation in the hills since the last war has brought its own local problems of trespass and damage for upland farmers.

Agriculture still dominates the upland economy, particularly in terms of employment. Agriculture also dominates the patterns of land use and landscape. Despite the improvement to personal incomes and services which may accrue from the introduction of other employment and from a more closely integrated pattern of different resource uses, the evolution of some form of viable agriculture, with its permanency of employment (which rarely exists in other upland jobs) must take place if the characteristic environment and a community in the hills are to be retained.

Continuing improvements in hill farming productivity will come from a variety of structural and especially technical improvements: from the further amalgamation of upland farms, from more resistant livestock breeds, increased stocking rates, better grass strains and pasture improvement by ploughing and other means. The need is seen for a closer integration of upland and lowland farms, for example, on the over-wintering of stock, and for more co-operation, especially in the use of machinery, and in livestock marketing. Agricultural extension work in the uplands (normally less effective than elsewhere) must be intensified, and some way found of improving the liaison between hill farmers and the many other groups with a stake in the way their land is managed. There will be a need for better collection and distribution services for the goods of upland farms. Many of these changes will involve more conflict with the widening resource interests of the hills; ploughing and enclosure of upland pasture has already met with considerable criticism from walkers and others who are concerned about the loss of free access, and change in the semi-natural upland landscape.[10] Further losses and changes are inevitable if productivity, and with it farm incomes, are to increase.

Forestry in the Uplands

The planting of bare ground with trees, both by the State and private organisations, has been concentrated mainly in the hills and uplands during this century. Here there are large areas of lightly used land, much of it marginal to most forms of hill farming, whereas in the lowlands, new afforestation has meant strong competition from intensive agricultural uses such as arable cropping and dairy farming.

In recent years, private interests have become more involved in buying land in the uplands, planting and managing it themselves or on behalf of clients attracted by the special tax provisions which apply as well as government grants. In many ways private interests have found it easier to purchase land in the uplands than has the Forestry Commission, which is circumscribed in its procedures and can only acquire land for planting when it is deemed to be of very low agricultural value by the Ministry of Agriculture. State forestry is therefore pushed onto the higher ground where hill farming is either static or on the retreat. In contrast, however, private forestry interests can bid in the market for hill farms against hill farmers.[11] Although in some areas of the National Parks, private planting programmes have been agreed with Park planning authorities and with the Forestry Commission in relation to Government planting grants and dedication schemes, these controls are really too loose to deal with the question of whether particular tracts of land should best stay in agriculture or be afforested, with their different implications for land holding, employment, and recreation activity. Nor have these measures been effective enough in protecting certain areas from the very real change commercial afforestation can bring to their scenic character and value.

The debate about upland afforestation is frequently emotional and often confused. Chapter 3 has already discussed how the emphasis in argument has oscillated over the years between the various benefits which are thought to accrue from large scale planting. The *economic* case rests on a comparison of the long term returns from poor land under trees or in sheep and other livestock farming. From time to time, both individual research workers and government have made estimates of the possible economic returns. The most recent attempt at an economic evaluation of upland forestry is the 1972 Inter-Departmental Report on cost benefit analysis.[12] This study confirmed that the long term interest rate which afforestation could justify was only about 4 per cent but calculations on allowances for recreational developments in the new forests suggested that this rate of return could well be lifted to about 7 per cent. Even though there has been, in recent years, a marked increase in the prices received for timber and timber products, it is probable that if these are discounted over the long time period (of 50 plus years) which is necessary to cover a conifer rotation period, the probable rate of return on afforestation in the hills and uplands will not be materially increased above a 4 per cent level just from commercial considerations alone. All of these studies suggest that the place of forestry in the hill country must be decided by considerations additional to those of an economic nature.

For a long time it has been argued that a country heavily dependent on imports of timber and timber products should try to increase the amount and proportion of these products produced within its own borders. This *strategic* argument is still important even though the 1972 cost benefit analysis rather minimised its value. The difficulty is that balance-of-payments situations in a country like Britain change quite dramatically during relatively short periods making long term planning uncertain. In addition, because the supplies derived from some of the main timber exporting countries of Scandinavia and Russia are only a small proportion of their total timber stocks, these countries are in a strong position to make changes in the amount and the prices of timber exported. If their export markets were threatened by protected forestry industries in their main customers, their own marginal prices could easily be lowered.

It has recently been suggested, particularly by some private forestry groups, that it is important to have a sizeable domestic forestry programme in Great Britain in order that large enough timber mills and processing industries can be established to develop economies of scale. British timber firms, it is argued, could then process both domestic and imported supplies of crude timber more economically.

In the post-war forest policy of 1945, considerable argument was developed on the ability of new plantations to *employ* more than the hill farming units they replaced. But the experience of upland afforestation since that time has not supported this case of high employment benefits; indeed, many of the settlements and housing arrangements made in hill forest areas consequent on this hope for increased employment have not proved successful. Some new forestry villages were poorly located, others were never really needed and some houses have recently been let by the Forestry Commission as self-catering accommodation where there is no demand for them by bona fide forestry workers. Even so, the 1972 cost benefit analysis concluded that, on balance, afforestation did provide rather more jobs in hill areas than hill farming (Table 13, Chapter 3). The ratio between new jobs in forestry as against agriculture varies from 1-2 in the south of England to nearly 1-3 in North Wales and more than 1-10 in the north of England. The calculations suggested, however, that the cost of providing each new job in State forestry was very much heavier than the cost of providing jobs in hill farming and the difference was at least twice as much. In the subsequent government forest policy statement, the provision of more jobs in an area was seen as an important aspect of future agreements to the public purchase of land for planting, and it is clear that the forestry contribution to regional development is now receiving greater emphasis.[13]

The rise and fall of criticism against afforestation in the hills and uplands has been very much linked with the heavy use of conifers and the unsympathetic handling of new forests in areas of undulating topography. The monotonous plantings, in rigid drawing board design, have often contrasted savagely with the random distribution of indigenous tree growth in the hills and their valleys. Many of the past mistakes remain, for forestry has a long term environmental effect. But State and private practice alike have improved: most new plantings are more carefully sited and designed, with the internal and especially the edge species selected so as to reduce the dislocation of form, colour and ecological environment that new plantings bring. Disguise of this kind, with hardwoods and shrubs that will survive the pioneer phase, must be used more widely in the afforestation of bare ground. In the replanting of established forests, there is more scope for improving the aesthetic quality of whole areas, using a greater variety of species and varying the felling regimes. But the opportunity for substantial and long term damage remains, so long as the means of persuasion to manage upland forests in these ways are so weak.

In Britain, we have been rather late in accepting the possibilities of recreational development in our forests and planning to increase their attractiveness to more than small numbers of people. That forests are popular destinations for holidays and day trips is shown by recent surveys and the reactions of public and private forest agencies has already been described in Chapter 3. The experience in those forests where special provision has been made, suggests that most kinds of informal recreation activity are quite compatible with commercial forestry operations. But it is erroneous to argue that commercial forestry generates *extra* recreation benefits that would otherwise not accrue from the use of hill land. For similar investment, the potential of much hill farmland for recreation must be as great if not greater than the same land under trees for it is only the forest margins that are presently used or in any way attractive for most people to visit. Substantial recreation as well as general amenity benefits may be foregone by further large scale afforestation of some accessible and scenically attractive uplands. That is unless or until we become more accustomed to tree-covered slopes and attracted by the prospect of forest recreation of the scale and quality which is common in North America.

Although private forestry groups are showing that they agree with, and welcome, the new stress on amenity and recreational development in upland forests, it is difficult to see how they will seriously contribute in these areas. Their investors and their management policy are geared to the production of commercial timber with the highest economic returns net of tax. Although private forestry groups will be keen to increase their income by letting out shooting and other game rights, these are bound to be selective, involving only small numbers of people. Moreover, most of the land which private forestry groups have recently bought in the uplands is a long way from centres of population.

What then is the balance of the argument for and against forestry as a major user of the hills and uplands? If the right policy is to develop and manage land uses which create and expand local employment, then forestry must rank high on the list of potential uses. Even so, its contribution to total employment may be low in some areas, and fluctuating as the labour requirements vary according to the stage of forest development, although labour demands will be balanced over the larger plantation areas. A more realistic goal for the long term may be one of combining forestry into a multiple use management policy for the hill economy. But the lack of a tradition of combined forest-and-farming holdings[14] (in contrast to many hill areas in the rest of Europe), the poor relationship, in practice, between land capability and land use, and the lack of any reliable means of influencing land assembly for different purposes, all hinder the achievement of this goal.

Water Conservation

The water resources of the uplands have been heavily exploited in the past: high rainfall and a mountainous topography with many natural lakes provided the obvious location for reservoir schemes to serve the thirsty conurbations of the drier lowlands, in the south and east and the industrial conurbations.

The demands for more water continue to rise — not so much to drink, but rather to satisfy the amenities of modern homes and to supply new industrial processes. Surprisingly (though in common with the use of some other rural resources) there is little concern or pressure to influence this demand; in Britain there has been a reluctance to link closely the cost of supplying water with the price paid for it by the consumer. Flat rate charges at least for domestic water supply are common, and these bear little relation to the volume used. Nor have there been incentives, except when severe shortages are forecast, for people to economise in their generally profligate use of water, or for water authorities to reduce leakages.[15] In a situation where demand is not directly influenced by price changes (and where forecasts may be based upon only a superficial understanding of those factors which influence water use)[16] it is obvious that estimates of future need will be high: the average daily use of 14 million cubic metres in 1971 is expected to double by 2001. A report by the Water Resources Board has suggested that 2.9 million cubic metres per day of extra water will be needed by 1981 together with an extra 9.5 million cubic metres per day by 2001.[17]

There are two different ways of approaching the problem of providing more water as populations increase and as more people live in cities with piped water supplies. The first is an extensive method of large scale storage reservoirs set in wet and hilly areas often far away from the point of consumption. In practice, this has been the traditional approach in Britain. Direct supply reservoirs, some built with little regard for the landscape of the valleys they have flooded, and cordoned off from public access, are a familiar sight in parts of the uplands, especially in the Peak District (where there are more than 50 reservoirs), the Lake District and Wales. They have been the cause of some nationalistic dissent (only recently surpassed in Wales, by the resistance to English second homes) and of local hardship in cases where farmers have lost all or part of their holdings in return for compensation payments quite inadequate to re-establish a viable enterprise elsewhere. Often, valleys have been bought up by separate water companies; the better valley bottom land was flooded, severing the regime of hill farming, and agricultural use of the new catchment restricted because of the need to keep reservoir water, treated only by filtration, untainted by organic matter. Afforestation was allowed around the banks of the reservoir, but otherwise the valleys became deserted by people and by animals.

The major alternative method to upland direct supply reservoirs relies upon the use and re-use of water abstracted from rivers nearer to the centres of demand, a process which places increasing emphasis upon the maintenance of adequate river flows and better water quality. Most new reservoirs and their extensions in the uplands and in the lowlands are now of the river-regulation rather than the direct supply type; there is much more concern for landscaping the lake margins and introducing acceptable designs for dams and other structures; there is a greater willingness to provide for some kinds of water and lakeside recreation, and few restrictions upon the use of surrounding land for normal agricultural practices including grazing.

In their proposals for the next three decades, the Water Resources Board concentrate upon extending the river regulation and abstraction approach; there are clear advantages for other river uses and users, for local improvements in water flows and quality will benefit many interests including those of navigation, industry (for abstraction and waste disposal), fishing and other recreation activity. This multi-purpose approach has been helped by the administrative reorganisation of the water industry whereby the segregation of supply, effluent discharge and the prevention of pollution which took place under the old system of river authorities, is now made good in the new structure of ten all-purpose regional water authorities which control water gathering, supply and quality on a more realistic scale.[18]

Other methods of meeting future demands for water seem, at least in the short term, to be relatively less important. Desalination of sea water is still too costly compared with other schemes and the plants are too small to make a significant contribution to needs. The environmental impact would be considerable. Although there have been several feasibility studies on the damming of major estuaries, only the Dee barrage scheme is to be realised, in the period 1981-2001.[19] Some effort is to be directed to the use of underground storage and the recharging of acquifers. But no economic reasoning has been applied to the effective demand for water: there are, as yet, no plans for the metering of supplies to domestic consumers, nor for the development of new technologies for water saving.

The plans are cautious about more water gathering in the hills. Up to 1981, only three new upland reservoirs are planned with an enlargement of an existing one in Wales; from 1981-2001, two more will be built and two enlarged. The influence of the old style, sterile single use reservoir is still strong and in recent years the case against more extensive flooding of upland valleys, especially in National Parks, has been hardening. This is in spite of the recreational and landscape advantages which accrue to some areas, and despite the apparent technical and economic inefficiency of flooding larger, flatter and more fertile tracts of the lowlands, as at Empingham, for water storage. Amenity and conservation objections have grown, and a number of upland schemes, as in Upper Teesdale,[20] and at Swincombe,[21] have sharply polarised national attitudes.

But agricultural arguments and those of cultural and economic nationalism have also intensified. Hill farmers have become increasingly bitter about the loss of valley bottom land and their case has been strongly argued by their own farmers' organisations and by the Ministry of Agriculture. In future, the value of the better agricultural land in the valley bottoms should increase further with the pressure for Britain to become more self-sufficient in temperate foods, and particularly in livestock products. Nor are the nationalist objections to water storage and distribution to those who pay only meagre rates to the communities from which it is derived likely to diminish; and the new Regional Water Authorities will need to give expression to these reactions in the decisions they take.

As a national strategy for water policy, the latest plans thus meet many of the demands of upland interests. But the beneficial effects of upland storage may still be underestimated. Jones, for example, in a study of the fortunes and reactions of farmers in a hill area of Wales who had been affected by the construction of a reservoir, showed that supplementary incomes received by farmers who remained (from milk and poultry sales and from camping) were considerable, and their situation was often improved by re-allocation schemes. Many local people benefit from construction work in the early years and from the new roads.[22] These benefits will not apply everywhere, but easing of the pressure for *new* upland reservoirs should not mask the fact that many more advantages could be gained from those that already exist, by overcoming the resistance of water authorities to landscape and other conservation improvements and to provision for recreation (and not only by clubs) and by greater co-operation between the varied interests concerned including the National Park and Planning Authorities, Sports Council, Countryside Commission, Forestry Commission, Ministry of Agriculture, Nature Conservancy Council, tourist boards and the recreation departments of Regional Water Authorities, and their consumer representatives.[23]

The changing structure and technical emphasis of the water industry shows that multiple-interest management and water re-use are now stronger elements of policy than the mere construction of additional sources of supply. But in the longer term, and in relation to the wider countryside, the recent strategy may be less satisfactory than it first appears, because it takes so little account of reducing wasteful consumption. It is very bad economics to provide additions in water supplies at a zero cost to the existing community, whereas the cost of creating new reservoirs or otherwise extending supplies is high and rising. Moreover, the system is designed to produce enough water to cover the drought situations that occur only once in 50 years. It is understandable that water authorities respond in this way, when they are vulnerable to very vocal criticism from those consumers who pay little towards the economic cost of building into the system a considerable amount of excess capacity.

Mineral Working and the Uplands

Just as the physiography of many upland areas make them naturally suitable for water catchment schemes, so do they offer, because of their age and geological complexity, a great variety of the minerals sought by modern industrial man. In many parts of the hills, often in National Parks, the small scale and uncertainty of individual enterprises with their scant regard for clearing up the mess, have bequeathed a landscape disfigured by waste and derelict machinery (although in some parts of the country, notably Cornwall, much of this is now valued as industrial archaeology).

The present contribution of the National Parks is considerable: three quarters of the total British production of fluorspar comes from the Peak District, together with significant and increasing amounts of limestone, and other minerals in less quantities.[24] Many of these minerals are wholly or partially processed on site giving associated waste, buildings and machinery.

For many centuries, most minerals of commercial use have been mined by underground methods and although this has caused serious local landscape problems by the raising of spoil heaps, the clutter of overground machinery and buildings and poor quality housing hurriedly built for miners, the problems are often on a reasonable scale. The major clash of interests in this century has come about by the development of open cast methods of mining where extensive land areas are disturbed. The use of large and efficient mechanical means of excavation has recently been associated with the discovery of new ways of extracting small percentages of minerals from large amounts of parent rock so that deposits of low-grade minerals have become economic to work. The present balance of payments situation, and the consequent pressure to use home rather than imported raw materials, will ensure that it is expedient, as well as technically and economically feasible, to exploit these low grade ores. It is known that copper deposits are present in parts of north Wales and Aberdeenshire; lead and zinc are likely in Cornwall and in the Lake District; tin is being worked in Cornwall and there is still some gold lying in parts of the Snowdonia National Park. Thus, added to the legacy of past workings, are new threats of exploitation on a very much larger scale.

This scale of possible new working is considerable. An example given by the Zuckerman Commission suggests that a typical open cast copper mine (containing about 60 million tonnes and with a useful life of 15 years) could occupy an area of 5 square miles including the mine, waste rock and a tailings reservoir.[25] The effects of noise, traffic, air and water pollution, and severe visual intrusion would be felt over a much wider area.[26]

Mineral working can bring social benefits and gains to the local as well as the national economy. But the job opportunities, for local people, are difficult to forecast in advance, and are likely, even at the construction phase, to be rather fewer than protagonists of mining schemes would argue.[27] Even so, substantial amounts of indirect employment (and for all age groups) may be generated in a community dominated by mining, as for example St. Austell is in Cornwall. Concentrated industrial activity of this kind will have ripple effects on the social and physical services provided for resident populations.

But what of the environmental implications? How far can the impact of possible new mining developments be reconciled with conservation goals, particularly in National Parks but also in other protected areas? The conflict remains largely unresolved; the Zuckerman Commission dodged it and was much criticised for doing so; the Sandford Report recommends a policy which, for the most part, accepts that environmental goals will be sacrificed if the national need is great enough.[28] In the major cases so far Government has acted in favour of mining; after a public inquiry and opposition from national park and countryside interests, approval was given for potash to be mined in the North Yorkshire Moors.

It is likely that, for some time to come, Britain will be unable to sterilise the economic worth of any land by a blanket prohibition on mining activity, although some of the Sandford Committee argued that mineral working would be entirely out of place in those parts of National Parks identified as National Heritage Areas.[29] But society is placing more and more value upon unspoilt countryside; decisions cannot be left so much to chance, to shortsighted interpretations of vague, if well meaning, policies. We must aim to make wiser choices on the scale and siting of new workings, enforce much more stringent conditions upon operation and after-treatment,[30] and pursue all possible alternative supplies, in materials as well as in locations, where these may exist. There seems to be little point, for example, in continuing to expand limestone production in the Peak District for use in aggregates when a wide range of other materials may be used.[31] Part of the problem lies in the fact that relatively little is yet known about the national distribution of many minerals of economic importance. Some fear that exploration, encouraged by government, will itself have damaging implications for the remoter areas. Automatic permission for exploration will, it is argued, dismantle the early warning system of conservation groups and lead, subsequently, to piecemeal exploitation.[32,33]

But where mining activity is ruled out on environmental grounds, and the people of poorer and remoter parts of the country denied these opportunities for increasing their incomes and welfare, it will be even more necessary to make certain that other forms of employment and income are developed in the hills to compensate for this relative deprivation. It is no answer to preserve beauty by insisting that the people who live in such scenery remain poor.

Where there can be no commitment to the inviolability of areas of high amenity value (and not only in National Parks), the case is strong for environmental impact statements to be prepared, to a common format worked out by government, in advance of mandatory public inquiries. The onus should be placed on those seeking approval to extract minerals to prepare a full account of the alternatives and of their intentions for restoration. These and many other issues of mineral working control, where the present system is acknowledged to be inadequate, are being considered by a Committee on Minerals Planning Control.

Recreation and Tourism

As the amount of day-tripping and holiday-making has grown since the 1950's, so have the claims that recreation and tourism offer the panacea for solving upland problems:

together, it is argued, they can bolster the frail and uncertain economy of hill farming; provide a *raison d'être* for new forests and make upland reservoirs more acceptable. In many ways, the uplands are seen as compensation for our urban mistakes; they have a special appeal to the minds of jaded city-dwellers, offering not only peace and solitude but the comforting illusion of man's dominance by Nature (however man-made and managed this may be). More and more, it is in this vein that the uplands are seen and sold.[34]

There is a pushing as well as a pulling effect towards the hills. As farming has intensified on the lowlands and other rural groups have feared for the survival of their interests under growing recreation pressures, the uplands (like the urban fringe) are increasingly seen as a convenient place to which recreation activity might be channelled.

But all these arguments oversimplify the pattern of leisure activity and the recreation potential of these areas; they may have been in part responsible for the counter reaction, certainly in National Parks, that recreation is already too dominant a use of the uplands. The improved fortunes of hill farming, the debate about the extent of upland afforestation and the new emphasis assigned to landscape conservation in National Parks demands a re-evaluation of the part recreation can play in the planning and management of upland environments.

It is difficult to gauge the scale of present recreation activity. For long, the uplands have been the chosen location of many traditional leisure pursuits which, like grouse and deer shooting, exist in symbiosis with other hill land uses. The uplands offer many advantages for the newer forms of outdoor recreation: the inherent attractiveness of an interesting cultural landscape superimposed upon great physical and biological diversity; considerable *de facto* public access, and features of specific value for such activities as climbing, caving, orienteering, skiing and fell walking. It is likely that the Peak District, for example, receives sixteen million visitors in a season, and has experienced more than a doubling of activity in less than ten years.[35] There has been a substantial growth, over the same period, in the educational use of upland areas by school and adult groups, with, for example, at least fifty outdoor study centres in the Snowdonia National Park alone.

Chapter 4 argues that the scale of future recreation activity cannot be forecast with any certainty; but it seems likely that a considerable proportion of the expected growth in home holiday-making, especially in second and weekend holidays, will fall upon the most attractive parts of the uplands. The increasing popularity of 'specific activity' holidays based upon such pursuits as sailing, pony trekking, and painting will also generate more use of the hills. As communications, especially by road, are further improved, day tripping will inevitably increase.

But it is clearly not possible to treat the uplands as a single recreation unit: some (and quite extensive) areas will always remain relatively unattractive to more than a minority of visitors, by reason of their inaccessibility and the harshness of their climate and terrain. Elsewhere, where the uplands abut connurbations and holiday resorts, and are highly attractive for short trips, recreation may have to be treated, in some areas, as a dominant claim upon resources.

Problems and Policies

Growing recreation and tourist activity in the hills has brought problems, particularly to those areas which are most accessible from cities. Farmers face the consequences of damage to their equipment and livestock,[36] there is congestion on rural roads and the straining of rural services. Ecologically, parts of the hills, inside and outside National Parks, have suffered from the unwitting disturbance and indiscriminate collecting habits of visitors. At peak times, local traffic is often severely disrupted along tourist routes by the influx of visitors who may find their own enjoyment marred by heavy traffic, and the environment they seek altered by the road improvements which their activities demand.

Yet not all the consequences of increasing leisure in the uplands are unwelcome, nor are all the problems intractible. The evidence of the few recent experiments is that a satisfactory compromise is possible whereby informal recreation activity (and the maintenance of traditional scenery) can be better integrated with other upland land uses. The success of schemes in State Forests such as Grizedale; and in the North York Moors, and in management experiments should encourage more practical work on the mechanisms by which upland interests can be harmonised. The Upland Management Experiment in the Lake District[37] has demonstrated that many local problems for farmers can be resolved by better visitor management: by more wardening; sign-posting of routes; repair of footpaths and stiles and improved information services. An experiment in the Peak District National Park has shown how local and holiday traffic can be accommodated along a route system by better management.[38]

These studies show how it is possible to mitigate some of the problems of upland recreation, but this can only come by more *positive* action whether this is designed to promote or to limit use locally. If motoring is to be curbed in certain areas then it is not enough to rely upon the restrictions imposed by an unimproved road system, provision must be made for motorless zones with access only on foot, or with adequate alternative means of public transport, perhaps by resurrecting old rail and canal services, as well as buses and bicycles.

There is room too, for making the most of the benefits which leisure in the hills can bring. The infrastructure required by tourists, for communications, water, sewerage, health and other services consumes a substantial (if not a major) part of the rate income in some upland and hill areas. Not all tourist spending benefits the local economy, for it may be lost to the exchequer (as from petrol sales) or to large, city-based catering and food firms. It is well known that day visitors especially contribute relatively little to the economy of their destination. But other studies have shown that for some of the more popular holiday regions, particularly the South West, the multiplier effect of tourist expenditure is significant,[39,40] and a substantial proportion of local income is earned from a variety of tourist services. In some areas, an increasing share of local farm incomes are being supplemented in this way. Davies, for example, has shown that 18 per cent of Cornish farmers take in holidaymakers and that most make up a quarter of their income in this way.[41] In a survey of Lakeland parishes, Capstick found that a third of all the farms ran some form of tourist enterprise — mainly a guest house. But these enterprises were largely confined to farms which were already commercially viable, and the study suggests that tourism alone, especially in the remoter uplands outside the major tourist centres, cannot support a population large enough for essential services and adequate rural life. The benefits are only likely to come when tourism can supplement a basic economy which offers year-round rather than seasonal employment.

To fulfil this role effectively, tourist development must be selective in type and location. Large scale, capital-intensive tourist facilities may, in the long term, be less effective than low cost self-catering schemes, for camping or for farm holidays, which not only allow more income to be retained locally, but require little or no new infrastructure and imply no permanent disruption of the local environment or community. Those schemes which interfere least with the economic and family activities of busy hill farmers, and those, like self-guided farm trails, exhibitions and open days which help to improve the mutual understanding of visitor and farmer may be the most desirable. Both the positive management of hill land for recreation, and greater attention to the ways in which farming can benefit from tourist and recreation activity demand a rather different approach over much of the uplands than has been the case so far, with rather less segregation of planning for leisure from other aspects of the upland economy. The needs of individual, and sometimes quite small, hill areas must be sensitively assessed; blanket policies, whether for the concentration or for the dispersal of tourist and recreation activity may have to be modified. Clearly, the social and physical environment in parts of the uplands will suffer if indiscriminate tourist development continues in an *ad hoc* way; equally, the recreation potential elsewhere will not be realised if it is seen only as an adjunct to farm incomes.

There are many conflicts between resource activities in the hills; the next chapter considers some of the institutional and methodological ways in which upland problems have been approached.

Notes and References

1. Country Landowners Association (1972) *The Uplands*, Regional Working Parties' Report.
2. Personal communication.
3. Raeburn, J. R. (1972) The economics of upland farming in Ashton, J. and Long, W. H. (eds.), *The Remoter Rural Areas of Britain*, Oliver & Boyd.
4. Classification maps exist but are not published.
5. Davidson, B. R. and Wibberley, G. P. (1956) *The Agricultural significance of the Hills*, Studies in Rural Land Use No. 3, Wye College.
6. It could well be that the total weight of mutton and lamb produced and the size of the wool clip would be above two-thirds of the existing total, but this is because of the rather larger size and weight of lowland sheep as against those able to live and breed in the hills.
7. Economic Development Committee for Agriculture (1973) *UK Farming and the Common Market: Hills and Uplands.* National Economic Development Office.
8. Country Landowners' Association (1972) *The Uplands*, op. cit. See also:
    Attwood, E. A. and Evans, H. E. (1961) *The Economics of Hill Farming*, University of Wales Press.
9. The E.E.C. proposals include compensation based on numbers of livestock kept or area farmed, rebates on the interest on capital loans for farm modernisation (including improvements made in order to obtain non farming income), grants for land improvement, pensions for older farmers and premiums for younger farmers.
    At the time of writing (January 1976) British Government assistance covers a variety of grants, for example towards the provision and improvement of farm services (such as water supply and roads) farm buildings, land clearance and drainage; a 'Payment to Outgoers' Scheme and a 'Farm Amalgamation Scheme'; hill cow and ewe subsidies. Hill and upland farmers are eligible for all other non specific grants, subsidies and price guarantees made available to all farmers by the Ministry of Agriculture and other government agencies. These are described in: Ministry of Agriculture, Fisheries & Food (1975/76) *At the Farmer's Service.*
10. Particularly on Exmoor: Sinclair, G. (1976) Open Landscape and Hill Farming, in MacEwan, M. (ed.), *Future Landscapes*, Chatto and Windus.
11. For example, the Forestry Commission succeeds in buying on average only between 30 and 40 per cent of the land for which it makes tenders across the hills and uplands of Scotland.
12. H.M. Treasury (1972) *Forestry in Great Britain: An Interdepartmental Cost Benefit Study*, H.M.S.O.
13. Ministry of Agriculture, Fisheries & Food (1972) *Forest Policy*, H.M.S.O.
14. Nor are there incentives to manage land in this way. The Country Landowners Association (op. cit) have argued that under existing financial arrangements, upland farmers cannot afford small scale forest operations although these would bring shelter and amenity, sporting and other benefits.
15. Leakages though to be as high as 20-30% with some authorities.

16. Rees, J. (1972) Overview: in special issue of *Town and Country Planning*, on the Future of Water Resources, Vol. 40(a), September.
17. Water Resources Board (1974) *Water Resources in England and Wales*, H.M.S.O.
18. For an outline of the new structure, see:
    Beddoe, J. E. (1972) The Management of Water in England and Wales: the Case for Reform, *Town and Country Planning*, Vol. 40(a), September.
    and a critique by J. Rees in the same volume.
19. Water Resources Board (1974) *Water Resources in England and Wales*, op. cit.
20. Gregory, R. (1971) *The Price of Amenity: Five Studies in Conservation and Government*, Macmillan.
    Chapter 4 discusses the Cow Green Reservoir case.
21. Dower, M. (1971) The lessons of Swincombe, *Town and Country Planning*, Vol. 39 (9).
22. Jones, W. Dyfri (1972) The Impact of Public Works Schemes on Farming: a case study relating to a reservoir and power station in N. Wales. *Journal of Ag. Econ.*, January 1972, Vol. XXIII, No. 1.
23. Regional Water Authorities are required to take account of the needs of recreation and the conservation of amenity and wildlife. The Water Space Amenity Commission has been established as the national advisory body.
24. Peak Park Planning Board (1974) *The Peak District National Park: Your choice for the future*, P.P.P.B.
25. Commission on Mining and the Environment (1972) *Report* (the Zuckerman Commission).
26. Dower, M. (1972) The Smile of Sir Val Duncan, *Town and Country Planning*, Vol. 40(11), November.
27. Zuckerman Commission, Chapter 6.
28. Department of the Environment (1974) *Report of the National Park Policies Review Committee (Sandford Report)*, H.M.S.O.
29. See Chapter 10.
30. Committee on Minerals Planning Control (Stevens Committee).
31. The Verney Committee on Aggregates is investigating this.
32. Government exploration grants are given for finding non ferrous ores under the: *Mineral Exploration and Investment Grants Act, 1972*. The Zuckermann Commission argued for automatic planning permission for the first phase of exploration.
33. Committee for Environmental Conservation (1972) *Report of 1972*, CoEnCo recommends a government sponsored or executed geological survey.
34. By, for example, the English Tourist Board in its advertising campaigns for second holidays.
35. Sandford Report on National Parks (op. cit.) paras 7.7-7.8.
36. Capstick, M. (1972) *Some Aspects of the Economic Effects of Tourism in the Westmorland Lake District*. University of Lancaster, Dept. of Economics.
37. Discussed in Chapter 12.
38. Peak Park Planning Board/Derbyshire County Council (1974) *Routes for People*.
39. See, for example:
    Dower, M. (1972) Amenity and Tourism in the Countryside in Ashton, J. and Long, W. H. (eds.), *The Remoter Rural Areas of Britain*, Oliver & Boyd.
40. Capstick, M. (1972) op. cit.
41. Davies, E. T. (1969) *Tourism and the Cornish Farmer*. Dept. of Economics, University of Exeter.

CHAPTER 10

Policies for the Uplands

The clashes of interest which emerge in the uplands seem to be fundamental: involving conflicts between economic and amenity values, between local and national needs and aspirations and between individual and community benefits. The debates in cases such as the A66 road improvement decision in the northern Lake District,[1] or the proposal for a major oil installation at Drumbuie, have sharply polarised opinion around these issues. For poor and thinly populated areas, a basic dilemma appears to lie in the degree to which the advantages which may flow from 'development' of various kinds should be sacrificed to the requirements of conservation.

Yet these symbolic clashes of interest may mask a situation in which the conflicts are much more subtle, and where the benefits and dangers of alternative courses of action are not clearly defined. This chapter examines some strands of thinking on these issues and looks at various institutional and methodological ways in which upland problems have been approached.

Needs of the Local Economy

The population of the uplands continues to decline. Many policies have been and are designed to stall this process, to improve the physical infrastructure, to prop up ailing services and to provide new employment which will encourage the young to stay and reduce outmigration of the unemployed. But the case for arresting depopulation is rarely defined clearly; it rests often upon an unspoken, emotional belief that such a process is inherently bad.

Grieve[2] and others have argued that there are cogent reasons for keeping people in the hills: not simply to offer opportunities for an alternative way of life to urban and suburban living, and to make full use of the social capital already invested, but to service the growing number of upland resource activities. Adherence to a blind principle of stemming depopulation (rather than keeping those who want to stay and are needed in the hills) may have been responsible for misguided efforts in the past. Some jobs have been provided in an unselective way, and have not always brought the permanency and confidence needed to sustain a viable community and service structure. Nor have they necessarily contributed to the conservation of the environment. Such, for example, has been the case in some mining activities and in certain large scale public works operations. Nabarro,[3] describing a number of recent construction projects in Anglesey and North Wales, concludes that unemployment was only temporarily relieved by the projects and rose to higher levels when they were completed, as men who had left their previous jobs, in farming and the slate industry, came back on to the labour market. Although, in the course of the projects, the local economy was revived, the effects were shortlived; nor did local services benefit from the temporary influx of people and jobs, for the schemes offered too little justification for investment in new schools or hospitals.

Nevertheless, projects such as these are often welcomed as socially beneficial for poor upland communities, defeating many objections on environmental grounds. But even if they were more frequent (and thus more likely to realise their claims of longer term improvement in local employment and incomes) they are too centralised to be of value to the more remote upland communities, and to those ageing, residual populations who suffer most from depopulation. It is in these areas that incomes and employment must be supplemented and the resistance to adaptation and innovation overcome. Smaller, more creative and more dispersed injections of new capital are required, in ways which will yield a sustained improvement in local social and economic conditions; and this may mean not only the creation of new jobs and better physical and social services, but more extension and advisory work.

One agency, the Development Commission, helped by its agent CoSIRA,[4] has tried to guide this smaller scale but integrated development of communities within the remoter rural areas. The Commission have a wide remit to study and provide funds for (although not directly organise) such activities as the development of agriculture, forestry, fisheries and other rural industry, the construction and management of roads, harbours and inland waterways. The Commission have interpreted their mandate in broad and flexible terms to cover any scheme calculated to benefit, directly or indirectly, the rural economy, so long as statutory provision for helping the particular scheme does not already exist.

Over the past ten years, the Council for Small Industries in Rural Areas, and its counterpart in Scotland, have developed a nationwide service of advice, instruction and limited credit for small manufacturing and service industries.[5] They have supported not only the traditional village craftsmen such as woodworkers, wheelwrights and saddlers, but also an increasing range of modern processing industries from plastics to electronics. Advisory work has expanded greatly, with more emphasis upon technical training and accountancy. The industrial loan fund operated by CoSIRA had grown to just under £2 million by 1972/73 and the tourism loan fund (restricted to Development Areas) to £3.5 million.[6] Some of this money has been used to provide factories in advance in those areas where increased employment or a wider range of jobs are needed to counter the damaging effects of change in the major rural industries as for example in the Lindsey part of Lincolnshire where large and highly mechanised arable farms now offer limited male employment. A recent problem has been the finding of sites for small scale industry against the opposition of village preservation groups — a type of rural conflict which is growing in those areas attractive for commuting, retirement and second homes.

Among their other work in research and survey, the Development Commission support voluntary or self-governing bodies such as Rural Community Councils and Women's Institutes, which can strengthen the social and cultural life of rural areas.

The stimulation of employment by the Development Commission and its agencies has been small scale, generated by local and individual initiative and guided by those with local knowledge and concern. It is possible to argue that other upland improvement policies with their reliance upon subsidies rather than more productive financial support, have not always been well conceived. It may be, for example, that the past relatively unselective system of hill farming support has arrested a faster rate of population decline, but at the same time has inhibited more efficient and positive multiple use of upland grazing resources. Likewise, the single-resource-based forest settlements of Kielder and Byrness suffered by their divorce from existing communities and other upland activities. Although the form of E.E.C. support for the hills is not yet known in detail,[7] the hope is that it will be less single-minded and that future upland policies will encourage the integration of farming with other income-producing activities, in some of the ways discussed in the previous chapter.

The Uplands and Amenity

Even if retaining people is seen as a fundamental goal of upland planning, there is no concensus view about the amenities of the hills and how they may be safeguarded. For some people, they represent the wild and open spaces, the noble elemental landscapes to which it will always be possible to retreat, away from people, exploitation and sophistication, to find a simpler way of life. Some of these are the seekers of wilderness on the American style. Others, the majority, with a less powerfully emotional view, want only to preserve what they see: a dramatic but well-tended cultural landscape with crops and animals and people working in the fields and villages. Yet neither of these two interest groups (and there are, of course, other views) are necessarily prepared to accept that most of what they value depends upon a viable local economy, a healthy social structure, and retention of the farming system. Few, even of those who espouse wilderness, would favour only wet and unused moorland. Nor would they want, except in the imagination, a hill land devoid of people and the services they sustain.

At the same time, it must be recognised that the uplands do offer scenery and wildlife of unique value which should not be denied to those who do not happen to live there permanently. Moreover, the traditional custodians of upland landscapes have not always treated these assets with the trusteeship they deserve: they have cleared forests, burnt the vegetation, encouraged their stock to overgraze the poorer pastures, impoverished the soil, allowed the bracken to encroach upon upland grassland and let their walls and buildings go derelict. In more localised areas of the uplands users have left, as we described in the last chapter, a landscape often disfigured by unsympathetic and single-minded activity in mining, afforestation and water catchment. A designation of protection for the landscape and its wildlife has not, alone, solved these problems, either in National Parks or Areas of Outstanding Natural Beauty. Indeed, it may have exacerbated them.

It is a situation of ideological and practical conflict in which compromise is difficult. Suggested solutions are often extreme and frequently simplistic. There is certainly a case for more control over those activities like afforestation and mining which can markedly affect the character of upland landscapes but pressure groups have not always helped by adopting rigid positions about the need to exclude them totally in situations where economic and aesthetic conflict is most acute. The calls for 'amenity payments' to upland farmers to maintain the greengrazed landscape of the fells may be severely under-estimating not only the practicalities,[8] but also a more fundamental resistance to 'landscape gardening'. They are certainly under-estimating the technical and structural problems farmers face in these areas.

But how can upland problems best be tackled and the many conflicts of interest not only defined but reconciled?

Policies for the Uplands

Despite the improvements that are being made in the ways in which different resources of the uplands are used (and some of these were discussed in the previous chapter) the overall attack on hill problems remains piecemeal. Over most of the uplands, those public and private agencies responsible for resource management operate in an independent way. Moreover, the scale and variety of land uses, with all their different implications for investment and employment and their vastly different time horizons, makes co-ordination of purpose and method difficult. The relative paucity of residential and commercial development to which planners elsewhere have traditionally brought some co-ordination of purpose, means that responsibility for the linkage of separatist policies in many areas rests, effectively, with no-one. Local and national agencies work alongside but often at odds with each other.

The Ministry of Agriculture and the Forestry Commission argue about agriculture and afforestation almost entirely by themselves, the Council for Small Industries in Rural Areas stimulates employment through local action but not directly through local administrative organisations and tourism is encouraged by national and other agencies working apart from the local planning authority.

It is more and more recognised that in the densely populated lowlands, there is a need to co-ordinate the activities of different resource users, to minimise conflict between them, and encourage mutual benefits to be realised. It is recognised that sectional resource interests cannot (nor indeed do they want to) be left, individually, to decide the fortunes of those who live, work, and play on their land. Yet in the uplands this has been and is still often the case, with mining companies and forest agencies acting as the arbiters of growth or decline in rural communities.

Because the uplands have seemed so apart from urban areas, linked by their common problems of climate and terrain, their extensive land uses and their fragmented, often urban-dominated administration, the theoretical case for specialist agencies has been strong. In parts of the uplands, attempts have been made to find ways out of a situation of conflict and uncertainty by introducing various kinds of institutional structure with defined and comprehensive aims, and with special means available for their implementation. Such is the case in the Highlands and Islands Development Board area, and to some extent in the National Parks; and was begun in the area of the ill-fated North Pennines Rural Development Board. The record of these strategies and the agencies established to execute them is a useful one in sorting out what may be some of the vital ingredients for a thriving upland system.

Rural Development Boards

These new agencies for sub-regional rural planning developed out of the Agriculture Act of 1967, which empowered the Minister of Agriculture, Fisheries and Food in England and Wales and the Secretary of State in Scotland to set up Rural Development Boards for particular areas of Britain. These Boards were designed to deal with the special problems and needs of these areas including

"difficulties in the formation of commercial units of agricultural land, the need for an overall programme for guidance in making decisions as to the use of land for agriculture and forestry so that these uses are complementary, the need for improved public services in step with development for agricultural and forestry purposes, and the need for preserving and taking full advantage of the amenities and scenery."[9]

The Boards were to be given powers to acquire land by agreement (but compulsorily if necessary), to manage, improve, farm, sell or let the land and to enter into transactions which promoted amalgamations of enterprises in the interests of the community. The Agriculture Act made provision for grants and loans for improving communications and services to farming and forestry dwellings and those to be used for tourism; there were to be additional incentives for local people to provide tourist facilities such as sites for camping and caravanning.

Most controversial of the new powers (and finally responsible for the demise of the one Board established) were those which gave authority for intervention in the process of land transfer[10] and land use change,[11] where proposals were considered to be detrimental to the improvement of farm structure or the best use of land. Where land was thought to be essential for a scheme of farm amalgamation or boundary adjustment then this could be acquired compulsorily by the Board, although these powers were carefully circumscribed with provision for local and national appeal procedures.

This legislation for Rural Development Boards followed a number of special reports and Government policy statements[12] which concluded that financial and technical changes within individual farms were insufficient to yield permanent improvement in a large rural area. It was recognised that in the hills and uplands where small farm units gave low incomes, voluntary sale and purchase of land was unlikely to produce a restructuring of the farming fabric that would be more efficient and more economic. The need was seen for some kind of authority which could monitor land sales, and intervene in the market to speed up the process of agricultural adjustment. Moreover, many upland farming advisors and research workers had been impressed with the way in which Sweden had conceived and implemented a programme of agricultural adjustment in hill areas faced with major technical problems in agriculture and forestry and a continuing absolute and selective rural outmigration. Considerable success has now been achieved by the Swedish Government, over the last three decades, through a system of State agricultural boards established to guide farm amalgamations and restructuring.

Only one Rural Development Board was established in Britain: for an area of 800,000 hectares of the Northern Pennines containing over 6,000 farms. But its progress was short-lived. Despite some support from farming and landowning organisations, and subsequent considerable public lament, a Conservative Government disbanded the Board in 1970 on philosophical grounds, and in response to local objections to interference in the private land market.[13] In some ways, events since 1970 have provided rather more justification for this kind of intervention than when the Board was established, for escalating land prices[14] and the institutional investment in land for agriculture and forestry have effectively prevented small farmers from voluntarily improving the size and efficiency of their holdings.

Another Rural Development Board was suggested for Mid-Wales, and although the proposal met initially favourable comment and agreement, objections before and during the public inquiry, which involved arguments about loss of freedom and lack of the need for such an authority, ensured that the Board was never established.

The advantages of unification in large land areas with similar resource and social problems, yet severed by a multiplicity of administrative units, were thus not enough to overcome the real and imagined weaknesses of the approach. In retrospect some of these were obvious. The justification and, indeed, the operation of the Boards arose too much from agricultural considerations; the lip service paid to other activities which appeared ancillary to the needs of hill farming, intensified objections to the undue emphasis of agricultural interests, whose representatives dominated the North Pennines Board.[15] The emphasis on restructuring agricultural holdings strengthened fears of compulsory land purchase at a time when farmers faced improving economic conditions. If the passage of time and the economic climate had increased the marginality of hill farming then the Boards might have been greater in number and have lasted longer. But agriculture in the hills has not been allowed to move right across the economic margin and many small upland farmers have been helped, by the changing pattern of livestock prices and by grants and subsidies, to remain in business. Their land increased substantially in capital value in line with all land values in Britain during the early 1970's.

Rural Development Boards brought a further administrative unit into the complex and crowded pattern of local government. They were also to be given powers which cut across those of other organisations, such as local and county councils and statutory undertakers, in the fields of service provision and tourism. Many of the activities of Rural Development Boards could, in theory, have been carried out within the existing local government structure.

Highlands and Islands Development Board

Established in 1965 by Act of Parliament, the Highlands Board has remained a more durable and more successful example of an upland multi-purpose planning agency. Its powers apply to 3.6 million hectares of highlands and islands in which only 7 per cent of the land is under crop and grass cultivation and 5 per cent in forest plantations: the rest is dominated by rough grazings for sheep and deer. Within this area are some 15,000 crofting units which offer only two days' work in a week: a major need is for more diversification of employment.

The Board has the basic job of "assisting the people of the highlands and hills to improve the economic and social conditions and of enabling the Highlands and Islands to play a very effective part in the economic and social development of the Nation".[16] The Board has wide powers to carry out projects, acquire and own land and buildings, promote activities and enterprises in various ways, including financially by way of grants and loans, and provide related advice and training. These powers of intervention allow the Board to influence almost all aspects of upland life and resource use, but its work has become increasingly selective, concentrated upon particular areas, such as the 'growth areas' of Fort William, Inverness and Caithness, and on particular activities such as fishing (where the Board have supported boat building and improved fish processing plants); bulb growing in the Hebrides; a wide range of large and small craft industries, new hotels and other tourist accommodation; and major developments like the aluminium smelter at Invergordon.[17]

In terms of emphasis it is significant that the Board has done rather more for the non-agricultural activities and possibilities of its area — in forestry, tourism and manufacturing — than it has for agriculture and horticulture. In 1968, the Board's powers were extended to include those made available under the 1967 Agriculture Act for Rural Development Boards (and these were not withdrawn when the North Pennines Board was subsequently disbanded). But the Highlands Board has elected not to use these powers, perhaps rightly assessing that even in the marginal uplands, the threat of compulsory land purchase would be strongly resisted by farmers and not encouraged by local rural organisations. Moreover, the belief seems to have been that the best role for an upland planning agency would be to strengthen the rural fabric which lies around the basic industries of agriculture and forestry, accepting that although improvements can be made to the structure of farming and other hill land uses, these would affect relatively few people in employment terms, and interference may generate destructive local resistance.

Perhaps because of its rather different pattern of local administration, Scotland has been more ready to accept a new multi-purpose organisation; but there are various other reasons why the Highlands and Islands Board has been successful. The North-west of Scotland had, for a long time, shown a steady relative worsening of its position, with the failure of many isolated improvement projects and a constant absorption of government resources. That the area was living on or beyond the physical, economic and social margins was accepted, and there was a readiness to try out a more comprehensive approach to its problems. The Board has been very selective in its work, recognising that although the difficulties of the Highlands may be superficially very similar, the specific needs of different areas must be tackled. The Board has thus used a 'Growth Zone' approach, particularly in relation to major industrial development, but has also helped other upland activities on many different scales from the small business to the large Aviemore centre. In some contrast to the Rural Development Boards, the Highlands Board has wisely concentrated on helping many parts of the rural fabric and has moved with great caution into agricultural improvements.

With the development of North sea oil and gas, it is difficult to forecast the future role of the Highlands and Islands Development Board, but clearly some organisation of this kind is needed if only to ensure that the consequences of rapid and uneven growth neither mask nor exacerbate the physical and social problems of this difficult region.[18]

National Parks

The Highlands and Islands are unique in Britain with their social and economic fortunes now very much in the balance and it would be rash to abstract more than very general guidance for other upland areas from the still limited experience of the Highlands and Islands Development Board. The ten National Parks in England and Wales,[19] established in the years following the National Parks and Access to the Countryside Act of 1949, have had more time to test their strengths and show their weaknesses. Both have been aired in the Sandford report, to which the government have now responded.[20] But perhaps predictably, the verdict is not wholly clear.

The parks were set up to conserve characteristic landscapes and provide for outdoor recreation (Fig. 6). Guided in their overall policies by the Countryside Commission (and formerly the National Parks Commission) the park authorities have carried out their tasks by using normal planning procedures, augmented by additional powers to improve the landscape and provide facilities for recreation. They have been able to buy land, although the amount acquired has been small: most National Park land is in private hands.

Until local government reorganisation, each park was administered by its own Board or by a committee of the local authority in whose area it lies, to which the government appointed a third of the members to ensure that the national interest was safeguarded. The

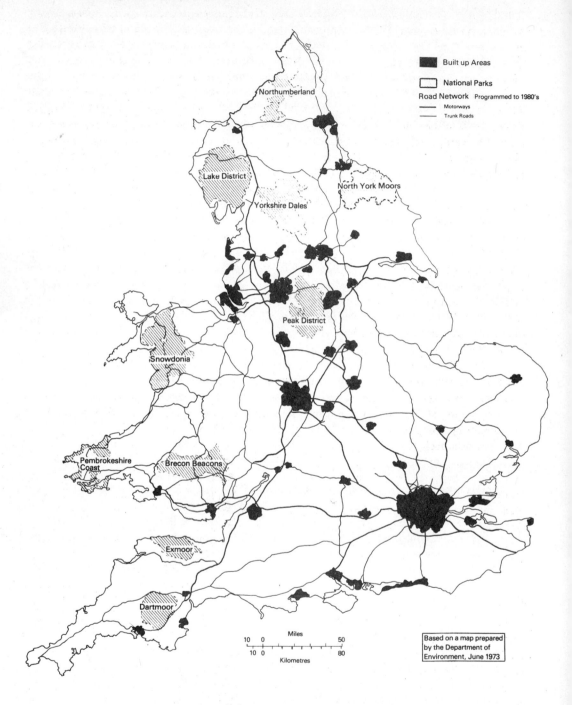

FIG. 6. *National Parks in England and Wales.*

administrative framework has now been revised so that each park is run by a single authority with a specialist officer. This is clearly an improvement upon the loose and often ineffective system established in the compromise discussions after 1949, especially for those parks like Snowdonia which fell in more than one county area. The revised administration was introduced in the hope that more staff and more money would be made available for the National Park purposes.[21] The present system is itself the outcome of compromise between two rival views as to how the National Parks should be administered: those who wanted independent National Park authorities, and those who argued for integration with local government. If it fails to meet the demands of the first group, the new system does at least recognise that although the parks may have special problems, their planning and management cannot be divorced (as in some ways the activities of Rural Development Boards were) from the other social, economic and environmental issues of their sub-region. Eddison, criticising the whole concept of separate authorities, has argued that the solutions to upland and National Park problems can only be found by integrated planning with their surrounding or nearby city regions.[22]

A new administration alone can do little to sort out the central and enduring problem for National park authorities: how to match the needs of conservation with those of development – not only for recreation, but for those who live and work in the parks. The wise and laudable goals of John Dower, accepted by the Hobhouse Committee[23] and embodied in the Act of 1949 seem as relevant today:

"A National Park is an extensive area of beautiful and relatively wild country in which, for the nation's benefit and by appropriate national decisions and action,

(a) the characteristic landscape beauty is strictly preserved,
(b) access and facilities for public open-air enjoyment are amply provided,
(c) wildlife and buildings and places of architectural and historic interest are suitably protected, while
(d) established farming use is effectively maintained".[24]

But conditions of social behaviour and resource demands have vastly changed both inside and outside the parks: the previous chapter has tried to sketch some of them. The goals are still right; the means of achieving them are now much more elusive. The record of the parks is a worthy one: they have done much to safeguard large areas of fine countryside. Resolution of some of the conflicts of interest has been locally very successful, but there have been major examples of failure. Many of the more difficult tasks of arbitration between competing claims upon the social and physical fabric of National Parks have been left for ill-defined national policies – on forestry, on mineral working, or on major road development – to resolve.[25]

A number of limitations of past national park planning have been acknowledged. There has been a growing realisation that local interests may not have been given sufficient weight. For various reasons – lack of time, staff, money and sufficient guidance – park authorities have concentrated on the day-to-day statutory control of development, at the expense of wider issues of policy-making. Relatively neglected has been the question of how the parks, as whole entities, can not only cope effectively with the pressures they face, but also develop the potential they harbour for more beauty and for more enjoyment. It is both the *strategic* decisions – for example, where and what new employment should be introduced; where stringent development control is most needed and where new recreation facilities should go

— and positive *management* policies, in particular, how a functional farming landscape can be safeguarded, that have suffered.

The Sandford Committee made many recommendations on these issues and the government have accepted some, notably that the emphasis in future must be on positive management to reconcile conflicts rather than on negative restrictions. They promise new powers for park authorities to make management agreements with landowners, and to acquire land by agreement for the purposes of preserving or enhancing the landscape.[26] The Landscape Areas Special Development Order is to be extended in area and scope so that the design, materials and now *siting* of farm buildings in all National Parks can be controlled.[27]

With more staff and finance and the promise of new powers, some of the deficiencies of past planning may be remedied, the more so since park authorities have to prepare special National Park plans which concentrate on management issues.[28] The Countryside Commission is now able to give much more advice than in the past on the objectives and methods of management for recreation and landscape conservation. They can draw upon the valuable experience of practical management experiments of the kind in progress in the Lake District which we discuss in Chapter 12.

Despite the somewhat confused status of National Park plans in relation to the new statutory planning system guidance has been given on their content and preparation.[29] National Park authorities will need to devise management strategies which separate intensive from lightly used recreation zones, define tourist corridors and multiple use areas. They are encouraged to introduce new schemes of recreation and traffic management, improved information and interpretive services and a wide range of visitor facilities. Park authorities are expected to negotiate special arrangements with landowners for particular tracts of landscape under which owners agree to manage their land in certain ways, in return for financial, advisory and other benefits. Examples of the terms of such an arrangement might be that the land is stocked in a particular way, that some rough pasture remains unimproved or that heather and gorse areas are retained.

But none of the new measures — of administration or plan-making or proposed legislation — provides a real answer to the growing practical and ideological conflict between recreation and conservation in National Parks. Park authorities have become increasingly unhappy and unclear about their dual role as protectors and providers. Certainly some have been reluctant to cater adequately for existing outdoor recreation demands, let alone encourage leisure activities, other than of a specialised and 'acceptable' kind. The view of most park authorities has been that as much informal car-borne recreation as possible should be catered for outside the parks, which assumes not only that sufficient provision will be made by other authorities, but also, and perhaps erroneously, that motoring and picnicking are as enjoyable outside these areas of finest scenery.

A central dilemma therefore is how to balance the needs of a viable agricultural economy which — incidentally — maintains the desirable upland landscape, and the need to offer to more than a minority, the opportunities of enjoying this environment. The Sandford Committee examination of National Park purposes made more explicit an assumption in favour of environmental conservation, which the government have endorsed for those areas where recreation and conservation are in conflict (although these have not been defined). It is impossible to achieve satisfactorily all the many goals for the uplands in the same area. In different parts of National Parks, different interests must be dominant and others secondary, accepting that, over most, the maintenance of farming in some form is likely to take precedence because it is so crucial to the social and environmental character of the uplands.

Some of the Sandford Committee argued for National Heritage Areas to be defined in those parts of national parks of the highest environmental quality where

> "conservation of environmental qualities would be the supreme objective, of national significance and taking precedence over all others".

> "no development or other change of use which would damage (their) qualities should be permitted without reference to Parliament".[30]

The areas were to be small, for it was envisaged that all forms of urban or industrial intrusion, such as quarries, reservoirs and settlements larger than a hamlet would be excluded. Access would be mainly on foot, horseback or bicycle. The accent would be upon positive management, to protect and enhance beauty as well as to preclude any deleterious change, through the operation of management arrangements over public and private land. When environmental management objectives could be secured, in this way, for a connected zone of land, designation of a National Heritage Area could follow. Those who argued against National Heritage Areas did so because they felt such a policy would hinder the better planning of the National Parks as a whole, absorbing valuable time and adding to the confusion of protective zonations and the agencies responsible for them. The government have rejected the idea.

Even so, as a goal for parts of the National Parks, the National Heritage Area concept seems a good one, whether or not the *label* remains. Among a number of basic requirements, the Countryside Commission argue for the virtual prohibition of development out of accord with National Park purposes in the most beautiful parts, to be breached only in the case of a most compelling national necessity.[31] But special protection for areas of the highest quality should not detract from two other needs: for action to conserve the landscape elsewhere (and in areas which may be wholly in private ownership) and for a corresponding emphasis upon recreational enjoyment in at least some parts of our National Parks. The notion of 'park hinterlands' which exist, for example, in French and American National Parks, may well be appropriate in Britain. Here would be a variety of recreation opportunities *within* a National Park, attractive in themselves, but providing an alternative to the penetration of more vulnerable environments. Here too, it may be possible for farmers to benefit more substantially from tourist enterprises such as pony trekking, linked to farm accommodation. There is a case for accepting atractions (like chair lifts) which could lengthen the tourist season and contribute greater local income, and those leisure developments — residential activity centres; interpretation centres — which could provide more stable ancilliary employment. More co-ordination is required between tourist and recreation policies for the parks. Although this would all mean greater demands upon central and local funds, extra finance could be raised in various ways: perhaps by road tolls or a tourist tax, and from contributions to park budgets by authorities which lie outside the area but contribute many visitors.

If we are to overcome our schizophrenia towards National Parks and evolve a system which can be identified in the public mind, then many kinds of visitor must be welcomed: to some parts at least. We cannot expect, as many hope, to promote further understanding of town and rural life between city-bred and countryman if the contact is severed at park boundaries with town and city people filtered off before they experience the environment of National Parks. There is room for many different kinds of informal recreation activity within the parks which relate to the environment, albeit in a different way from fell walking.

With most of our national interest focussed on economic growth, it is right to reiterate and emphasise conservation goals. But these will be realised only if they are wholeheartedly accepted by more than a few campaigners and this may mean that they must be justified, and to a large extent 'sold', as a viable and attractive policy for those who live and work in the National Parks and those who visit them from the town. People are not the only threat to conservation. The government have not yet shown how, in practice, the conservation priority can be realised for they offer no strategy and they have failed to introduce more effective controls over those activities, like afforestation and mining, which in parts of some parks constitute a much more severe danger to their beauty and integrity. Perhaps the time has come to accept, in practice as well as in principle, that our National Parks *are* very different from most of those in the rest of Europe and in America and cease to compare their standards of protection so readily with elsewhere. Either we must evolve a framework which best fits the British situation (and designate more parks especially in the south and east) or go on seeking very limited areas which more closely fit the National Park ideal on a world scale.[32]

Resource Planning Studies

A number of recent studies of upland problems have sought to find both a method and a set of solutions which might be applied more widely. These have ranged from the broad academic appraisal, through the fundamentally economic approach to more detailed, experiments in planmaking.[33] The last, notably in the North Pennines, have tried to bridge the gap between ideal strategies and what might be workable in practice.[34]

We discuss in more detail, in Chapter 11 the approach adopted in the North Pennines Study. Although all upland problems were not considered with equal emphasis,[35] the study has shown that integrated, multiple-use solutions are needed and can be generated within the complex framework of upland activities; and that an approach which incorporates these may be of more long term benefit than the discrete policy-making by major upland interests which now takes place. But the proposals are, as yet, untried in practice. The success of implementation rests not only upon the feasibility of the policies, and some improvement in the powers and finance available for upland management, but also upon all the persuasive skills public negotiators can muster.

Moreover, it has seemed possible, in the North Pennines Study, to devise a method of joint working which allows many upland interests to participate in plan-making, although the approach will need to be streamlined before it can be adopted more widely. In some ways, the search for a systematic and conclusive planning method has revealed many of the fundamental dilemmas of upland planning: real uncertainty about the future and the implications of national and international policies; the need to question traditional assumptions about the dominance of certain attitudes and interests, the size of particular upland industries and about the ways in which remote communities may best be sustained. It is these issues that must be resolved before there is any further refinement of methodology. It would be wholly wrong, as House has argued,[36] to reduce upland problems to an exercise in logistics and compromise, where much more extreme policies may be locally or temporally needed.

Conclusions

The uplands offer harsh and complex planning environments. It is difficult to be rational about the wise use of resources where issues of survival — of animals, men and communities

— are at stake. Even so, in such marginal situations, we would do well to adopt a cautionary attitude to resource exploitation.

Human welfare must, in most cases, take precedence over a concern for the look and feel of the upland environment, but the two may be much less sharply differentiated than upland policies have suggested. Many problems, as we have tried to show in these chapters, stem in large part from the fragmentation of policies among a multiplicity of single-purpose and single-minded agencies so that, for example, unselective agricultural support programmes continue although they may not be achieving the most desirable objectives; the wider potential of forestry or tourism in the hills does not seem to be realised; urban and industrial development is divorced from rural resource planning so that any mutual benefits of association remain unexplored.

It is tempting to search for 'cure-all' formulae: the creation of specialist agencies which will ensure that separatist policies are co-ordinated[37] or the application of new techniques which can dictate, once and for all, the optimal pattern of upland activities.[38] Components of all these solutions may be needed, with more facilities for co-operation and better understanding of the upland resource system. But it is not likely that any one will offer the total answer. There are few reasons why local government could not take on the extra powers which are needed, for example, to control some of the activities of extensive land uses, so long as this is coupled with a broadening of attitudes and function within the main resource planning agencies. Analysis of resource capability, even if techniques of data collection progress far enough to allow it, may be too inflexible a tool to cope with the changing values and aspirations of society. Spurious objectivity may dangerously mask the crucial decisions.

More sophisticated plan-making, more powerful administrative units will not alone compensate for a failure to identify the range of political choice that exists. The need is first to clarify the many roles that the uplands might have to play in the twenty-first century; only then is it possible to set objectives for individual resource interests.[39]

Notes and References

1. Countryside Commission/Lake District Planning Board (1972) *West Cumberland Trunk Road Study*.
2. Grieve, R. (1972) Problems and Objectives in the Highlands and Islands, in Ashton, J. and Long, W. H. (eds.) *The Remoter Rural Areas of Britain*, Oliver & Boyd, and see other chapters in this volume, for example, by J. Gareth Thomas: Population changes and the provision of services.
3. Nabarro, R. (1973) Do Public Works Help in the Uplands? *New Society*, 29 November.
4. Development Commission (1974) *Change and Development in Rural Areas*, H.M.S.O.
   Council for Small Industries in Rural Areas, *Annual Reports*, H.M.S.O.
   The Development Commission was established under the Development and Road Improvement Funds Acts of 1909 and 1910.
5. The work of CoSIRA, which is an amalgamation and development of the earlier work and organisations of the Rural Industries' Bureau (begun in 1921), the Rural Industries Committees of individual counties and the Rural Industries Loan Fund (started in 1940), has been limited to settlements in rural Britain of not more than 10,000 population and to firms employing not more than twenty skilled persons. These restrictions have been applied with flexibility and are, at the time of writing, under review.
6. Development Commission (1974) *Change and Development in Rural Areas*, op. cit., p. 16.
7. This was the position at November 1974.
8. See, for example, the discussion of the Upland Management Project in Chapter 12 which looks at the implementation of rural policies.
9. Sec 45(2), 1967 Agriculture Act.
10. Except among family members; excluding residential property.
11. The conversion of more than 4 ha. or one ownership in 12 months.

12. Some of these were the Hill Farming Acts, 1946 and 1951, the Agriculture Act, 1957; the White Paper on 'The Development of Agriculture', August, 1965; the Agriculture Act, 1967; the Mid-Wales Investigation Report of the Welsh Agricultural Land Sub-Commission, December, 1955 (Cmnd. 9631); *Depopulation in Mid-Wales*, H.M.S.O., 1964; White Paper on 'The Scottish Economy, 1965-70'; Darling, F., *The Future of the Highlands*, Thomson & Grimble, 1968.

13. Coupled with a number of nationally unpopular decisions about afforestation as in Langstrothdale, Yorkshire Dales National Park.

14. At least until July 1974.

15. Whose membership was appointed by the Minister of Agriculture.

16. The Highlands and Islands Development Board. Act of Establishment, 1965.

17. Highlands and Islands Development Board: *Annual Reports.*

18. See also Grieve, R. (1973) Regional Planning in Scotland, *The Planner*, Vol. 59(9), November.

19. The 10 parks cover 9% of England and Wales, there are no National Parks in Scotland.

20. Department of the Environment (1974) *Report of the National Park Policies Review Committee*, H.M.S.O. (Sandford Report). *Ministerial Conclusions on the Report of the National Park Policies Review Committee*, circular 4/76, H.M.S.O. 1976.

21. For a discussion of the old system of administration and its inadequacies see:

    Countryside Commission (1971) *The Reform of Local Government in England and Wales: National Parks (Longland Report)*. Under the Local Government Act 1972 (and operative from April, 1974) each park has a single executive board (in the Peak and Lakes) or committee with two-thirds of the members appointed by the county councils in whose area the park lies, and one-third appointed by central government.

    In the past, the Exchequer has grant-aided 75% of the cost of recreation facilities and services, and the Countryside Commission has contributed substantially to the cost of information services. But most other costs (and running costs) have been borne locally. Under the new system, more finance will be contributed from central government in the hope that total expenditure will rise. But this is not guaranteed if local authorities now contribute less to National Park activities as, for some parks, is proving to be the case (January, 1976).

22. Eddison, T. (1971) National Parks Reform, *Town and Country Planning*, Vol. 39 (9).

23. Ministry of Town and Country Planning (1947) *Report of the National Parks Committee* (Hobhouse Report), Cmnd. 7121, H.M.S.O.

24. Ministry of Town and Country Planning (1945) *National Parks in England and Wales* (Dower Report), Cmnd. 6628, H.M.S.O.

25. The government have rejected the recommendation of the Sandford Committee that forestry in National Parks should be brought within normal planning control arrangements. There is still no government policy on mineral working in National Parks; the proposal that applications for new or extended mineral workings should be automatically 'called in' for ministerial decision has not been accepted. Arrangements for negotiation on road improvements in National Parks are still inadequate; local highway authorities are not bound to consult National Park Authorities. Government policy on major routes promises that none will be constructed through a National Park, nor will there be any upgrading of existing roads, *except with compelling national need.*

    Department of the Environment (1976) *Ministerial Conclusions on the Report of the National Parks Policies Review Committee*, H.M.S.O., Circular 4/76.

26. Changes are proposed in the rules for the disposal of land in lieu of Estate Duty or Capital Transfer Tax which will enable owners to offer land to National Park Authorities.

27. Arrangements will be made for financial assistance to farmers and landowners who incur extra costs as a result of the application of the Landscape Areas Special Development Order to all National Parks.

28. Under the Local Government Act 1972, Park authorities must prepare, within 3 years of 1.4.74 a National Park Plan to be reviewed at 5-yearly intervals.

    Only the Peak Park Planning Board has a statutory responsibility for structure planning, other park authorities may have some delegated planning powers.

29. Advice on the preparation of National Park Plans is given in:

    Department of the Environment (1974) *Local Government Act 1972: National Parks*, Circular 65/74, April 19.

30. Department of the Environment (1974) *Report of the National Park Policies Review Committee*, H.M.S.O. chap. 20. See also chapter 21.

31. Countryside Commission (1976) *National Park Policies*, Countryside Commission Statement, January 12.

32. National Parks have been defined by the International Union for Conservation of Nature and Natural Resources as having the following characteristics: relatively large size, containing natural ecosystems of special interest, 'not materially altered by human exploration or occupation'; protected and

managed by the 'highest competent authority of the country'; and open to visitors, under special conditions, for inspirational, educative, cultural and recreative purposes'. Though this definition recognises the dual purpose of conservation of nature and human use, the National Parks of England and Wales are criticised by members of the Union for lacking adequate protection of their natural communities or cultural landscapes and being periodically invaded or threatened by invasion from hydro-electric installations, mining developments and other forms of urban-industrial intrusion.

See Dasman, R. F. (1973) Classification and Use of Protected Natural and Cultural Areas, I.U.C.N. Occasional Paper No. 4.

33. See for example:

Robinson, D. G. (1972) Comprehensive Development, in Ashton, J. & Long, W. H. (eds.) *The Remoter Rural Areas of Britain*, Oliver & Boyd.

Select Committee on Scottish Affairs (1972) *Land Resource Use in Scotland: Vol. I (Report and Proceedings of the Committee)*, H.M.S.O.

Whitby, M. C. (1972) Economics, Planning and Remote Rural Areas, *Recreation News Supplement*, No. 7, August.

34. North Riding Pennines Study Working Party (1975) *North Riding Pennines Study: Report*, North Riding County Council. Further upland studies have been conducted: in parts of the Peak and Yorkshire Dales National Parks by a team from the Ministry of Agriculture, Yorks and Humberside Economic Planning Board, Department of Trade and Industry and of the Environment, within the North Pennines study area, by members of the Department of Land Economy, Cambridge; and also in Northumberland and Durham by the County Planning Departments.

35. It was acknowledged that more emphasis was given to environmental issues than social and economic factors.

36. See the Report of a Seminar on Upland Planning by Laurie Brett in *Recreation News Supplement*, No. 7, August 1972.

37. The need for specialist upland agencies has been argued, for example, by the North Pennines Study team; the Select Committee on Scottish Affairs who suggest a 'Land Use Council' – a central forum on rural resource affairs – to be supported by a 'Land Use Unit' staffed by professional rural planners. R. J. Green argues for a Rural Development Authority with administrative and executive powers for planning and development, supported by a Rural Development Fund, in chap. 10 of *Country Planning*, Manchester University Press, 1971.

38. Land Capability Analysis (as practised in the Canada Land Inventory Programme under the Agricultural and Rural Development Act (A.R.D.A.) 1963) has been seen as fundamental to the solution of upland resource problems.

See for example:

Statham, D. C. (1972) *Land Use Changes in the Moorlands of the North York Moors National Park*, Centre for Environmental Studies University Working Paper No. 16.

39. An experiment in upland planning for multiple objectives (but not recreation) is reported in:

Ministry of Agriculture, Fisheries & Food (1972) *The Dinas Conference.*

Part IV: Planning and the Rural Environment

CHAPTER 11

The Development of Rural Planning

The early chapters of this book discussed the objectives and practices of some of the most important planning systems operating in the countryside which are concerned with the manipulation of natural and semi-natural resources. In these chapters, and in our case studies of the urban fringe and the uplands, we have argued that land use planners[1] have been only marginally involved in most of these planning systems: it is 'resource' planners — in the agencies of government and among landowners and tenant land managers — that have been responsible for generating and controlling changes which contribute to the present function and appearance of the countryside. Away from built up areas, the rural environment we enjoy, or suffer from, is the outcome of their planning programmes, yet for none of them is the creation of it their primary task. Many problems arise at the interstices between separate areas of action, but no one group of planners has taken responsibility for the over-view. No-one has adopted a concern for the total fabric of the countryside.

This and the next chapter explore the case for a greater practical concern with the rural environment *as a whole* and discuss the ways in which this might take place, both in policy-making and in practice. This chapter reviews the response of resource planning systems and the town and country planning system to the changing countryside.

Recognition of conflict

Previous chapters have shown how recent developments in the traditional rural activities, particularly in agriculture, together with growing public concern for greater protection of the rural environment and for more recreation have generated new conflicts. Some of these conflicts are transient and can be resolved by fairly limited public or private action. Other conflicts are frivolous and reflect an unhealthy resistance to rural change and over-concern for preserving the *status quo.* But some conflicts are rather more basic to the survival of a countryside which people can, and want to, live in and visit.

Over the last decade many of these conflicts have been recognised. Their general nature has been explored in a large number of conferences which have varied in their subject matter from a global concern for the environment[2] to very local habitat problems.[3] Powerful interest groups have emerged, working for agriculture, forestry, nature conservation, mineral exploitation, water supply and other activities each pursuing fairly independent policies to meet single-purpose objectives. The conferences did much to bridge some of the gaps in understanding:

"The worlds of town and country thus met, and the talking had to start — but without the benefit of much common language, and with attitudes already hostile."[4]

In preparatory work and in conference discussion, co-ordination of purpose and method may have been accepted but the ways of achieving this in practice were less obvious.[5]

Since the talking of the sixties, the approach has been to do three things: to create new legislation and planning systems to cope with new areas of rural activity; to widen the remit of existing resource planning systems; and to structure government in such a way that conflicts might be exposed and co-operation encouraged.

A good many improvements in legislation and in the organisation of resource planning agencies have taken place since 1965, resolving in part, and in theory, many of the inefficiencies of single-purpose action. There was, for example, special legislation in the Countryside Acts to provide for some of the new recreation demands, while Section 11 of that Act placed a duty on all Ministers, government departments and public bodies, in the exercise of their functions 'to have regard to the desirability of conserving the natural beauty and amenity of the countryside'. This clause allows wide scope for interpretation, and so far has not been markedly effective, but it does at least draw attention to the possible consequences of ill-considered action. Other clauses in this Act recognise that some resources like forests and reservoirs, primarily planned for one purpose could well be used for others such as recreation.

The British system of water conservation was rationalised with the introduction of river authorities in 1963; the 1968 Transport Act allowed redundant commercial waterways to be restored for amenity use. The Civic Amenities Act of 1967 encouraged more tree planting and gave firmer protection to existing trees. The 1967 Agriculture Act recognised that certain upland areas, with severe social, economic and environmental problems, should be tackled by co-ordinated action — in agriculture, forestry and tourism — and that such areas should be guided by a Rural Development Board. The Ministry of Agriculture itself began to expand its services to farmers to include advice on amenity matters. The scope of other national agencies, such as the Forestry Commission and the Central Electricity Generating Board, was similarly widened.

After the Planning Advisory Group[6] had made its recommendations, a new planning system was introduced in 1968 which gave land use planners opportunities not only to be involved at all in the countryside, but to make a more positive contribution towards the planning of it. The Redcliffe-Maud proposals for local government reform[7] reflected an acceptance of town and country interdependence and promised a more realistic structure of local decision-making. Although no formal machinery was introduced, the idea of regional planning, embracing town and country, grew.

At central level, successive governments have attempted to improve the co-ordination of urban and rural environmental policies by departmental restructuring. The Ministry of Land and Natural Resources was in some ways an ideal, if shortlived, improvement. In 1969 co-ordination was once more encouraged by the creation of a Secretary of State for Local Government and Regional Planning, with responsibilities for housing, local government, planning and transport. All these areas of government, together with others, including water conservation, historic buildings, sport and recreation, landscape and wildlife conservation are now united in the Department of the Environment, created in 1970.[8] This structure, retained by successive governments, has been generally welcomed as a significant improvement in approach, although other major agencies with influence upon the rural environment — the Ministries of Agriculture and Defence, the Department of Trade and Industry — lie outside the D.O.E. Even so, the evolution of 'super Ministries' which is advocated by some[9] may be less effective in achieving greater rural harmony than the widening of aims and interest within existing ones, and especially within those agencies of government, like the Forestry Commission and Nature Conservancy Council with executive as well as advisory responsibilities for the management of rural land.

In all, the legislation, the restructuring and the debate of the mid and later sixties reflected a welcome growth of interest in rural matters and the need for a less blinkered viewpoint on the part of resource planners. In practice there has been some success; alliances have been made, mutual understanding professed. Yet few of the improvements of the sixties have lasted; some proposals, like local government reorganisation were implemented in a different form; others, like the water planning system, have been subsequently changed again. The advisory services of the Ministry of Agriculture have been curtailed; the Rural Development Boards have failed.

In many ways, as we have tried to show in previous chapters, attitudes among resource interests have hardened since 1970. The permanent erosion of sectional interests remains a myth and although there have been local expressions of compromise, real integration between the planning systems of the countryside has proved elusive.

It is tempting to argue that only the activities of land use planners have widened, for the new planning system introduced in 1968 (and consolidated in 1972) does, in theory, offer a new approach. The rest of this chapter looks at some of the ways in which the statutory planning system and the planners who operate it might make good some of the deficiencies in a still disparate framework of rural interests.

The limitations of post-war rural planning

In the field of urban planning, the inadequacies of the system introduced in 1947 were recognised early on; the Planning Advisory Group was set up specifically to examine them. Although many of P.A.G.'s criticisms — on public participation for example — are as relevant in the countryside as in the town, there was only cursory comment upon the limitations of the old planning system for rural areas:

> "... Our general impression is that country planning, outside Town Map areas, has tended to become a neglected aspect of planning work and the present development plan system tends to discourage a more positive approach."[10]

Amplifying this view, it is possible to suggest that there were three particular inadequacies of the system for rural planning: in attitude, in the conception of the rural environment and in the tools available for implementation.

First, the over-riding urban emphasis of the post-war system provided no encouragement to planners to be involved in rural matters outside villages and town map areas, and even here their concern was with visual rather than with functional, social or economic issues. Travis[11] argues that the remoter rural areas, especially, suffered from small and poor planning staffs, and even these had an urban orientation.

Secondly, the conception of the rural environment — like that of the town — was one of assemblages of land *uses* each occupying a discrete area, each capable of being planned for separately, simply by zoning areas for particular uses and ensuring that these areas remained in the use (mainly agriculture) for which they were zoned. But, as previous chapters have tried to show, *resource interest* is a more important concept than land *use*, for land in one use may nevertheless be valued by many different interests. Moreover, rural problems do not arise simply from the way in which land is used, in the broad sense, but from the way in which that use is practiced. It is the day-to-day operations of resource management — the kind and frequency of tree felling; the type and timing of insecticide spraying; the nature and intensity of recreation activity — which are crucial in the generation of rural conflicts. Their resolution depends upon modification of these practices rather than the wholesale protection or rearrangement of land uses.

Thirdly, the 1947 planning system provided almost no means of influencing resource management practices of this kind since most agricultural and forestry operations were (and still are) exempt from planning control. The major alternative method of securing a public interest in land management, through public ownership, was neither feasible nor desirable at the scale on which it was required.

The new planning system

The 1968 Town and Country Planning Act introduced a new system of development planning which was designed to overcome, in various ways, the inadequacies identified by P.A.G. in the old system. These were not, however, the inadequacies for planning rural areas. They were those, derived largely from urban experience, of delays in decision-making, of insufficient public participation and of the unsatisfactory negative rather than positive role of planning in creating a good environment.

The new system approaches these problems by procedural improvements to reduce delays, by new statutory requirements for tapping public opinion while proposals are still being formulated and by revisions in the form and content of plans. Urban and county structure plans and their dependent local plans will deal with a much wider range of subject matter than land use and, in a more positive and constructive way, they will link the social, economic and environmental facets of urban and rural systems.[12]

Predictably, most comment on this revised system has come from observers and practitioners of urban planning. But it is possible to outline, at least in theory, what seem to be the main advantages for rural planning.

 First, rural areas are not only to be drawn into the sphere of development planning but in a much more purposeful way than was possible under the old system. *In theory*, it is no longer possible for rural areas to be treated as 'white land' and thereby excluded from policy-making. Instead, all parts of a structure plan area, whether urban or rural, must have a planning policy.

Secondly, the new style plans, together with a two-tier structure of counties and districts will do much to clarify the nature of planning at different scales. Far greater distinction can now be drawn between policies which are strategic and those which are practical, between the long term view and the short. In urban areas, this kind of reform, involving a return to detailed local development planning and civic design, may have come as a backlash to more than a decade of emphasis upon urban strategies guided mainly by transportation decisions. For countryside planning, which in the past has fallen short of both the strategic view and the positive local approach, this development has important implications. A strategic approach forces planners to look ahead at the agencies and nature of future change rather than concentrate solely upon trying to maintain the *status quo*. At the same time effort must be focussed upon the implementation of broad-brush policies. Hookway[13] has argued that a major difference between structure planning and local planning in the countryside will be in their different emphasis upon management: county planners will be strategists while those working at district level will be concerned essentially with 'environmental management'. Detailed local plan policies for resource use and protection will be vital if strategic decisions are to be implemented, as we argue elsewhere, in connection with national parks, nature reserves and green belts.

Thirdly, the complexity of the countryside is now recognised. The new procedure, in contrast to the old, recognises that other rural planning systems exist and are the major arbiters of change in the rural environment. It is not enough, therefore, for planners merely to consider the rural implications of urban decisions at the end stage of their *urban* planning process. Realistic plans for rural areas must include the actions of other rural activities and the policies of other rural planning systems. Not only are land planners encouraged to use the special powers at their disposal for positive action (for example, under the Countryside Act) but they are also urged to draw into the ambit of the new style plans those activities, like agriculture, over which they have no direct control, but whose practices profoundly affect the function and appearance of the countryside. The intention is that land use planners may 'influence' even if they cannot necessarily 'control' management operations, though the mechanisms of persuasion by which this influence can be secured are only vaguely spelt out.

Finally, provided that the models of the Development Plans Manual for specifically 'urban' and 'county' structure plans are not too closely followed, the new system offers real scope for linking town and country policy-making, and for treating both environments as one planning arena. Moreover, the inclusion of rural areas within a wider planning framework should ensure that some attention is paid to the *process* of their planning; so that, as for urban areas, alternative strategies are generated and evaluated, and attempts are made to guide, as well as to react to, change. For too long, rural planning has remained immune to the influence of developing methodological rigour in urban planning. Analysis, creativity and flexibility in policy-making are as relevant in the countryside as in the city.

In theory, therefore, the philosophy and powers of the new planning system overcome many of the deficiencies identified in its predecessor. It seems to provide just the planning framework required to integrate the separate aims and methods of many different rural resource interests.

The System in Practice

But advantages in theory do not always work out in practice. It is perhaps rather early to review progress in the operation of a planning system so recently introduced.

At the time of writing, few rural structure plans have been submitted for approval (although a number are now at the stage of public consultation) and in the absence of approved structure plans, there can be no statutory local plans.

Even so, a number of structure and local plan studies and reports have been produced since 1968, and a proportion of these are concerned wholly or in part with rural areas. Some of these have been experimental studies which themselves partly influenced the form of the new planning system. All allow some, albeit sketchy, assessment to be made of the realities and development of plan-making for the countryside; although it is already clear that the new system raises fundamental problems on the scope and role of planning, whether in town or country.

Experience since 1968 has revealed many complexities in the concept and operation of new style plans, particularly in the process of structure planning with its ambiguous relationship to the wider activities of corporate and community planning.[14] The danger remains of a cumbersome statutory procedure inhibiting the operation of relevant and flexible plans. Meanwhile, local government reform, geographical and administrative, has raised other difficulties which apply as much to rural as to urban areas. Taken in combination with the final outcome of the various proposals for geographical reform, the new planning system allows rather less integration of urban and rural planning in some areas, especially around the conurbations, than would have been possible if local government boundaries had been redrawn along the lines suggested by Redcliffe-Maud. The situation may have been improved for smaller cities and towns, but for most of the conurbations, the boundaries of metropolitan authorities have been tightly drawn, severing them from their immediate rural hinterland, and in some cases, from their surrounding Green Belts. The omission of any statutory recognition of the regional level in planning is a further weakness of the present system of reform. Planning at this level could ensure that urban and rural policy-making is integrated.

There are problems, in the two-tier system of counties and districts, of conflict and lack of action. Despite the theoretical advantages, the scope exists for damaging disunities to develop between strategic plans and their local implementation, the more so since many advisory local plans are likely to be operative in advance of approved structure plans. Nevertheless, the opportunities are also there for much greater co-operation than in the past.[16]

Public participation in the planning process was a major issue in restructuring the system; yet real participation, in contrast to *post hoc* consultation, remains limited and time consuming. In the countryside, there has been some progress with the involvement of particular rural interest groups on some aspects of policy-making: most counties have countryside committees of one form or another. But the real participation of those who own or work most of the land over which rural policies will apply has only recently been tried (in experiments in the Lake District and the Bollin Valley) and there are clearly difficulties.[17] Moreover, there are many visitors to the countryside, and others who have an interest in how the rural environment develops, who remain largely unrepresented and unconsulted in the process of planning. Some of these people may have been surveyed at a local beauty spot, but it is difficult to see how they can be brought more effectively into plan-making, especially at a strategic level. The difficulties of personal identification with large scale problems and extensive areas may be even greater in the country than in the town.

Approaches to planning the rural environment

Aside from these common problems, a very varied treatment of rural issues is beginning to emerge from the plan-making so far carried out both in advance and in the spirit of the new system. It is clear that at *regional* and *sub-regional* level, more attention is now devoted to countryside matters. But there is so far no agreement either on content or on the degree of detail at which rural issues should be treated. Some studies, like the Strategic Plan for the

South East,[18] do little more than provide a broad zonation of territory which would formerly have been classified as 'white land'. In this case a zonation is made on the basis of agricultural land significance and an arbitrary criterion of environmental quality, but the development of workable policies for the zones has been left to the lower level of structure planning.

Other studies, notably those in Nottinghamshire/Derby,[19] and for Coventry, Solihull and Warwickshire[20] cover rural issues more thoroughly, treating them, as they do urban problems, in a systematic way: setting goals, analysing the resource and activity base and generating various strategies. Both of these studies, in their adherence to a logical process of planning, and particularly in their development and application of 'potential surface' techniques have made innovative contributions to plan-making for rural areas.

There is similarly little general agreement among *structure* plan studies on what their rural content should be and how policy-making should be tackled. All show some improvement upon traditional development plan statements, but for some, like Leicestershire,[21] the countryside still features as an afterthought. Other authorities, the majority so far, have chosen to treat rural issues more fully, yet quite separately from the urban component of their plans. Their work, in Derbyshire for example,[22] perpetuates a view of the countryside not fundamentally different from the past: one in which rural areas must at all costs be defended from the town, and where protection from development is a primary goal. So far, it is only in South Hampshire[23] that the potential of the structure plan format for planning urban and rural environments *as one* has been exploited.

On the basis of experience so far, it is too early to draw firm conclusions about the benefits of the new planning system for a more comprehensive approach to rural problems, at least at structure plan level and above. No consistent differentiation of content or treatment has emerged between the different scales of planning; there are few common features among structure plans apart from a generally increased attention to analysing and describing the components of the rural system. With few exceptions, there is little evidence of a new approach to policy-making and implementation which might make good some of the deficiencies in post-war rural planning identified earlier in this chapter.

It is at local plan level that a clearer picture seems to have emerged of the real problems and potential for change in rural areas, and where some attempt has been made to integrate rural interests.[24] Notable studies at this scale have been the series of experimental rural planning exercises, jointly initiated by the Countryside Commission in East Hampshire in 1966 and developed subsequently in Sherwood Forest and the North Pennines.

Integrated Resource Planning Studies

In retrospect, a number of studies of areas of rural conflict which took place in the early sixties seem to have been important in shaping later work, not necessarily in terms of the methodology used, but because of the integrative approach adopted towards policy-making and the involvement of a number of different agencies and disciplines. The particular value of these studies, for example on Broadland[25] and the uplands,[26] was the benefit they showed could accrue from 'working together' — not only in the assembly of facts and figures but in the understanding of conflicting viewpoints and the development of compromise solutions. The Broadland study especially showed this. The work of the Land Use Study Group on the uplands was much wider in scope, yet more detailed on methodology. By attempting some objective comparison of the relative values of different combinations of rural land uses, the study was able to suggest a way of improving upon decision-making guided only by subjective speculation.

The conclusions of both studies were broad and their recommendations were of strategic or national, rather than local, significance. Both concentrated heavily upon the analysis of problems and conflicts so that suggestions on policy, and especially on methods of implementation, were less clearly worked out. More detailed were the planning studies of five estates on the Solent shores of South Hampshire, prepared by consultants participating with the landowners.[27] These plans, which were later adopted by Hampshire County Council as part of their development plan, provide another example of integrated rural planning, and of the possibilities for partnership between planners and landowners.

In all these studies, the approach was a practical attempt at the realities of rural conservation: the harmonisation of resource interests, with the minimum of conflict.

The East Hampshire Study[28]

A rural planning exercise in East Hampshire provided a better example of what rural conservation could mean and how it might be practiced.

The East Hampshire Area of Outstanding Natural Beauty, a tract of some 150 square miles (350 km^2) of chalk downland east of Winchester, is an area of prosperous arable farming. With its rolling well-wooded appearance, this is attractive countryside, suitable and popular for a variety of the informal recreation activities. The overall intensity of recreational activity is not high although certain areas like Old Winchester Hill and Butser Hill are well used. But the potential for increased recreation pressure is clearly there as accessibility from London to the south and west of England continues to improve and, more especially, as the city region of South Hampshire grows. Wildlife interest over much of the area is limited by the poverty of natural habitats on land so intensively farmed, but there are small areas of chalk grassland, fertile river valleys, and beech hangers on the scarp slopes of the east.

Many aspects of rural policy-making — settlements, communications, mineral working — had already been decided before the conservation study began.[29] The team was therefore free to concentrate upon the present and future interactions between five major resource interests — agriculture, forestry, recreation, wildlife and landscape conservation.[30] For each of these interests the A.O.N.B. was zoned according to differences in character and value. There was speculation, for each interest, on the likely future changes that would take place — the increasing intensification and specialisation of agriculture; expansion in the volume and variety of recreation activity; the growth of interest in wildlife conservation, for example. Present clashes of interest and the likely conflicts resulting from further developments in the major activities of agriculture and recreation were explored in what was perhaps the most interesting part of the East Hampshire method. On the basis of these 'interactions', the relative acceptability of new activities and developments among different rural interests was gauged. In this way, such activities as chemical spraying, field drainage, tree felling or the introduction of new footpaths or country parks could be accepted or rejected by each of the five main interest groups for each of the many zones into which the A.O.N.B. was divided.

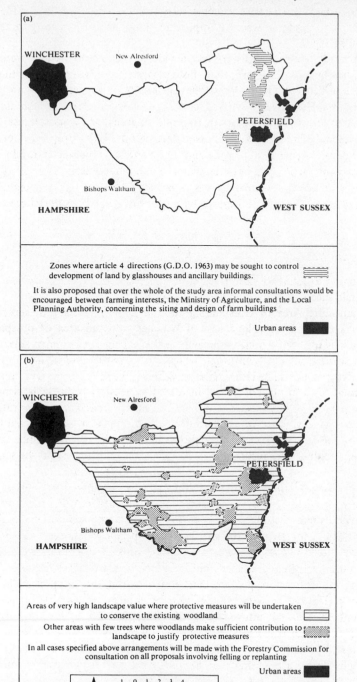

FIG. 7. *East Hampshire Area of Outstanding Natural Beauty*
(a)   Agricultural policy
(b)   Forestry policy

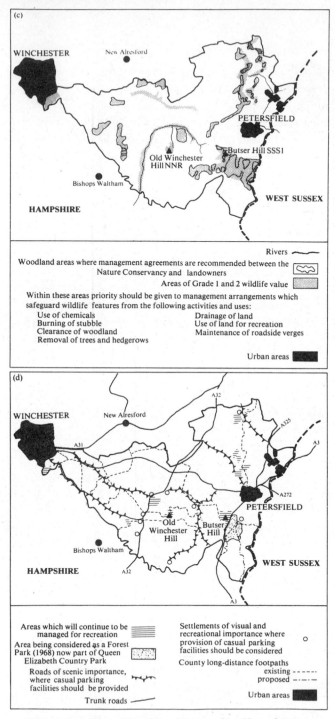

FIG. 7. *East Hampshire Area of Outstanding Natural Beauty*
(c)   Wildlife Conservation policy
(d)   Recreation policy

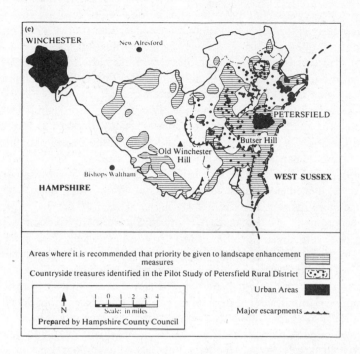

FIG. 7. *East Hampshire Area of Outstanding Natural Beauty*
(e)   Landscape policy

The results of these analyses were synthesised in the generation of 'policy zones' (delineated on grounds of resource quality) within which certain activities were considered to be more or less acceptable and for which, therefore, policies of promotion or restriction might apply. In some zones, where for example landscape or ecological values were high, it was suggested that priority should be given to these interests; conservation measures, such as planting in field corners were to be encouraged, while damaging practices — such as hedgerow clearance — should be restricted. Elsewhere, in zones of high agricultural quality, it was accepted that recreation activities might need to be curtailed, if not wholly diverted to areas of poorer farming.

For some zones, where values were high for several interests and direct policy conflicts could be anticipated, more detailed studies were recommended. This applied particularly to those areas where novel methods of implementing policies were advocated; where, for example, measures for control and action available under the 1947 and 1962 planning legislation were inadequate to deal with the kind of policies proposed. In these areas, it was suggested that positive action might be achieved not simply through development control or by public ownership, but perhaps by special management arrangements (Fig. 7).

Inevitably, there were weaknesses in the approach and methods of the East Hampshire exercise.[31] It was recognised, too late, that those who held most of the power on implementation — the local farmers and landowners — had not been directly involved in the process of plan-making; their representatives had been consulted only when the study was substantially complete. Clearly, if policies (as they were in East Hampshire) are to involve activities and practices over which the planner has limited or no statutory control, and where government agencies can exercise only limited influence, then the preparation of plans for rural areas cannot be their task alone: those affected by the policies should be a part of the planning team. A proportion of the failure of a subsequent attempt to implement the East Hampshire plan in part of the A.O.N.B. can be attributed to the lack of support for a study carried out in isolation from locally represented interests.

The plan-making techniques too, have been justly criticised. Although improvements were made upon previous work in a number of areas, notably perhaps in the evaluation of ecological interest, there was no overall compatibility of resource evaluation methods. The assessment of future demands upon the area was crude, especially for recreation, on which considerable progress has been made since 1968. The statements of acceptability were based upon broad value judgements; given more time and more skills, these might have been verified by some more rigorous analysis of costs and benefits.

The resource problems tackled in East Hampshire were relatively simple; large areas of policy-making were already decided and although conflict did exist between the interests and would probably intensify in future, the problems were not intractable. The test of such an approach must be the degree to which it is replicable elsewhere, and especially in areas of rather more diverse and tangible rural conflict. The New Forest Study[32] provides an example of how the approach, modified and developed, can be applied at a more detailed level, with rather fewer, though perhaps more directly conflicting, resource interests. Here, the concern is with resolving conflict by more effective resource management, particularly for recreation, an approach which largely ignores (perhaps unwisely) the implications of policies at the strategic level.

But in both the New Forest and East Hampshire the conservation goal is fairly clear: the need is for some means of protecting what is left of a semi-natural landscape threatened by changes in land management and the influx of new and potentially damaging uses. Elsewhere, conservation may depend much more upon establishing viable social and economic structures as a pre-requisite for recreation, landscape and wildlife policies. Larger scale studies of the East Hampshire type have subsequently taken place in other very different rural environments: in Sherwood Forest, flanked by the industrial areas of Nottinghamshire and South Yorkshire; and in the North Pennines, where — in the latter case especially — social issues are far more prominent and rather more tangible conflict exists between the needs of local communities and those of visitors and preservationists. In both of these studies, the experience in East Hampshire has been widened, to incorporate more interests, and deepened, by devoting more attention to the processes of analysis and synthesis in the course of generating policies.

The Sherwood Forest Study[33]

In 1969, as a follow up to the East Hampshire work, a joint planning study was begun in the smaller (145 km^2) but more complex area of Sherwood Forest between Sheffield and Nottingham. The principal contributors to the Study, and the interests represented on the working party were Nottinghamshire County Council and the Countryside Commission,

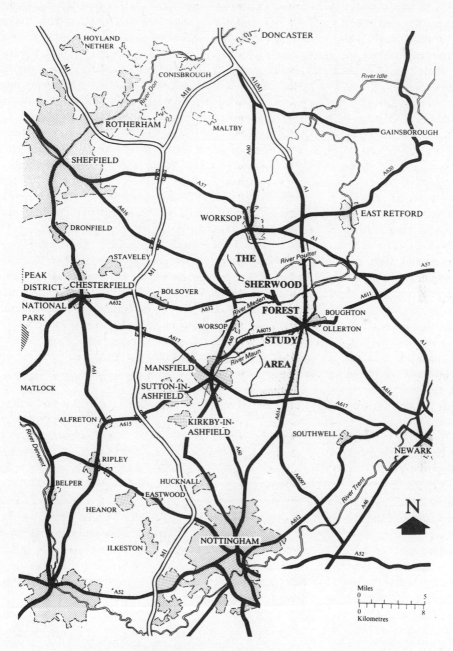

FIG. 8. *Sherwood Forest Study*
(a)   Regional Setting (prepared by Nottinghamshire County Council)

	LANDSCAPE	AGRICULTURE	FORESTRY	RECREATION/TOURISM	NATURE CONSERVATION	MILITARY TRAINING	TOWNS	COALMINING/INDUSTRY	ROADS
AGRICULTURE	Prairie farming. Loss of trees/hedges. Unsympathetic buildings. Loss of forest identity.								
FORESTRY	Alien conifers. Rigid plantation boundaries. Felling problems.	Forests harbour agricultural pests.							
RECREATION/TOURISM	Litter. Impact of cars	Trespass. Fire damage to crops and animals Removal of rights of way. Unattractive modern farming.	Fire damage to young trees. Conifer plantations of lesser attraction.						
NATURE CONSERVATION		Loss of natural habitat i.e. hedges, tree clumps, Pesticides, Stubble burning.	Coniferous plantations less attractive for Flora & Fauna. Conservation versus cropping.	Erosion by feet & cars. Damage to plants. Reduction of natural habitats.					
MILITARY TRAINING		Major conflict i.e. damage to crops and animals.	Fire damage to trees Plantations too dense for fieldcraft.	Major conflict between visitors and guns and tanks.	Erosion. Some damage to flora by tanks, etc. Noise frightens wildlife Preserves land from other incursions.				
TOWNS	Air pollution. Unattractive modern development—urban fringe problems.	Fire. Trespass. Air pollution. Damage to crops and animals.	Air pollution.	Air Pollution. Unattractive modern development	Pollution, Urban extensions reducing natural habitat.				
COALMINING/INDUSTRY	Pollution subsidence Absolute visual conflict	Pollution subsidence.	Pollution subsidence.	Pollution Poor environment.	Pollution subsidence.	Terrain and cover interfered with.	Pollution. Subsidence poor Environment.		
ROADS	Unsympathetic design and scale of engineering Improvements.	Access problems on minor roads.	Access problems on minor roads.	Large lorries & heavy traffic versus people. Tourist traffic on minor roads.	Noise danger to wildlife. Reduction of habitat.	Large Military vehicles and dangerous crossing.	Environmental problems—people versus traffic.	Subsidence	
WATER SUPPLY		Pollution of rivers and aquifer	Possible pollution.		Lowering of water table.		Pollution.	Lowering of water table.	Lowering of water table.

Legend:

☐ No apparent conflict

▨ Conflicts which could be substantially overcome

▦ Apparently insuperable conflicts

Prepared by Nottingham County Council

FIG. 8. *Sherwood Forest Study*

(b)   Diagrammatic representation of levels of incompatibility between land-use and resources together with the Department of Environment, Forestry Commission, Nature Conservancy (now Council), Ministry of Agriculture with consultants from Manchester University — a wider group than in East Hampshire, reflecting both the differences and the greater scope of problems to be tackled. Moreover, to improve upon this limited representation of official agencies which was identified as a major deficiency of the East Hampshire exercise, a second and larger working party was involved in the Sherwood Plan. In the development of final recommendations, public reaction was sought to a preliminary outline of policies.[34]

As in East Hampshire some areas of policy-making, for example on settlements, had already been decided and this allowed the teams to concentrate upon the conflicting rural interests of agriculture, forestry, nature conservation, recreation and the landscape. But in all of these the problems and opportunities of Sherwood Forest were significantly different from those of East Hampshire.

The landscape of Sherwood, like its land use pattern, is diverse, with old and new forests and sandy heaths, the landscaped parklands of once extensive estates and tracts of open agricultural land dominated by the paraphernalia of industrial and mining development. This is an area of arable farming (especially for barley) which is undergoing many of the structural and technical changes common to other arable areas. Conifers have been planted on a substantial scale, replacing the old broadleaved parkland trees. The whole is fringed by collieries and their spoil heaps; and these, with new industries and communications now invade the Forest Area bringing air and water pollution as well as considerable visual intrusion. Water is extracted from the underlying sandstone aquifers which will need to be recharged as demands continue to grow. Large areas have been used for military training, and the future of these remains in debate. The whole area, with its historic associations and attractive remaining parklands, is an increasingly popular location for informal recreation (for which there is presently inadequate provision) and offers largely unexplored tourist potential.

Growth and change in the major land uses, and the erosion of much of the old forest cover has increased the fragility of the landscape and reduced ecological values which now rest in the remaining areas of ancient oak forest, the heaths, and the wooded estates. A complex pattern of land ownership adds to the conflicts generated among all these interests.

The approach to generating policies in the Sherwood Forest Study was considerably more rigorous than in East Hampshire. Building upon a method applied in the Nottingham/Derby Sub-Regional Study,[35] the team tried to assess the *potential* of rural resources to meet the wide range of present and future demands upon them. Assessments of resource capacity to accommodate particular uses allowed competing activities to be evaluated in different parts of the area, and the most suitable locations to be identified for each. A parallel exercise looked at the nature and scale of present and future demands within each major activity. Matching the two operations allowed the demands for land and water resources by different rural interests to be compared, and converted, both to areal measures of resource needs, and to specific locations. Using the example of recreation, Zetter has described the application of this 'potential surface analysis' to the Sherwood area where it was valuable in devising both general policies — for example, the identification of zones where agriculture or recreation or forestry should dominate — and specific proposals, for example on the location of new recreation facilities.[36]

The policies which emerged from the Sherwood Forest Study, like those of East Hampshire, stressed the multiple-interest management of rural land as an important means of resolving conflict, especially among the more compatible activities of forestry, recreation and wildlife conservation. But it was recognised that multiple use would not always work: opportunities for combining recreation activity and farming for example, were thought to be limited in this area.

Compared with the Hampshire downland, intrusions of industrial activity are a much greater problem in Sherwood and physical control measures (as part of a new protective designation for the area) figure more prominently in the policies. Even so, most of the recommendations for action involve measures which lie outside the statutory framework of physical planning but which bring into the ambit of the plan a wide range of management approaches relating to: agricultural and forestry practice; to landscape conservation and enhancement; to traffic and to information services.

The study goes further to suggest a permanent and widely represented advisory committee to guide the implementation of many aspects of the plan, particularly for recreation. In keeping with its format along the lines of a local District Plan, 'action areas' are identified for more detailed study, and the proposals are ranked on the basis of their priority in a programme to the 1980's.

The North Pennines Study[37]

In 1971, the Countryside Commission, pursuing further its aim of trying to devise new approaches to planning in different rural areas, initiated a joint plan-making exercise in the North Pennines. This involved, directly or indirectly all the relevant statutory organisations, many voluntary bodies and representatives of the landowners and occupiers, all co-ordinated by the North Riding County Council.[38]

The study area of 525 square miles (1,361 km²) included part of the Yorkshire Dales National Park and fell wholly inside the area temporarily administered by a Rural Development Board which was later disbanded. Its problems were fairly typically those (which were outlined in Chapter 9) of a relatively remote upland region with a poor natural resource base: marginality in farming; low incomes and inadequate social and physical services; pressures for afforestation and other land use change; unique if as yet unexploited values for recreation and wildlife.

The approach was firmly objective-based — aims were defined, in a Delphic way, for a whole range of upland interests although there was an acknowledged concentration upon environmental rather than social and economic factors. The subsequent method adopted the principle if not the detail of potential surface analysis: problems and opportunities of the area and its activities were exposed and many 'options' were generated by which the problems might be alleviated and the opportunities realised. These options were then evaluated against the original (now weighted) aims[39] and grouped (perhaps too soon and too conveniently) into three exclusive 'illustrative' strategies in which priority was accorded, in turn, to the local economy, to landscape and wildlife conservation and to recreation.

It is clear from the attempt to reach a compromise that views about desirable priorities for upland areas were strongly polarised both within the planning team and the consultative committee, reflecting the more complex situation which this study faced, without the obvious dominance (as there was in East Hampshire) of environmental goals. Nevertheless, a 'preferred' strategy of comparable and feasible policies was generated from the reactions of the consultative committee to the priority of different aims and the suitability of the options to meet them.

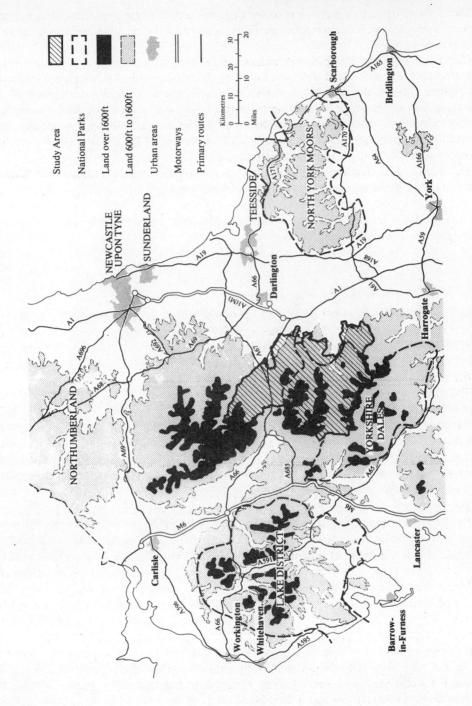

FIG. 9. *North Pennines Study: Regional Setting*

The breadth of the study and its limited time-scale have meant that, in some ways, the final policies appear disappointingly vague compared with the logic and relative sophistication (at least among rural studies) of the method. The work argues not so much for more refinement here (although the evaluation of alternative policies is obviously still a problem) as for a more objective way of building into the plan-making exercise, and at an earlier stage, the real attitudes and priorities of its consumers. A consultative committee, of arbitrary composition, cannot adequately mirror these. Most of all, the study revealed a fundamental need to clarify the aims of upland policy-making, nationally and internationally, and to set out the ways in which these might be achieved or thwarted by future events. Sadly, there was insufficient time in the North Pennines Study to develop alternative social and economic scenarios for the future of Britain and Europe, with their different implications for upland problems and opportunities.[40]

Conclusions

Although the emphasis has changed, the aims of all these experimental studies were twofold: to develop the methods of rural planning and to prepare realistic proposals for planning and managing their particular areas of countryside.

On the first, progress has undoubtedly been made in those aspects of environmental planning outside the settled parts of the countryside. The later studies, particularly in Sherwood Forest, have met a number of the technical criticisms of earlier work in East Hampshire — perhaps to the point at which further major improvements would now yield diminishing returns in a situation where time and skills are limited. But as viable rural plans, all are, as yet, unproven. Some, like the Sherwood Study have been adopted by the relevant local authorities. In all areas, individual proposals on which there was widespread agreement will probably be implemented. But the more controversial policies, and especially those which *in combination* make up an integrated approach to rural problems, remain untested. The next chapter looks at various components of these plan-making exercises and tries to assess their contribution, along with that of recent work at other scales, to our understanding of the countryside and our ability to tackle some of its obvious environmental problems.

Notes and References

1. That is, those concerned with the statutory activity of town and country planning.
2. For example European Conservation Year 1970, United Nations Conference on the Human Environment, 1971.
3. For example, symposia on road verges and hedgerows have been among a number organised by the Nature Conservancy Council.
4. Dower, M. (1972) Who Plans the Countryside? *Town and Country Planning*, Vol. 40.
5. Johnson, S. P. (1973) *The Politics of the Environment*, Tom Stacey.
    Kennet, W. (1974) The Politics of Conservation, in Warren, A. and Goldsmith, F. B. (eds.), *Conservation in Practice*, John Wiley.
    See also: Lowe, P. (1975) The Environmental Lobby, *Built Environment*, Vol. 1 (1, 2, 3).
6. Planning Advisory Group (1965) *The Future of Development Plans*, H.M.S.O.

7. Royal Commission on Local Government in England (1969) *Local Government Reform*, Summary volume; H.M.S.O. Cmnd. 4039.

8. Davidson, J. M. (1974) Countryside Conservation: Some National Perspectives, in Warren, A. and Goldsmith, F. B. (eds.), *Conservation in Practice*, John Wiley.

9. Weller, J. (1968) *Modern Agriculture and Rural Planning*, Architectural Press, Chapter 1.
   See also:
   Wibberley, G. P. (1975) Changing Landscape: the Threats and the Remedies, *The Countryman*, Winter 1975/76.

10. Planning Advisory Group (1965) op. cit.

11. Travis, A. S. (1972) Policy Formulation and the Planner, in Ashton, J. and Long, W. H. (eds.) *The Remoter Rural Areas of Britain*, Oliver & Boyd.

12. For details of the 1968 Act provisions and the nature of Structure and Local (District, Action Area, Subject) plans see for example:
    Ministry of Housing and Local Government (1970) *Development Plans: A Manual on Form and Content*, H.M.S.O.

13. Hookway, R. J. S., personal communication.

14. There have been many critiques of the structure plan procedure; see especially:
    McLoughlin, J. B. and Thornley, J. (1972) *Some Problems in Structure Planning: a Literature Review*, Centre for Environmental Studies, Information Paper 27.

15. Department of the Environment (1971) *Local Government in England: Government Proposals for Reorganisation*, White Paper, H.M.S.O., Cmnd. 4584.

16. Hague, M. (1972) Structure Plan Opportunities, *Journal of the Royal Town Planning Institute*, Vol. 58(9).

17. See discussions of the Upland Management and Bollin Valley Experiments in the next chapter.

18. South East Joint Planning Team (1970) *Strategic Plan for the South East*, H.M.S.O.

19. Nottinghamshire County Council *et al.* (1969) *Nottinghamshire/Derby Sub-Regional Study*.

20. Coventry City Council *et al.* (1971) *Coventry-Solihull-Warwickshire: A Strategy for the Sub-Region*.

21. Leicestershire County Council (1971) *A Strategy for the Countryside*.

22. Derbyshire County Planning Department (1972) *Countryside Plan: An Interim Strategy for the Countryside*.

23. South Hampshire Plan Advisory Committee (1972) *South Hampshire Structure Plan*, published by Hampshire County Council.

24. The first two of the studies discussed in the rest of the chapter correspond to 'subject' plans at the district scale; the findings of the North Pennines Study emerge as subject policies more appropriate at structure plan level.

25. Nature Conservancy *et al.* (1965) *Report on Broadland*; see also:
    Broads Consortium (1971) *Broadland Study and Plan*, Norfolk County Council.

26. Department of Education and Science (1965) *Report of the Land Use Study Group: Forestry, Agriculture and the Multiple Use of Rural Land*, H.M.S.O.

27. Leonard Manasseh and Partners (1969) *North West Solent Shore Estates: Study and Plans*, Leonard Manasseh.

28. Hampshire County Council (1968) *East Hampshire A.O.N.B.: A Study in Countryside Conservation*.

29. Hampshire County Council (1968) *Country Conservation Policy*.

30. The planning team was composed of officers from five public bodies: Hampshire County Council; National Parks Commission (now Countryside Commission); Nature Conservancy (now Council); Forestry Commission and Ministry of Agriculture.

31. For a review of the study in its political context see:
    Dower, M. (1969) Politics of Countryside Planning, *Town and Country Planning*, Vol. 37(3).

32. Hampshire County Council (1970) *Conservation of the New Forest*.

33. Sherwood Forest Study Group/Nottinghamshire County Council (1973) *Sherwood Forest Study*.

34. Sherwood Forest Study Group/Nottinghamshire County Council (1972) *The Future of Sherwood Forest*, Public Consultation document.
    The larger working party represented the following: Council for the Protection of Rural England; Country Landowners' Association; Ministry of Defence; National Coal Board; National Farmers' Union; National Trust; Regional Sports Council; Royal Forestry Society; Timber Growers' Organisation; Trent River Authority.

35. Nottinghamshire County Council *et al.* (1969), op. cit.

36. Zetter, J. A. (1974) The application of potential surface analysis to rural planning, *The Planner*, Vol. 60(2).

37. North Riding Pennines Study Working Party (1975) *North Riding Pennines Study: Report*, North Riding County Council.
    See also Chapter 10.

38. Organisation of the study was structured in the following way: a *steering* group on which was represented the local planning authority (N. Riding C.C.); Countryside Commission; Department of the Environment; Forestry Commission; Ministry of Agriculture; Nature Conservancy; a *working* party which included representatives of all these organisations and of the Game Conservancy, Institute of Geological Sciences and the Yorkshire River Authority; finally, a *consultative* committee which included representatives of local district councils and of such organisations as the Council for the Protection of Rural England; Country Landowners' Association; National Farmers' Union; Ramblers' Association and other sporting, naturalist and community bodies.
39. Aims were ranked by a vote among rural groups represented on the Consultative Committee.
40. See also: Countryside Commission (1975) *The North Pennines Study: Methods Report*.

CHAPTER 12

Problems in Rural Planning

Although experience of rural plan-making, and more so of implementation, is still so limited, it is clear that a number of crucial issues have emerged which will continue to face those who must prepare and carry out new-style plans for rural areas. Four seem especially in need of resolution: the way in which rural problems are conceived; methods of analysis and plan-making; the nature of rural policies, and the means of implementation.[1]

The Conception of Environmental Problems

The basis of the new approach in East Hampshire and subsequent studies was in their view of the nature and function of the rural environment, and the wide scope of rural problems and opportunities they perceived. They saw the countryside, not as a great 'green jelly' which could absorb and reform unchanged around new urban developments,[2] but as a dynamic environment, reacting not only to urban-generated activities but to rapid internal change. But in most other studies the goals and objectives and indeed the policies formulated for rural areas reflect a prevailing conception of the countryside which (despite the new terminology of 'conservation') is not fundamentally different from the traditional 'white land' notion of 1947.[3] The countryside is seen as a milieu utterly different from the city although, as we argue in other chapters, much is now threatened by new kinds of rural industrialisation. Countryside problems are seen largely in terms of the clash of obvious urban and rural interests, particularly over the loss of land for development. Policies therefore concentrate upon the careful siting of urban growth and the stringent control of new building.[4] But this view ignores the kind of conflicts discussed in the first part of this book, which arise *within* the countryside between rural interests, and which sometimes outweigh the influence of more direct urban pressures. It is, moreover, a view which inhibits (because it assumes there cannot be) a closer integration of urban and rural activity.

Where deeper rural conflicts are recognised, and this is a growing feature of new plans, the tendency is again to polarise urban and rural differences and see conflicts largely in terms of recreation. Greater attention to this new facet of the rural environment is a common theme among recent plans. Perhaps predictably, because of the nature of their sponsorship, it has been emphasised in the analysis and policy-making of the experimental studies.

The danger is that for some authorities *rural* planning is rapidly becoming synonymous with *recreation* planning, the more so since this almost alone among the extensive uses of rural land involves the powers of public planners in a directly executive way. The counter assumption seems also to hold true: that those whose legal job it is to control other rural activities should have the greater say in their planning. Yet this concentration upon recreation, although it has provided a *raison d'être* for planners to step outside the urban fence and the village envelope, reflects again a reluctance to see the countryside other than in terms of discrete and short term problems. The emphasis in recreation analysis and policy-making is thus placed upon deficiencies in provision, the need for segregation from other activities and for single use facilities built to definable standards, rather than upon opportunities for integration, for multiple use and for flexibility.[5]

In all but a few of the recent rural studies, discussion of the long term future of the countryside, how it will change, what new demands will be placed upon it, is bypassed in favour of this analysis of present problems. Yet to plan implies some vision of the future, a willingness to suggest how it might be and to offer some choices. There is now more attention to forecasting the numerical change in particular demands, particularly for recreation, but much less concern with a reasoned, if qualitative, discussion of the effects of other changes — in leisure, in the market for land, or in urban and industrial processes.

Rural Planning Methods

Some of the most significant developments in planning over the last decade have been made in the techniques of analysing, explaining and forecasting urban systems.[6] But little of this new approach has rubbed off on rural planners.

One reason is the continued severance of urban and rural planning tasks and teams with the emphasis of interest and skill upon urban matters and a consequent perpetuation of traditional ways of looking at the countryside. Another, perhaps more positive, explanation for the failure of rural planners to keep pace with technical and philosophical developments in urban planning has been, until recently, their resistance towards attempts to analyse systematically those elements of rurality which are held to be so intangible as to defy much quantification. This has been the case in descriptions of rural resources and activities and more especially in forecasting their future state and in their evaluation both internally and in comparison with other resources and activities.

Progress has been made in describing the various elements of the rural system and on forecasting change in particular activities such as recreation, but here as with other rural interests, predictions may still be too little qualified by the wider implications of national and international developments.

A particular problem acknowledged in the East Hampshire exercise was the difficulty of comparing the value of tracts of land for different activities. The criteria upon which individual evaluations were made were not only fundamentally different (employing, for example, physical, biological, visual, managerial and other factors) but were also related to value scales which varied from national to local significance. Moreover, some represented inherent and relatively permanent values, others were transitory.

It is difficult to see ways round this problem, unless all rural interests can express their values in comparable terms — money, for example[7] — but this too has many dangers, and for some interests, notably landscape and informal, dispersed recreation activity, it is doubtful whether a solution along these lines is possible. Even if it is, the development of a more integrated planning approach to rural resource problems must go on while research is in progress. There is certainly a need to increase objectivity (although subjectivity can never be eliminated) but it would be foolish, in the search for monetary values, to curtail the very valuable work which employs other criteria such as that on the measurement of resource attractiveness for recreation;[8] or on landscape[9] and wildlife evaluations. The need is for rapid, cheap and reliable resource evaluation techniques to be developed *on all fronts*, to suit particular circumstances, and not just for further refinement of those methods which may have limited application. Some rural plan-making exercises do reveal imbalances in the technical effort devoted to different rural interests.[10]

Over-emphasis upon the analysis of one component of the system (such as landscape or recreation) may be an inefficient use of manpower; it may also lead to inconsistencies in priorities at the stage of policy-making, based only upon imbalanced data collection.

Perhaps more important now is the need to refine techniques of synthesising rural values (however they are derived) as for example Statham, arguing for land capability analysis, has tried to do for upland resource interests,[11] and Weddle and Pickard devised in their method of 'least social cost' analysis.[12] The potential surface techniques applied to rural problems in the Sherwood Study offer some way round the comparability problem, not least because, like cost benefit analysis, they provide a framework which may itself be more important than detailed statistical accuracy and objectivity in individual fact-finding exercises.

> "The technique involves a systematic assessment of the potential of an area to accommodate a particular form of development. Firstly, it entails the identification of those factors that in combination constitute an ideal location, in terms of a set of defined aims and objectives. It measures the occurrence of these factors and maps them as a surface. The surface itself can be visualised as a contour map with high points (the peaks) being areas of highest potential, and low points (the valleys) being areas with little or no potential. The method can be seen as a development from the sieve map in that, instead of defining areas that are not suitable for a particular use, it identifies potential in a positive way and grades the suitability of areas, thus enabling priorities of location to be established."[13]

There are still, as Zetter describes, many problems to be resolved in potential surface analysis, but the techniques seem to offer a workable approach to the generation of alternative policies, and their evaluation, in situations of rural conflict.[14] Perhaps the real value is that this method forces those who prepare plans to formulate and discuss long-term and short-term objectives making the reasoning explicit at all stages of plan-making. The definition of goals, for so long *assumed* in rural planning now rightly demands much more attention, but most work is still preoccupied with finding solutions for the short-term, where aims and objectives are assumed to be obvious and remain unexpressed. Not only may these implicit assumptions be misguided, the danger is that short-term problem-solving policies will be outstripped by events while more durable alternatives, which anticipate future change, are ignored.

The definition of longer term aims, so that they can be translated into working objectives, is not easy. There is a need to use traditional 'Delphi' methods in a more rigorous way, and to experiment with surveys and gaming techniques. Encouraging the consumers of plans to think about aims and objectives, and not merely to react to final proposals, is likely to be a more fruitful approach to public participation, as the North Pennines Study has shown.[15]

No method, no set of techniques, however rigorous and sophisticated can replace the creative and essentially political process of generating policies and deciding, in particular circumstances, the priority to be accorded to different interests. In the rush to catch up with technical progress in urban planning some rural plans have suffered on this score: planners have perhaps believed that detailed analysis alone will define appropriate action, or — more dangerously — that sophisticated analysis will mask the weaknesses of policies generated quite independently.

Aside from the need to improve specialist techniques, the more general methodological issue of the *process* of planning may have been neglected in rural studies.

It would be ridiculous to suggest that planning in the countryside, any more so than in urban areas, could or should follow a rigidly compartmentalised procedure in a mechanical and uncreative way. Nevertheless, to plan any environment presupposes that some attempt will be made to guide the course of future events on the basis of some analysis of the present, and that in the course of this process, some alternative 'futures' will be suggested with their relative merits and defects explained. The simplified model "survey-analysis-plan" is no longer adequate as our understanding of the complexity of planning systems increases.

There have been many attempts to codify the various stages that planning could involve; Sarly has developed one such theoretical model from a wide review of the literature in planning, in operations research and in general management.[16] Nine main stages are included:[17]

1. Problem recognition;
2. Data collection, analysis and forecasting;
3. Description of the planning system;
4. Determination of constraints, opportunities, goals and objectives;
5. Design of alternative plans;
6. Evaluation of alternative plans;
7. Decision making on policies;
8. Implementation;
9. Review.

Several writers have suggested the procedures which might be adopted for rural planning and the kinds of information which should be collected but these do not necessarily add up to a comprehensive or logical process of planning. Smart[18] has argued that the approach advocated in much official advice is a fairly conventional one where compartmentalised policies are worked out for different resources and activities such as landscape, minerals, water and recreation. This may work for the remoter rural areas, but it is too superficial 'for a city regional context, where there are dynamic relationships between urban and rural activities'. Barrow[19] suggests that the countryside, certainly in the city region, can only be planned as one with urban areas; the urban planning framework and the techniques of demand and resource analysis commonly used in planning urban areas can also be applied to rural problems, as they have been in the structure plan for South Hampshire.[20]

For the more remote countryside, Statham[21] has suggested the components of an integrated planning approach:

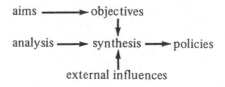

These simplified stages summarise a whole series of different steps, but Statham argues that the process is basically similar to that used for urban situations 'except that the constraints and parameters are mainly defined by ecology, and the resources and activities which are studied are often not subject to control by planning legislation'.

There are other obvious differences (even though many may be only temporary) between urban and rural environments and these must condition, in practice, the way in which they are planned. Certainly, the special importance in rural areas of ecological principles and techniques of resource management may well provide an argument for continuing to approach the detailed planning of town and country in a slightly different, though not totally discrete, manner.[22] Even so, the broad stages of planning outlined by Sarly would seem to be appropriate to both environments.

Yet many rural planning studies reveal little evidence of a structured approach and indeed little enthusiasm for describing, in any detail, the plan-making process adopted. Few studies include a discussion of goals, more detailed working objectives or the derivation of these. Almost no importance is attached to the generation or evaluation of alternative planning strategies. Not all studies show how their proposals might be implemented and few include proposals for monitoring and reviewing their progress.

It would be undesirable, and no doubt impracticable to suggest that all rural plan-making exercises adopted the same working process; but there are dangers in the continuation of a generally unstructured approach. An imperfect understanding of the rural system does not make for effective policy-making. Creative policies are suspect unless they can be justified and worthless until they are implemented. Finally, there can be no development of approach or methods upon which future studies can draw.

Rural Policies

Policy-making for rural areas has, as the new planning system encourages, become more comprehensive and more positive. The proposals in a number of rural studies, notably for Cheshire[23] and South Hampshire[24] range widely over the more familiar ground of rural settlement planning and protection from development to positive social and economic policies on rural transport, housing and employment, and to policies on land management: for reclamation, for tree planting and other means of landscape reconstruction, for traffic management, and for information and advisory services on countryside matters.

But many studies do not include such policies. In practice, most reflect the conventionally negative approach to the countryside discussed earlier, which sees only the need for restrictive measures, applied through statutory development control procedures, for curbing urban growth and the incursion of other activities such as mineral working or recreation. Emphasis is thus placed upon protecting from development those areas of highest agricultural and amenity value with these and other features of the rural environment acting more as constraints upon new development than as positive guides to its location and form. In the protected areas, concern is with the visual rather than also with the functional. Where more positive policies are included, they relate largely to extensions of public ownership, particularly for recreation land.

There are two other common features of the current approach. First, the areas of policy-making — for recreation, settlements, communications, agriculture, forestry and other activities — are discrete. Firm policies often relate only to the definable statutory jobs of local planning authorities, although this emphasis may inhibit the evolution of just the kind of integrated policies which rural areas require. There are few attempts to co-ordinate local authority policies with those of other policy-makers, in government and outside, and others who will shape the future countryside. One lesson of the experimental work in East Hampshire and elsewhere must be that local planning authorities in isolation are relatively powerless to harmonise conflicting resource interests. Policies must involve many different activities and interest groups where planners may have little or no direct influence by control or ownership.

Secondly, there is some reluctance, even among the more progressive authorities, to re-examine the persistent elements of planning dogma in the light of changed circumstances. Few rural studies, for example, question either the values or the real success of Green Belts in their area. Reiteration of the designation and its policies for development control is common although, as Chapter 8 discusses, it may be wrong to assume that desirable objectives are being achieved in this way. It is a preoccupation with strategic land use zonations of this kind that still dominates rural policy-making. The need for workable environmental management policies is largely ignored. Perhaps even more important is the necessity to co-ordinate the strategic and the local management scales of planning. Just as strategy alone may be unworkable, it would also be wrong to assume that the countryside can be planned by a series of schemes for short term management prepared with little concern for the implication of wider strategic policies.

Implementation

The test of any plan must be its success in implementation but it is too early yet to judge the outcome, in practice, of most recent rural planning work.

Chapter 1 discussed how, in many respects, the planning record in rural areas has been highly successful: but for the controlling influence of post-war planners, we would not have such an open, pleasant and flourishing countryside. However, the forces for rural change are now very different; the attitudes, methods, policies and *tools* of planning must likewise be modified. There is certainly a need for better understanding of the rural system; for much more thinking about the agencies and nature of future rural change; for improvements in the way we identify and attempt to resolve rural problems, but the fundamental requirement is for effective *action*: for implementation as well as plan preparation.

How can rural policies be realised?

There are already many means of achieving rural planning decisions, whether these involve agencies of central or local government, the owners and managers of rural land, or other organisations and voluntary groups. Earlier chapters have, however, drawn some distinction between the more persuasive mechanisms adopted by certain resource planning agencies, like the Ministry of Agriculture with, until recently, its system of guaranteed prices and special grants, or the Forestry Commission with its system of forest management agreements, and those methods available to land planners, which rely more heavily upon controls backed by legal sanctions.

There have been two main tools used by statutory land planners for the implementation of their policies in rural areas: direct executive action which usually involves the public acquisition of rural land, and the imposition of controls upon the activities of other individuals and agencies, often within specific protective zonations of land. The case has been argued strongly for these mechanisms to be more widely used in rural areas: for public ownership and management to grow, and for statutory controls to be applied to some activities which are presently exempt from planning restrictions.[25]

But, for various reasons, extensions of this kind are likely to be limited; alone, they may anyway provide an inadequate defence against many of the less desirable features of present rural activity. Nor do they necessarily allow a more positive approach to the solution of rural problems and the guidance of rural change. In the same way that new kinds of policies are now required, rather different and more persuasive methods of implementation may also be needed. The danger is that opinion will continue to be polarised between these two approaches of compulsion and persuasion — of 'sticks' and 'carrots'. Meanwhile planners, recognising their lack of effective influence outside the built countryside, will continue to limit the scope of rural policy-making to a few selective activities like recreation, and shelve any concern with the total fabric of the rural environment.

A few studies have made the case for a wider view, suggesting that planners may be able to exert a more positive influence on the rural environment via measures ranging from advisory and information services; the promotion of voluntary codes of practice, and financial incentives to more formal arrangements for land management. In a plan for the Cheshire countryside,[26] policies for planning control are only one group of a much larger set of policies involving other local authority departments, landowners, developers and voluntary groups.

In theory at least, it might be more helpful to think in terms of many mechanisms available for the implementation of rural policies, ranging from more direct public intervention to the improvement of goodwill. The potential of some of these is discussed in turn below.

Extensions of public land ownership

Recent legislation has considerably increased the opportunities for public action in the countryside, for example, in tree planting, traffic management and the establishment of various kinds of recreation facility. The 1968 Countryside and Planning Acts both encourage (though do not demand) a more positive approach on the part of local authorities, while agencies such as the Forestry Commission and Regional Water Authorities now have added powers to own and manage land and water for purposes other than those which are their primary task.

The response of local authorities has been encouraging: indeed, the acquisition of land for country parks has probably been the most tangible achievement of new style planning in rural areas. But the extension of land acquisition alone to achieve a better distribution of rural recreation areas, and more especially to realise other (non-recreational) rural planning objectives may be limited, unless land nationalisation takes place on a much larger scale, and for purposes other than development.[27]

It is true that compulsory purchase powers are available to acquire rural land for various purposes but these have hardly been used and the tenor of present opinion suggests they are unlikely to be on any scale. Moreover, while land prices stay high and local authorities and government agencies suffer tightened budgets, the opportunities for greater public ownership of rural land, as well as the political acceptability of it, will not increase. Nor, except in particular circumstances, is it a wholly satisfactory mechanism for achieving greater harmony among rural interests.

In theory, the policy would work — as it partly does on the Dutch polders, or in the Tennessee Valley — if public resource agencies could manage rural land in such a way that its multiple interest was recognised and rival claims were met. But there is no guarantee that public resource agencies would be so enlightened; earlier chapters have been critical of national land holding bodies such as the Forestry Commission and the Nature Conservancy Council; and we could be equally so of the Ministry of Defence. Recent government policies for particular aspects of resource management and water conservation still have many limitations. Extensions of ownership among single-minded public agencies pursuing a narrow range of policies could worsen the situation and encourage a more rigid and exclusive system of rural land zoning. There are also other disadvantages which may be anticipated. The experience of countries, particularly in Eastern Europe, where extensive state ownership of rural land is common suggest that public land holding agencies, because of their size and administrative complexity, become resistant to change. Their rigidity stifles innovation; mediocrity in land management increases, with a corresponding decline in quality and variety which are features much valued in the British countryside. It can also be argued that present national resource agencies would be ill-equipped in terms of experience to take on the management of rural land on a large scale or in highly fragmented parcels. There are problems at the local level:

> "If we take the matter of care for rural beauty, public ownership seems, far too often, to mean lower standards. There are real problems in persuading committees to spend taxpayers' money, often without clear statutory directive, on something as abstract as trying to improve rural beauty . . ."[28]

But there are parts of Britain such as the uplands and the urban fringe where the fragmentation of administration, the disinterest of private landholders in environmental trusteeship, make public action vital. In these areas, some extension of public ownership, where firm control over land use and management can be exercised without institutional problems, may provide the only administrative framework for tackling resource problems. We argue strongly in Chapter 8 for the extension of public control to parts of the fringes of major conurbations for resource management. The case has been made elsewhere for more public ownership of some upland areas (especially within National Parks[29]) and to reclaimed estuarial land, at least in the early stages of development. Outside of these areas, extensive and permanent public ownership is less desirable and likely to remain politically unpopular. But this is not to argue that there should be no strengthening of the public interest in the ways in which private land is used and managed.

A much more urgent task is the better management of all publicly owned land, whether in farms held by local authorities; alongside roads, railways and watercourses; or the extensive holdings of central government departments.

Extensions of control by regulations

Since 1947, most of the British countryside has benefitted, in appearance and in the functional efficiency of its major industry of agriculture, by control over development. This control has been exercised through the refusal of planning permission for a variety of activities or by the imposition of conditions upon the way in which particular developments are carried out. Special controls, for example on farm building designs, have been operated in certain areas such as the National Parks,[30] while in others, such as Green Belts, and Areas of Great Landscape Value, the nature of their protective designation has ensured a more rigorous application of normal development control procedures. This does not, however, apply to all protected areas. When proposed development affects a Site of Special Scientific Interest, local planning authorities will consult the Nature Conservancy Council, but they are not bound by Conservancy views. Moreover, those activities which do not require planning permission are not the subject of such consultation although they may prove as damaging, if not more so, to nature conservation interests.

Normally, the activities of government departments and statutory undertakers, in town or country, lie outside this control system although they are required to notify local planning authorities of their intentions, and Section 11 of the Countryside Act places a responsibility on all public bodies to

> ". . . have regard to the desirability of conserving the natural beauty and amenity of the countryside."

But the Countryside Commission cannot enforce this requirement and events show that even in National Parks its efficacy is limited in situations of direct conflict.

The major land activities of the countryside are largely exempt from planning control, both in the scale and extent of their land use and in the detail of their day-to-day management operations. It is true that in some areas, and for some activities, extensions of control have been successfully operated by the use of Article 4 Directions, Discontinuance Orders and other means. There are special procedures whereby a local authority can impose protective controls upon threatened environmental features, through for example, the use of Tree Preservation Orders.

The case is frequently made (implicitly in much writing on rural planning) for the scope of development control to be widened, and for amendments to be made to the General Development Order to exclude some of the activities it presently contains, making their practice subject to planning permission. Predictably, many landowners and their representatives see otherwise; they maintain that extensions of control are neither desirable nor practicable. Nevertheless, cogent arguments have been made for certain activities, notably large scale afforestation, the erection of farm buildings and the ploughing and improvement of moorland, to be controlled in this way. There is evidence to suggest that some farmers might prefer regulations to incentives (financial or otherwise) in other aspects of landscape conservation such as the retention of cover — primarily perhaps because this imposes an equal burden upon all operators.[31]

But much current opinion, borne of local frustration with the working of the present system of development control, argues against major extensions of this means of policy implementation. The Dobry Report which reviewed the Development Control system, favoured a more speedy and less detailed treatment of many development decisions, although it recognises the need for greater control in special environmental areas (especially the National Parks, Areas of Outstanding Natural Beauty and Heritage Coasts);[32] few of the recommendations have been accepted by the Secretary of State for the Environment.

Statutory control is not suitable for all the activities which planners would like to influence. In many cases, local authorities do not have sufficient staff, skills or experience to arbitrate (and farmers especially are fond of arguing this). Other disadvantages are more permanent. It has been argued elsewhere in this book that it is often resource and activity *management* operations which generate and sustain rural conflicts; control will be too slow, unwieldy and costly a means of influencing many of these operations, especially in farming, where decisions are required rapidly and frequently. It would not be economically (much less politically) feasible to operate regulations such as Article 4 Directions or Discontinuance Orders on all rural activities or in every case where some public interest is at stake and some extra influence desired. Requirements — of minimum standards of landscaping or cover, or of approved colours — would fall unfairly upon different operators in a very competitive industry. Such measures would be difficult to justify at times of financial stringency and there are always problems of enforcement. Less onerous could be the proposal of the Council for the Protection of Rural England for a system of compulsory notification of intended change to particular landscape features (such as some hedgerows, stone walls, areas of downland and heath).[33] But it would be difficult enough at present to argue for new planning jobs; more important might be the depressive effects of such a scheme upon existing goodwill among landowners towards conservation measures.

Nor do control mechanisms alone necessarily encourage the *positive* approach to integrated resource management that is needed. Tree Preservation Orders, for example, are not adequate mechanisms for creating and maintaining the kind of 'new agricultural landscapes' discussed in Chapter 7. They are ineffective in the conservation of individual trees or groups, and of hedgerows. They are too inflexible to encourage farmers to undertake a comprehensive tree planting and management policy on their land.

As was argued for the extension of public ownership of rural land, there would seem to be scope for *some* widening of the sphere of legal control. For certain types of rural activity, regulations and control mechanisms could provide a relatively cheap and effective means not only of implementing strategic policies for the countryside, but also of ensuring that preventive action can be taken at the local level of environmental management. Certainly, it would be unwise to *reduce* the degree of control exercised over development in the countryside.

But 'carrots' as well as 'sticks' are needed; other ways of strengthening the public interest in private land must be sought, even if more control by regulations becomes the ultimate sanction. The rest of this chapter looks at the possibility of financial incentives, management agreements and various kinds of voluntary arrangement.

Financial incentives

It is possible to think of various ways by which those who incidentally contribute to the rural environment might be persuaded to maintain or enhance those features which may be unnecessary in the efficient working of their enterprise.

Recent discussions have focussed especially on farmers, with the case increasingly being made for some mechanism by which farmers are not only compensated for the damage they incur from other rural activities, but are offered financial inducements to act in a more positive environmental way.[34] However, the form these incentives might take is rarely spelt out. Some have argued for direct money payments for small jobs done in the interests of amenity, reasoning perhaps that such inducements, in a form less binding than other legal arrangements, would be more appropriate both to the needs of farming and of landscape conservation.

So far, there is limited experience of how a system of this kind could work in practice, and more especially, its long term efficacy in the retention and enhancement of whole landscapes. There have been a number of recent incentive schemes, operated by local authorities, voluntary bodies and others to encourage the planting and retention of amenity trees.[35] But the scale has been small, and this effort alone cannot keep pace with the loss of tree cover in the lowlands. Locally, there have been successes, but usually among those farmers already concerned about environmental values, or in situations where restrictions and incentives are part of normal tenancy arrangements.[36]

The most useful work so far, in gauging the reactions of farmers to *ad hoc* financial persuasion has been carried out in the Upland Management projects, initiated by the Countryside Commission in 1969, using the experimental powers of the Countryside Act. In parts of the Lake District and Snowdonia, project officers have persuaded farmers to allow a variety of maintenance jobs (the repair of walls, gates, stiles) to be carried out, with some positive works (such as tree-planting and signposting) all designed to improve recreational opportunities and the appearance of the landscape. In return, the costs of materials and labour were met by the experiment.[37] No legal agreements were negotiated; farmers simply undertook verbally to do or allow certain jobs with a verbal assurance of payment.

The original motives for and aims of the experiment were mixed and, to some degree, obscure. A number of elements can be discerned. There was acceptance of the fact that the work of upland farmers must continue if recreation and tourist assets are to be retained. At the same time it was recognised that many features of the upland landscape were suffering from recreation pressure and a general lack of maintenance which could be attributed to the marginal nature of the farming economy, with its declining labour force. Moreover, it was seen that repair of these features, and the provision of new facilities, might be done at relatively little cost and with benefits to the local economy if farmers and other local people, rather than public bodies, could be paid to do the work. A longer term by-product was originally seen to be some increased understanding, on the part of farmers, of the needs of visitors, and greater enthusiasm for positive involvement in the management of an attractive as well as a functional landscape.

In both areas, the experiment appears to have been successful, judged on the criteria of jobs done, money spent and improvements in understanding between farmers and the national park authorities. This is particularly so in the Lake District.

It would be wrong to generalise about the likely success of financial incentives from these experiments. The attitudes of farmers have hardened as the need for economic efficiency has increased and most would be unable to accept that they should become 'landscape gardeners in the public service'. Recent evidence of farmers' views suggests, perhaps surprisingly, that direct grants for retaining and enhancing landscape features are not popular with the majority who fear more bureaucratic interference.[38] It may be that before farmers in some areas can be persuaded to undertake positive land management measures, they must be compensated for damage incurred. The Country Landowners Association have, for example, suggested the notion of 'negative rents' to be paid to farmers in popular upland areas.[39]

A subsequent experiment, following on from those in the uplands, confirms the reluctance of landowners in more prosperous farming areas to be persuaded in this way. In the Bollin Valley, south-west of Manchester, landowners face all the problems and uncertainties of farming on the urban fringe,[40] yet it is mainly their actions, as in the uplands, which shape the landscape and opportunities for public access. An experiment here, designed to enhance the landscape and improve access, has found landowners less willing to respond to financial incentives. Their co-operation, in allowing tree planting and repair work, has been achieved only after a considerable period of negotiation and assurances of greater control over public recreation. Here, as in the Lake District, experience has shown that persuasion may need to rely not only on financial inducements but also upon the effective removal, into public management, of some of the traditional and burdensome responsibilities of private land ownership, such as the maintenance of rights-of-way.[41] But most important is the role of a project officer in these experiments: someone who can provide the link between farmers and public agencies and organise the labour for amenity work. Experimental work of this kind is now being developed further on the north western and eastern fringes of London.

Alone, piecemeal financial incentives (and their equivalent 'in kind' of free labour or materials[42]) have many limitations. But this is not reason enough to abandon them for no one mechanism offers the panacea for implementing rural policies. Incentives must be used where they are most effective: in situations of relative marginality,[43] and where they can be co-ordinated in schemes for whole tracts of countryside which will make a measurable and lasting impact upon the landscape and its opportunities.

Management agreements

The scale of environmental renewal needed over much of Britain means that other more certain and durable methods of persuasion must be found. Management agreements for particular stretches of countryside offer one, as yet largely untested, possibility.

The idea of management agreements as a means of securing some public interest in the way in which rural land is used is not new: many examples exist under present legislation covering timber production, nature conservation, public access and the protection of field monuments.[44] Some of these have already been described in earlier chapters. The majority, though not all of these agreements are legally binding upon successors in title to the land, and most carry the sanction of compulsory public purchase if an agreement is not honoured. In return for their co-operation, and to compensate for restrictions placed upon their freedom, landowners are paid a consideration.

Some of these agreements — especially those concerning access — can involve local authorities, who are also empowered in a more general way, to make agreements relating to land use or development.[45] But the use of this mechanism of regulating rural land use has been limited, partly perhaps because alternative, less involved, procedures have been available, or because the mechanism itself may provide only a temporary solution. Agreements of this kind are enforceable against successors in title only if they are negative; positive agreements must usually be renegotiated with each new land holder.

Even so, the limited use of agreements covering the wider aspects of rural change may simply reflect the lack of interest and influence of planners in country areas, and their conservatism in the use of unfamiliar methods. Most of the credit for showing the relevance of management agreements (already a familiar tool of other rural resource planning systems) to town and country planning is due to Hookway.[46] He argued that the agreement

> "has proved to be an acceptable procedure to link private management and public planning, covering production, scientific conservation and one aspect of recreation. Surely it has a wider and greater potential, which should include the conservation of rural beauty."

Yet, for various reasons, none of the existing forms of agreement provides an adequate mechanism for controlling or guiding environmental change in rural areas in a comprehensive way. First, most relate to specific resources or activities rather than to the more general environmental consequences of these: upland landowners, for example, may agree *not* to restrict public access, but they can still, by their management practices, alter the appearance of countryside which people want access to.

> "Some protection of valuable landscapes may result from the (different) kinds of management agreements . . . But this can only be incidental, fortuitous and partial as the enabling powers relating to those agreements are not primarily directed to landscape aims."[47]

The protection of landscape should be possible outside access areas.

Secondly, in most cases, the desirable management approach to rural land in which interests other than those of landowners are at stake, will involve positive as well as negative action, that is grazing sheep, planting trees or repairing barriers, as well as *not* improving, *not* felling or *not* ploughing. The requirement that local authorities should negotiate the complicated terms of a positive agreement with changing and perhaps unwilling landowners provides no incentive for doing so initially, and no guarantee of continued success.

Thirdly, at present, there are no powers of compulsory purchase for many aspects of environmental change, including landscape conservation outside designated areas. In these uncertain circumstances, it is not likely that hard pressed local authorities will enter into financial commitments which may be very different with each new agreement and for which, although an agreement will benefit non-local residents, there is no financial aid from central government.

To overcome these barriers to the wider use of a potentially useful mechanism for landscape conservation, the Countryside Commission has proposed new powers for 'landscape agreements'.[48] Under the terms of a landscape agreement an owner would manage his land in accordance with a detailed plan in return for payments from other parties to the agreement, normally one or more local authorities. The Commission argues for financial aid from the exchequer towards these payments where the agreement benefits visitors as well as local residents, and for reserve powers of compulsory purchase (taking the form of a 'landscape order' similar to an 'access order' which can now be used to enforce an access agreement).

Even so, the notion of *landscape* agreement is perhaps still too narrowly framed unless, in practice, agreements can incorporate measures designed to safeguard and improve other aspects of the rural environment for which there are, at present, few encouragements. For example, there are no formal arrangements which might persuade some owners to carry out a co-ordinated programme of tasks to improve the recreational attractions of an area, although these may only incidentally enhance the landscape. The laying out of farm trails, parking and picnic areas or the installation of lavatories could all figure in a more widely defined 'countryside agreement'.

Such agreements could also be negotiated for those tracts of country, which may not lie in National Nature Reserves or Sites of Special Scientific Interest, but within which special management operations are needed to safeguard a variety of environmental values. This might be the case in an intensively farmed area where further decline of ecological values could be arrested by, for example, the cessation of stubble burning or the planting of particular types of vegetation. Agreements of this kind might also be appropriate for land from which minerals are being extracted, for water catchments, and more generally for the fringes of expanding cities.

New legislation along these lines could considerably enhance the influence that public authorities are able to exert on private activity in parts of the countryside, and allow policies to be implemented in a more effective and cheaper way than the traditional means of public purchase and management. But successful implementation of management agreements will depend upon the willingness and enthusiasm of local authorities to co-operate with the private sector in this way, to take on the extra administrative work, and to spend the necessary money (which will represent a long term financial commitment).

Most of all, it rests upon the goodwill of landowners and, as we have seen, their response is likely to be greater in marginal areas. It is in more prosperous farming regions that the means of safeguarding environmental values, and of creating new ones, seem so elusive. For many landowners, long term restrictive covenants can only be seen to prejudice the realisation of future profits from improvement or diversification of their enterprise. Their existence will probably depress land values.[49] Landowners may only be interested if payments are considerable, and if agreements are negotiated for shorter periods. Both measures are likely to discourage the involvement of public authorities on any scale.

For all these reasons, the power of management agreements and of *ad hoc* financial incentives will remain limited, the more so while they are divorced from other accepted and longstanding measures which persuade landowners to change the countryside.

Other measures

The linkage of environmental programmes with arrangements for farm improvement is already common in several European countries. In theory, it seems sensible that government grant and subsidy arrangements designed exclusively to increase food production should be manipulated, as they are in schemes for private forestry, to take account of the wider values society places upon the management of rural land. These grant and subsidy arrangements — for ploughing, draining, hedge removal, fertiliser application — have, in the past, contributed substantially to the environmental losses sustained particularly in lowland Britain. The Countryside Commission suggest that

> "public involvement in improving agricultural efficiency should be dependent on the implementation by the farmer of a landscape plan, itself framed with agricultural efficiency in mind. This would promote the creation of new landscapes in those very areas where official action was promoting landscape change."[51]

But there are practical and ideological difficulties. It is clearly easier, in those countries with a much less adequate pattern of farm structure than prevails in Britain, to reap environmental benefits as part of land reconstruction programmes involving the redistribution of holdings. The Ministry of Agriculture have stressed the unfairness, as well as the administrative problems, involved in introducing selectivity (either by withholding or augmenting grants in some areas) to what is presently a universally available system of financial support for agriculture. Yet other planning systems, including the control of development, do this in a different context for most other industries and it may be that inflexible attitudes rather than practicalities are the fundamental impediment.

More acceptable means of persuasion (and penalty) in environmental matters may lie in some manipulation of the fiscal system relating to rural land. The costs of abiding by amenity covenants which imposed restrictions and also requirements of positive action could be met, in addition to direct payments under the covenant, by concessions under various taxes (including capital transfer tax and the proposed wealth tax).[52] But, as we have argued earlier, the effects of these taxes may be to intensify land management and reduce investment in the long term, diverting funds away from amenity management. Tax concessions may not even compensate for these problems.

All these various incentives, from individual amenity payments to manipulation of the fiscal system offer, in combination, some way of increasing the public interest in private land which may prove to be more acceptable than statutory controls, more feasible than public ownership and in the long-run more effective than a reliance upon voluntary action. But this will only be the case if the awareness and sympathy of rural interest groups towards environmental problems is strengthened. A greater willingness to act voluntarily must rest upon a continuing programme of persuasion which, initially, involves no legal commitment and which is heavily backed by information and advice.

Voluntary arrangements

If sufficient goodwill exists, there may be no necessity for any financial incentive to persuade different interests to co-operate in a defined way. A number of informal agreements, voluntarily negotiated, exist for various practices which affect the appearance and function of the countryside although, like the agreement on forestry in some National Parks,[53] not all have worked well. More successful has been the Pesticides Safety Precautions Scheme, negotiated between the government, user representatives and the manufacturers of agricultural chemicals.

Local liaison arrangements, voluntarily agreed, may work, especially where more formal control mechanisms may be threatened. Lloyd, for example, discusses the farm building notification scheme operated in the Dedham Vale Area of Outstanding Natural Beauty between farmers' representatives and the local planning authority which has so far provided a successful alternative to the use of Article 4 procedures.[54]

A number of codes of practice have recently been developed for use in the countryside, but these — like the conservation, water safety and mountain codes — apply mainly to the participants in particular recreation and education activities; they are designed to protect the interests of those on whose land the activity takes place rather than influence the actions of land managers themselves. The Straw Burning Code does try to do this, although it has not yet achieved universal acceptance in practice. But again, until alternative uses can be found for straw, the threat of more formal byelaw control (already introduced in some counties) may be enough to encourage voluntary adherence to the code.[55]

Voluntary action of these kinds is unlikely to achieve large scale improvements on the ground. It seems to be most effective in reducing, locally, some of the undesirable consequences of land management and there is probably scope for more informal agreements and codes of practice — for example on the type and timing of chemical spraying. Their creation alone may allow opposing groups to meet; if nothing else, their development shows just how slim is our knowledge of the real implications of many management operations.

Information and advice

A wide range of information and advice is needed to support all the implementation methods so far discussed. Nevertheless, improvements in these services alone could provide considerable and rapid environmental gains for several reasons.

First, the damage done to particular rural values by some management practices, results as much from ignorance — about the appropriateness of alternative operations, their timing or method of execution — as from any conscious design. There is a widespread lack of knowledge about the interests at stake in particular tracts of countryside, which relatively limited and unsophisticated information services could redress.

Secondly, no obligation, legal or voluntary, is placed upon the recipients of information and advice to act in ways which may differ from their normal practice: the management experiments in the uplands and in the Bollin Valley, discussed earlier in this chapter, show that this principle of freedom from obligation is important to many land managers. Moreover, local councils who are reluctant to allocate scarce funds to the negotiation of risky management agreements may be more easily persuaded to support the provision of additional information where they already have some experience of its worth.

Thirdly, the infrastructure of effective information and advisory services for a wide range of land management issues already exists. To take as an example, the case of farmers, there are at least three major sources of information available to them. The Ministry of Agriculture provides a comprehensive system covering administrative and legal as well as technical matters. Although the advisory services have now been restructured with, some would argue, a reduction in the scope of free advice on offer, the breadth and detail of information available through regional and local representatives of the Ministry of Agriculture is still extensive. The National Farmers Union, at national and local levels (and the Country Landowners Association) provide further sources of specialist advice on aspects of agriculture and landholding. The commercial sector continues to expand the range of advice to farmers and landowners which is given on a fee-paying basis, and also freely, in association with the promotion of goods and services.

In recent years, several attempts have been made to graft onto this extensive network, information and advice on environmental matters. The interest and roles of the Ministry of Agriculture have widened since European Conservation Year 1970 with, for example, specialist in-service training courses for advisory staff which include discussion of landscape and wildlife matters. But for a department that wields such power over the rural environment, surprisingly few non-agricultural specialists are employed. Until those with environmental skills are recruited, there can be no widening of the scope of agricultural suppport or the range of official advice and information on environmental matters given through the Ministry of Agriculture, and agencies like the Forestry Commission.

There is now evidence of some broadening of the curricula by which land managers and those in the land-linked professions are trained, but this is uneven. There has been an expansion of interest in undergraduate and postgraduate teaching on conservation and environmental studies, and considerable increase in the environmental content of planning courses;[56] but few colleges of agriculture or forestry schools yet devote much teaching time to other rural issues.

Practitioners and others are exposed to a growing body of information and advice from many voluntary groups such as the County Naturalists' Trusts, the Council for the Protection of Rural England, the Farming and Wildlife Advisory Group, the Royal Society for the Protection of Birds and many others. All these sources are augmented by advice from journalists and broadcasters, in popular as well as specialised items and programmes.

But more could still be done: by means of joint advisory leaflets and exhibitions, such as have been prepared for farm buildings,[57] and perhaps for more award schemes, not only for well designed rural buildings, but for many other aspects of land management, which could generate publicity. Some local authorities already provide information and advice, directly and through publications, on many aspects of resource management, new style plans for rural areas could well provide the focus for much more co-operative advice. A problem of co-ordination remains. There is a confusing multiplicity of advisory sources and no easily identifiable reference point.

But farmers are by no means the only group who may need and benefit from new kinds of information. It is probably a truism to say that the average planner (and the urban community he is most likely to represent) has less knowledge and understanding of the practices of farmers and landowners than these groups have of the wider environmental preferences of society. In order to persuade those with day-to-day responsibilities for land management to act in ways which take account of the multiple interest of their assets, planners and other critics must themselves speak a common and practical language. There are signs that local planning authorities and others are attempting to improve their credibility and influence in relevant rural disciplines and practice by increasing their exposure to literature and discussion on landowning views and problems, and by employing specialists – agriculturalists, estate managers, ecologists, foresters and others.[58]

The problem remains that in contrast to much agricultural information, knowledge on many environmental issues is slim and uncertain. Fresh and convincing data in support of arguments for modifying land management practices must be found, and in circumstances which replicate the real world. Moreover, in the longer term, the most tangible results of improved information and advice may flow from attempts to *involve* managers and their advisors, in a direct and practical way, in estate planning demonstrations where the aims of different rural interests can be explored. The Silsoe Study was the first of a number of experiments where compromise plans which try to optimise economic efficiency in agriculture and forest management with wildlife and landscape conservation, have been prepared for real enterprises by multi-disciplinary teams.[59] Although, in some cases, these studies have generated positive improvements to the local environment, their number and representation is too limited to assess the wider value. Even so, realistic demonstrations of this kind will carry more weight than emotional pleading.

They suggest, too, that if landowners cannot be persuaded, for personal satisfaction or from a sense of trusteeship, to undertake amenity tasks which yield no profit or which may even reduce profitability, then indirect means of increasing environmental values must be sought and appropriate information and advice made available. There are various supplementary enterprises on agricultural land – game management, forestry operations, provision for certain recreations – which can yield some profit, but which can also, and incidentally, bring about improvements to the landscape and its wildlife.

Conclusions

Previous chapters have argued for a more positive attitude towards the resolution of conflicts of interest in the countryside and the guidance of rural change. We have suggested three broad approaches by which these goals could be implemented. First, there is a need for more positive action by public bodies – national resource agencies as well as local authorities – which will involve some extensions of public ownership in certain rural areas. Secondly, some rural practices, which at present lie outside the statutory planning system, could usefully be brought within the framework of control. Lastly, alternative legal and informal arrangements must be developed to regulate those activities which are likely, for various reasons, to remain beyond the limits of planning control.

Most of the current debate centres upon the desirability and feasibility of these last two methods of securing a greater public interest in the management of private land. At least two conflicting strands of opinion emerge.

First, there is the stand adopted by some planners that the rural industries of agriculture and forestry, like industry elsewhere, should be subjected to a system of legally enforceable controls, although there is uncertainty about the precise form and application of these. This view springs from a variety of attitudes which appear to include questions of equity, simplicity and bureaucratic tidiness. It is also a view which reflects the scepticism many planners have for informal arrangements where there can be no recourse to legal sanctions, where precedents and administrative difficulties may be frequent, and where opportunities exist for the abuse of public funds. It is a view held by some who see landowners, already too privileged in their freedom from interference, as seeking only to augment that freedom at public expense.

The contrary view is as uncompromising. It may take the form, on the part of some landowners, of an over-riding suspicion of public bodies, planners especially, and no willingness to co-operate in schemes which they see can only damage their interests. They would strongly resist further controls, and demand public payment for all land management tasks carried out in the interests of amenity. It is a view more subtly expressed by protagonists of the cause of what are seen to be under-privileged rural groups. Upland farmers, for example, are considered by some to have suffered unfairly at the hands of the public and their institutions, and thereby deserve compensation, not only in continued freedom from planning controls but also in a good measure of financial support for their activities in maintaining characteristic landscapes for the benefit of others. There are, moreover, those landowners whose view of amenity is fundamentally different from others in society: who believe they are creating, along with a functional landscape, one that is also visually satisfying.[60]

For neither group is the present law adequate. The former argue for greater obligations to be placed upon the private owner; the latter want present laws (designed, they would argue, for quite different circumstances) to be changed in ways which relieve them of unnecessary commitments (such as the management of public rights of way).

But resort to legal wrangling can only reinforce the gap between these extremes and narrow the middle ground of compromise, eroding the foundation of goodwill upon which co-operation can be fostered. It is no longer feasible to assert, in a simplistic way, that the rural landowner must follow the same rules as the industrialist: there are substantial differences between them. But it *is* possible to argue that the landowner, like the industrialist, has wider social obligations beyond his immediate concern to run a profitable and pleasurable enterprise for his own benefit. Like the urban industrialist, but on a much larger areal scale, he is responsible for creating 'environment' as a by product of his actions; with that responsibility should go a commitment that his operations improve rather than degrade the environment. In other words, society increasingly expects those who control resources, to care for them in a manner of trusteeship rather than exploitation. We want and expect owners to maintain their land 'in good heart' even though we admit that they should not have to do this without considerable help.

"Whatever the moral obligations and legal restrictions, some voluntarily incurred, the ownership of land is, and in the foreseeable future is likely to remain, the most potent factor in determining its current management and future use. In particular, it alone can secure the creative use of land as opposed to the simple and often frustrating denial of change . . . in our enthusiasm for plans and projects, we can too easily find ourselves giving insufficient weight to what ownership can achieve, or conversely, what can be achieved only with the understanding and willing cooperation of the owner or owners of the land involved."[61]

This chapter has argued for some expansion of public ownership, and for widening the sphere of planning control, but the principal argument is for more co-operation between public and private interests with values at stake in rural land, stimulated and maintained where necessary by financial help, and strongly supported by effective, freely accessible information founded upon continuing research and experiment. There is a particular need for more experimentation with different implementation mechanisms in such a way that the real effectiveness of them can be assessed. This will imply a willingness to spend money, not only on experiments but also in the form of temporary and permanent incentive payments.

The argument is not for all 'sticks' or all 'carrots', but for a measure of the two — for a variety of implementation methods to suit a wider and more sensitive range of policies for the countryside.

Notes and References

1. In common with the rest of this book, our discussion concentrates upon the non-built rural environment and thus does not review progress on other aspects of planning in the countryside. It would be misleading to suggest that environmental problems are the only, or indeed the most important components of countryside planning which must embrace many social and economic issues not emphasised in this book, nor in most of the studies on which this review of progress is based.

   More detailed reviews of recent studies, mainly at sub-regional level and from an urban viewpoint, are given in:

   Jackson, J. N. (1972) *The Urban Future – A Choice Between Alternatives*, Allen & Unwin, University of Birmingham Urban and Regional Studies, No. 3.

   Cowling, T. M. and Steeley, G. C. (1973) *Sub-Regional Planning Studies – An Evaluation*, Pergamon, Urban and Regional Planning Series Vol. 6.

2. Wibberley, G. P. (1971) Our Green Jelly, *Town and Country Planning*, Vol. 39 (7-8).

3. There are exceptions, see for example:

   Cheshire County Planning Department (1971) *Policy for Rural Cheshire*, Cheshire County Council.

   South Hampshire Plan Advisory Committee (1972) *South Hampshire Structure Plan*, Hampshire County Council.

4. See for example:

   Derbyshire County Planning Department (1972) *Countryside Plan: An Interim Strategy*, Derbyshire County Council.

   And a review of this:

   Davidson, J. (1973) Derbyshire Countryside Plan, Recreation News Supplement, No. 8, March.

5. See also Chapter 4.

6. See for example:

   McLoughlin, J. B. (1969) *Urban and Regional Planning: A Systems Approach*, Faber.

   Friend, J. K. and Jessop, W. N. (1969) *Local Government and Strategic Choice: An Operational Research Approach to the Processes of Public Planning*, Tavistock Publications.

   Chadwick, G. (1971) *A Systems View of Planning*, Pergamon.

   Wilson, A. G. (1972) *Papers in Urban and Regional Analysis*, Pion.

   Roberts, M. (1974) *An Introduction to Town Planning Techniques*, Hutchinson.

   And for a more philosophical discussion:

Wilson, A. G. (1973) How Planning can Respond to New Issues, in Cowan, P. (ed.), *The Future of Planning*, Heinemann.

7. Maclean, H. A. M. (1970) The Island of Mull: An Experiment in Land Use Planning, *Recreation News Supplement*, No. 2, November.

8. Zetter, J. A. (1973) *Planning for Informal Recreation at the Local Scale: Sherwood Forest Study*, Countryside Commission, CCP.69.

    Zetter, J. A. (1974) The Application of Potential Surface Analysis to Rural Planning, *The Planner*, Vol. 60(2).

9. See, for example, the bibliography on *Landscape Evaluation* prepared by Peter Tolhurst, Department of Town and Country Planning, University of Manchester, March, 1972; and

    Dunn, M. C. (1973) *Landscape Evaluation Techniques: An Appraisal and Review of the Literature*, University of Birmingham, Centre for Urban and Regional Studies Working Paper.

10. See, for example:

    Coventry City Council *et al.* (1971) *Coventry, Solihull, Warwickshire – A Strategy for the Sub-Region*, Supplementary Vol. 5: The Countryside.

11. Statham, D. C. (1973) *Land Use Changes in the Moorlands of the North York Moors National Park*, Centre of Environmental Studies University Working Paper, No. 16.

12. Weddle, A. and Pickard, J. (1969) Least Social Cost Analysis, *Journal of the Town Planning Institute*, November.

13. Sherwood Forestry Study Group (1974) *Sherwood Forest Study*.

14. Zetter, J. A. (1974) Application of potential surface analysis to rural planning, *The Planner*, Vol. 60(2), February.

15. The question of aims is further discussed in:

    Chadwick, G. (1971) op. cit.; and, related to particular studies, in:

    Coventry City Council *et al.* (1971) op. cit., and the:

    North Pennines Study – Methods Report (1975) published by the Countryside Commission.

16. Sarly, R. M. (1972) *The Planning Process*, Planning Methodology Research Unit Working Paper No. 2, University College London, School of Environmental Studies.

17. These stages are merely descriptive, to be operational they would each require considerably more definition. Nor is their order fixed; for example, the recognition and operational definition of problems may have to *follow* rather than precede any analysis of the planning system. Likewise, the formulation of goals may be seen as the initial task in some studies, or as a continuing one in others, with refinement at various stages.

18. Smart, A. D. G. (1968) Rural Planning in the Context of the City Region, *Report of Proceedings, Town and Country Planning Summer School*, University of Manchester for The Town Planning Institute.

19. Barrow, J. F. (1970) Recreation and Rural Resources in the South Hampshire Structure Plan, *Recreation News Supplement*, No. 2, November.

20. South Hampshire Plan Advisory Committee (1972) op. cit.

21. Statham, D. C. (1972) Natural Resources in the Uplands, *Journal of the Royal Town Planning Institute*, Vol. 58, December.

22. For a discussion of resource management and planning, see Chapter 5. The differences between town and country as environments for planning purposes are discussed further in the final chapter.

23. Cheshire County Planning Department (1971) op. cit.

24. South Hampshire Plan Advisory Committee (1972) op. cit.

25. See Chapter 7 which discusses farm building control, and Chapters 3 and 9 which discuss controls upon afforestation.

26. Cheshire County Planning Department (1971) op. cit.

27. The Community Land Act (1975) allows local authorities to acquire land for future development (at existing use value) to be held in 'land banks'. This *may* provide interim opportunities for some positive rural planning on the edge of towns: see Chapter 8 on the Urban Fringe.

28. Hookway, R. J. S. (1967) The Management of Britain's Rural Land, *Proceedings of The Town and Country Planning Summer School*, Belfast.

29. See Chapter 10. The Sandford Report argues that powers of compulsory purchase ought to be available for land over which the retention of visual beauty as well as public access may be important, to be used in cases where voluntary negotiations fail:

    Department of the Environment (1974) *Report of the National Park Policies Review Committee* (Sandford Report), H.M.S.O. (paras. 9.14-9.19).

30. Landscape Areas Special Development Order; see also Chapter 7.

31. Westmacott, R. and Worthington, T. (1974) *New Agricultural Landscapes*, Countryside Commission, Chapter 7.

32. Dobry, G. (1974) *Review of the Development Control System; Interim Report*, H.M.S.O.

Dobry suggested that in Special Environmental Areas, the Special Development Order procedure could be used, making certain classes of development, now permitted under the General Development Order, subject to planning permission; Article 4 Directions could be used to achieve tighter control in some other areas.

33. Council for the Protection of Rural England (1975) *Landscape – The Need for a Public Voice*, C.P.R.E.

    Under the notification system farmers would have to give their District Planning Authority 6 months' notice of intentions to remove the features. Failure to notify ensures liability to a fine. During the notification period, local authorities can decide upon the conservation value of the threatened features and take any necessary action.

34. See, for example:

    Fairbrother, N. (1971) The Countryside and Urban Recreation, *Proceedings of The Town and Country Planning Summer School*, Southampton.

    Royal Society of Arts (1970) *Agriculture Forestry and Land Management* Report No. 1, 3rd 'Countryside in 1970' Conference, London.

    Phillips, A. A. C. and Roberts, M. (1973) The Recreation and Amenity Value of the Countryside, *Journal of Agricultural Economics*, Vol. 24(1).

35. Formerly available under the Countryside Act 1968, finance for treeplanting by local authorities is now available under the Local Government Act, 1972.

36. For example, schemes have been operated on smallholdings in Buckinghamshire and on some Crown Estates, whereby tenants have been paid to retain and plant hedge and other farm trees.

    For a discussion of the progress of treeplanting in several counties see: Lloyd, R. (1974) *Planning and Agricultural Land Management*, unpublished M.Phil. Thesis, University of London, Chapter 7.

37. Project Officers were employed by the Ministry of Agriculture and worked to briefs agreed by the Countryside Commission, the park planning authorities, Department of the Environment and the Ministry of Agriculture. The projects continued with project officers employed by the National Park Authorities in the Lake District and Snowdonia. See:

    Countryside Commission (1976) The Lake District Upland Management Experiment, CCP 93.

38. Westmacott, R. and Worthington, T. (1974) op. cit., Chapter 7.

39. Country Landowners' Association (1972) *The Uplands*, Regional Working Parties Report.

40. Hall, A. (1973) The Bollin Valley Project, *Recreation News Supplement*, No. 9, July.

41. See the discussion in Lloyd, R. (1974) op. cit., Chapter 7.

42. For difficulties and opportunities in this field, see:

    Countryside Commission (1972) *The Use of Voluntary Labour in the Countryside*, CC.

43. Areas within which there are marginal farming zones on a regional scale, such as the uplands and urban fringe; and the marginal parts of individual farms: wasteland of field corners, or the boundaries of holdings.

44. "A management agreement may be described as a formal written agreement between a public authority and an owner (lessee or occupier) of an interest in land who thereby undertakes to manage the land in a specified manner in order to satisfy a particular public need, usually in return for some form of consideration", para. 3 of Countryside Commission (1973) *Landscape Agreements*; CCP-61 which also describes the different kinds of existing agreements in Annex A.

45. Under Section 52 of the 1971 Town and Country Planning Act.

46. Hookway, R. J. S. (1967) op. cit.

47. Countryside Commission (1973) Landscape Agreements, para. 8.

48. Countryside Commission (1973) op. cit. The proposal has been reiterated in:

    Countryside Commission (1974) *New Agricultural Landscapes: A Discussion Paper*, CCP 76A, and apart from the notion of orders, was supported by the National Park Policies Review Committee reporting in 1974.

49. Lloyd (op. cit.) reports a decline in the willingness of landowners to negotiate Nature Reserve Agreements since the early 1960's. For a note on farmers' generally unfavourable reactions to Management Agreements, see also:

    Countryside Commission/Lake District Special Planning Board (1976) *A Study of the Hartsop Valley*, CCP 92.

50. For example: The Netherlands, Germany and Sweden.

51. Countryside Commission (1974) *New Agricultural Landscapes: A Discussion Paper*, CCP 76A, para. 12.

52. As at January 1976 Fiscal means are further discussed in the report on *New Agricultural Landscapes* op. cit. and its companion *Discussion Paper*, and in:

    Lloyd, R. (1974) *Planning and Agricultural Land Management*, op. cit. Rating of agricultural land may provide one answer to underuse on the urban fringe.

53. See Chapters 3 and 9.

54. Lloyd, R. (1974) op. cit., Chapter 6.
55. 1972, revised 1973, Straw Burning code, agreed by National Farmers' Union, Ministry of Agriculture and the Fire Brigade. See also:
    National Farmers' Union (1973) *The Use and Disposal of Straw*, Report of a Working Party on Straw Disposal, cyclo.
56. See, for example:
    Newbould, P. J. (1974) Conservation in Education, in Warren, A. and Goldsmith, F. B. (eds.) *Conservation in Practice*, John Wiley.
    Davidson, J. (1971) Countryside Planning at University College London;
    Riley, J. (1971) Education in Rural Planning at Manchester University; both in *Recreation News Supplement*, No. 5, November.
57. See Chapter 7.
    The National Agricultural Centre at Stoneleigh, Warwicks. houses a permanent display of farm buildings.
58. The case has been argued for local planning authorities to employ 'agricultural liaison officers': those, trained agriculturally, to act as intermediary in negotiations between planners and landowners. See, for example:
    Davidson, J. M. (1974) Recreation Management, in *National Parks – The Challenge to the New Authorities*, Report of the Annual Conference of National Park Planning Authorities, Great Malvern.
    The Countryside Commission also argue for executive landscape staff to be employed by local authorities to carry out the work of creating new landscapes, see:
    New Agricultural Landscapes: A Discussion Paper, op. cit.
    Lack of spare labour may often be the main impediment to more voluntary action on amenity jobs by landowners.
59. Royal Society for the Protection of Birds (1970) *Farming and Wildlife: a Study in Compromise.* (Report of the Silsoe Conference).
    Subsequent studies are described in detail in the reports of the *Dinas Conference*, 1972 (organised by the Farming and Wildlife Advisory Group) and the *Cowbyers Conference* 1974 (organised by the Agricultural Development and Advisory Service and the Countryside Commission). These studies are critically discussed in Lloyd, R. (1974) op. cit.
60. Westmacott, R. and Worthington, T. (1974) *New Agricultural Landscapes*, op. cit.
61. Cripps, J. (1972) *Whose Countryside*? Town and Country Planning Association Conference on Planning and the Countryside, February 1972.

CHAPTER 13

The Future

Throughout this book, our concern with the countryside has been a very selective one; we have made little comment on social issues or the problems of rural settlements because our main emphasis has been upon the interactions of resource use with the fabric of the rural environment. We have tried to explore some of the ways in which rural resource systems function, the conflicts of interest and attitude that exist and some of the successes and failures of intervention.

The countryside emerges as an environment quite unlike the image of it people might wish to retain. In places, it is bleak and lacking variation, the scene of new forms of industrial dereliction. Elsewhere, there is evidence of the insidious decay of once-thriving environments where, within a generation, the sight and sound of natural things will be lost. Above all, it is an environment of rapid change characterised, in its function and appearance, not by permanence but by real uncertainty, and this despite the comforting fact that a quarter of England and Wales is covered by some form of protective designation.

Most writers must labour against a background of political and economic change and their repercussions for society. But recent years have seen an acceleration of policy changes which affect the structure and function of rural organisations. These include British entry into the European Economic Community;[1] the reform of local government; major reviews of some important areas of rural activity; and changes in taxation. Fluctuating and generally worsening economic conditions at home and abroad, the energy crisis and world shortages of raw materials combine to make it difficult to forecast even a short term future for the countryside.

Limitations of the Present Approach

Although, in several chapters, we have discussed the solutions that are being and could be applied to environmental problems in the countryside, we have not sought to be prescriptive. Even if it was possible to identify adequately the causes of conflict and define desirable objectives for the management of rural resources, there is unlikely to be a single blueprint for action. The need is not so much for more money or more powers or better organisations (although all these are necessary) as for greater understanding of the ways in which the countryside is changing and a willingness to think at all about its future.

We have found much to criticise in the present approach to rural problems, both at national level and locally. It is characterised by a plethora of agencies who respond to change rather than guide it, who often react to short-term problems with single-purpose solutions, so that for example, in policies for rural traffic or the siting of major developments in the countryside, general principles which could be more widely applied are not developed. Moreover the present approach is too selective. Planners concentrate upon 'fitting in' major developments such as motorways and reservoirs while the open countryside between is neglected. Other agencies are concerned with preserving the best, often at the expense of ignoring the rest, whether the context is scenery, food producing land, recreation assets or habitats for wildlife. In theory, the interplay of conflicting ideas should lead to constructive and workable solutions; in practice, the action of most rural resource planning agencies is so piecemeal and single-minded as to inhibit the kind of integrated policy-making many rural areas seem to require. It is the totality of the rural fabric that suffers most from the dislocation of independent interests.

Another effect of the piecemeal concern of resource planners, in the agencies of central and local government and among a wide range of rural interest groups, is to polarise our thinking about the countryside and its problems at two levels: the national and the very local. Yet the countryside with which people identify is often most clearly recognised at an intermediate scale — as tracts of land less extensive than a county, but normally larger than a single ownership unit. Executive responsibility for the care of areas on this scale is either absent or divided. Government programmes for expansion in the agricultural and forestry industries, dictated largely by national and international economic circumstances, are implemented at the very local level by means which influence the individual farm and forest owner. Countryside recreation policies are implemented mainly through the local scatter of public and private parks. The environmental implications of such national strategies as exist (and these are often vague) on mineral working or the conservation of water supplies or the protection of wildlife are not usually assessed for a particular landscape type, or a river basin or several miles of coastline — tracts of countryside in which the most acute resource conflicts may emerge, and where there may be greater opportunities for harmonising different interests, in contrast to the smaller scale of a mine, a reservoir or a nature reserve. Efforts may be made, at this very local scale, to absorb or to enhance intrusions, but they must often rely upon disguise, upon cosmetic treatment, upon the details of design. Wise resource management is more than this. It must depend on more than one farmer's concern for the appearance of his holding, while his neighbours strip the landscape of its cover; on more than one country park in a zone of neglected, inaccessible Green Belt; on more than one amenity wood along a horizon of young conifers.

Not even in the tracts of land over which there is some unifying protective policy (such as the National Parks) is there necessarily a concern for the rural fabric or more importantly, the means to enhance it. It is true that some intermediate scale is now being recognised in the new range of organisations which will represent the interests of a number of rural activities: the Regional Water Authorities, Regional Advisory Committees of the Forestry Commission, a strengthened regional framework for the Nature Conservancy Council, and the suggested Regional Councils for Sport and Recreation.[2] But some of these bodies are consultative rather than executive and all, despite their co-ordinating aspirations, will be dominated by a single different resource interest. Nor are the interests of landscape conservation or rural recreation yet adequately represented at regional level for the Countryside Commission has no effective regional organisation. The relatively poor treatment of rural environmental issues in regional planning strategies demonstrates further the administrative and technical gap at this level.

In theory, only the measures of the statutory Town and Country Planning system encourage a truly corporate approach to rural issues, and offer some way of reconciling conservation and development. But as we have discussed in Chapters 11 and 12, with some exceptions, the progress in practice has been lamentably slow.

What then may be needed?

Our conclusion is that at least three developments must take place: in our understanding of rural values; in forecasting the future; and in attitudes towards implementation.

Rural Values

The myth of an unchanging countryside has been largely destroyed by the pattern of recent events. The problem now is to dispel the apathy and the complacency which arises from a belief that the countryside will somehow still survive, and in ways not fundamentally different from its present form.

It is tempting to follow those who argue that, left to itself and to the traditional custodians of rurality (especially the farmers), a functional countryside will emerge as it did in the Middle Ages and again after enclosure which will, in time, be accepted and enjoyed. But there are differences in the present situation not least in our capacity to change very much more rapidly than before and more fundamentally, so that semi-natural systems are not only modified but extinguished. There is change, too, in the number and variety of demands we place upon countryside resources; and in the gradual erosion of the philosophy and means of their trusteeship. The landlord/tenant system which supported the custodial approach of past land managers has been replaced by a new generation of owner/occupiers whose prime concern is with productivity of the land rather than its visual or ecological nature. At the same time, farmers are becoming less important as leaders and activists in the affairs of their localities; the growing size of their operations and the international nature of their technical and economic contacts are weakening the bonds with their own communities. They belong, moreover, to an industry which has enjoyed not only a sustained period of success since the war, but a kind of public reverence unparalleled in most other industries and many countries — a dangerous belief that farming can do no wrong. It is true that other changes have brought into the rural community those with a powerful voice for conservation, but they have limited means of action. The pace of change, the structure of land tenure and the dislocation of resource planning responsibilities do not encourage the evolution of an environment which can satisfactorily absorb new demands without the loss of its own integrity.

Equally, it would be dangerous to follow too eagerly the arguments of those who seek mainly to preserve or resurrect a countryside which has lost its function and which, in a paternalistic way, is assumed to be of universal value. The conservation of a thriving, useful and satisfying rural environment implies creative change to meet a diversity of tastes.

In many ways, we need to define and apply a new 'land ethic' — a commitment to the trusteeship of resources. But conservation does not lie at the top of everyone's priorities, and it would be wrong to assume that much action will flow from uncompromising, emotional campaigns which deny the need for political choices, and the demonstration of feasible and equitable means of achievement. There are many and more pressing claims upon national and local finance; rightly, most politicians are preoccupied with questions of social and economic welfare. But a lack of money or manpower is probably not the reason for apathy.

Much could be done with modest increases in expenditure on rural land management, and by a reallocation of present funds. In contrast, there seems to be no lack of enthusiasm or financial support for urban sports developments, for this is a field with which politicians can identify and where they can see clearly the potential benefits (even if these are not always realised) for those they represent. Most public concern for rural conservation rests firmly among those already privileged in their living, working and playing environments. The urban pressure groups which strive to improve conditions for those less fortunate as yet find no counterparts in the countryside. But without a more widely represented public interest in rural issues, the level of political concern and the prospects for action, will remain low.

Forecasting the Future

The increasing number of countryside studies is a welcome indication of the growing interest in rural issues. But the mood is still one of cosy optimism, a concern to resolve present conflict rather than to anticipate the future. To conserve any environment so that as many as possible of the demands upon it may be satisfied presupposes some vision of what the future might be. Ashworth has written, in the context of urban and rural planning:

> "Either we believe in the long-term identification of possible goals and the choosing of policies to lead us some way towards them, or the word 'planning' is a dead letter.

> ". . . we must acknowledge a triplet of questions . . . What do we want? What do we need? What can we have?"[3]

Much of the present analytical work in rural planning, particularly on the evaluation of resources, will greatly improve our understanding of rural systems and help to define the limits of what is possible in rural areas. But such studies, however rigorous, cannot adequately identify what we may want or need from the countryside. Policy-making cannot be reduced to acreage standards for recreation provision, or a necessary percentage of cover for new landscapes. Rather do we need a more fundamental understanding of private and community responses to rurality, which must involve psychological, medical and other approaches.

Present uncertainties do not permit firm forecasts of the demands which individual rural activities will make in future. In their absence, we can only speculate about the consequences of a whole range of economic and societal changes: the implications of short-term crises in the balance of payments situation and in the supply of energy and other raw materials; the effects of cuts in public spending and of inflation and new taxes on land ownership and management; the implications of Common Market policies; the longer term consequences of social change in the patterns of work, leisure and family life, and, not least, the possible outcome of a continuing decline in the British birth rate.[4]

External economic change in Europe, and in the world supply and price of many raw materials, especially oil, has had a growing impact upon rural policies, notably in agriculture but also in the development of energy resources. We have argued (in Chapter 2) that the pressure to intensify food production at home in an effort to improve the level of self-sufficiency in temperate products will increase. This will accelerate those changes in the function and appearance of the countryside which we have discussed in Chapter 7.

Many conservationists fear that the rapid development of oil, where planning considerations are already being shortcircuited in the interests of expediency, could bring to

British coasts, not only in Scotland, a whole new range and scale of industrial developments. The incentive to exploit all our own resources of energy and minerals could mean the reworking of many coal mining areas, probably by opencast methods, bringing new dereliction at a time when funds available for the restoration of land degraded by past working are limited. The extensive mining of low grade ores could become a major environmental problem in the uplands (Chapter 9).

It may be, then, that we should envisage, by the end of this century, a totally utilitarian countryside of extensive industrialised farm zones, punctuated by mining and refining developments and severed from each other and from the high density conurbations by swathes of countryside which carry motorways, pipelines and overhead wires, rapid transit routes and sonic boom corridors. Alternatively, if we forecast a major recession or pursue the notion of intermediate technologies, it is possible to imagine a countryside based upon subsistence farming with scattered self-contained communities in a new agrarian landscape. Agriculture could once more become labour-intensive and the drift from the land reversed.[5]

It may be idle to speculate upon such extreme rural futures; it would be misguided if we failed to solve the obvious problems of today because of a preoccupation with the future. But experience suggests that we may continue to be caught out by our inability to think ahead and by our unwillingness to experiment. The major national resource planning agencies, as we have discussed, seem to be committed to policies for the short term, rather than equipping themselves for alternative possible futures. Their actions are often dictated by traditional preoccupations (such as the apparent shortage of good agricultural land) and traditional assumptions (about, for example, resistance to dietary change, or the continued supply of raw materials) just as conflicts between resource interests are often resolved by recourse to traditional positions of power. Mellanby has argued that if the commitment to high energy, high technology farming were abandoned, and some dietary change occurred Britain could service all her food needs in the long term, on less land, and with less dependence upon imported materials.[6] There is no evidence that policy-makers are assessing the rural implications of other possible longer term changes: in the distribution of population and the growth of small towns; in travel patterns and the provision of public transport; in the effectiveness of environmental pressure groups; in the development of synthetic proteins for human consumption.

The failure to think ahead may also affect the short term. The wider implications of particular decisions, made for other purposes, have not always been followed through and this may happen again with the introduction of new systems of taxation and of public land ownership. Generally higher levels of taxation upon larger landowners, imposed by the capital transfer tax and the proposed wealth tax (which could bring about a substantial change in the ownership of rural land) will discourage spending upon non-profitable and longer term landscape measures such as amenity planting. The uncertainties involved in fiscal change and land nationalisation together with inflationary pressures, which force landowners to protect their cash and capital assets, could encourage a less productive and less intensive approach to land use in some areas. The trusteeship responsibilities that rightly go with land ownership could well be forsaken in the pursuit of short-term goals.

Implementation

As important as forecasting what could or should happen in the countryside, is the suggestion of practical ways in which its future might be guided. Even if plan-making is improving, any evidence that real guidance is taking place on the ground is slender. We have not considered that the solution of environmental problems can be brought about by the operation of market forces alone, nor do we advocate the wholesale application of public ownership and controls to rural land management. There are many examples in the world where market forces are allowed to dominate planning and the effects are well-known. It means that urban development will go for the cheap sites which are usually agricultural land of high quality close to cities. Farms are fragmented in such a way that the costs of agricultural production are increased, and many holdings will become either much too small for efficient use, or large and monopolistic. It means that the most favourable parts of a countryside get too many urban and rural developments while the remote and more difficult areas are left to suffer the full rigours of selective rural migration and poverty. An alternative to *laissez-faire* is complete control with full administrative machinery and legal powers whereby each case of permanent land use change is decided by public servants. Because of the large number of transactions in land, no country could afford the massive civil service which would be needed to implement this degree of control, nor would it tolerate the inevitable delays.

Between these two extremes is a range of possible mechanisms for achieving policies in the countryside, some of which we discussed in the last chapter. The search for a single approach is likely to be fruitless; there is room for much more variety in methods of implementation and in ways which ignore the traditional preferences and prejudices of institutions.

Throughout this book, we have tried to examine the aims and methods of different rural planners, looking especially at the role of those who operate the statutory town and country planning system. Many of the problems that we identify in particular environments like the uplands and urban fringe, but also at the level of national policy-making and execution, stem from the lack of co-operation between these different planners, not only in their values and objectives for rural resources, but also in their ways of achieving these. Perceptions of the function of countryside remain fundamentally different: for the Ministry of Agriculture it is almost exclusively a food factory; for the Countryside Commission it is a milieu whose landscape qualities must be safeguarded and where outdoor recreation must employ or contribute to those qualities. Means of implementation are also opposed. Thus, the Ministry of Agriculture, as well as farmers, dislike obvious means of public intervention; physical planners, suspicious of financial inducements, have tended to favour legal sanctions.

Rural environmental management comprises many tasks and different means of implementation will be needed for each. Regulatory powers under the planning system have worked well in specific areas of protection, such as in the National Parks and Areas of Outstanding Natural Beauty where they have provided a form of 'preventive care'. Their ambit could be extended. But the countryside has suffered from too little *remedial* action in the treatment not only of scheduled dereliction but of other less spectacular tracts of worn out or neglected countryside where the notion of 'General Improvement Area' may be as appropriate as in the town. These areas need rehabilitation of their degraded fabric and *creative action*, sometimes on a grand scale. Both require a whole range of implementation devices.

Many groups and individuals have suggested administrative ways in which the values and planning methods of resource interests could be better integrated. Some have argued for a return to the idea of 'super' ministries responsible for many rural functions.[7] More recently, others have suggested temporary or permanent co-ordinating committees of rural interests.[8]

It is tempting, as some of the suggestions imply, to argue that rural problems can be resolved by fairly simple bureaucratic re-organisation, and there are obvious anomalies in the present structure of government agencies. Why, for example, should the agricultural and forest industries, accorded their own ministry and largely exempted from planning controls, be treated so independently? How can a special department of government, established to co-ordinate environmental matters, be made to function adequately when activities such as farming or energy development lie outside its sphere of interest? Why are policies for countryside recreation so closely linked (and at times restricted by) conservation considerations to the virtual exclusion of questions of social need?

It is possible to think of some new arrangements. A more sensible remit for the Ministry of Agriculture would include not only social welfare (a growing European influence) but environmental conservation insofar as agriculture and forestry are concerned. Such widened responsibilities would need to be reflected in policies and in advisory and research programmes. They would require additional staff with a greater range of skills than presently exists in the Ministry — including ecological, landscape and even dietary specialists.[9] We have suggested similar modifications of the responsibilities of the Forestry Commission in Chapter 3. To overcome the inhibitions of frequently conflicting bedfellows, there may be a case for *separate* national agencies for the promotion of sport and recreation in town and country, and for the conservation of landscape and its natural and manmade components.[10] The limitations of the Department of the Environment (not least the mood of complacency its very existence may breed) could be partially remedied by the creation of Ministerial responsibility for environmental management and the monitoring of environmental impacts of the work of all other ministries.[11] But the environment is still a political 'lightweight'; new structures will not work without new attitudes.

At the local level, some realistic structure must be evolved to initiate and carry out the kind of environmental tasks of protection, rehabilitation and creation we have discussed earlier (especially in Chapter 7). We have argued that a greater degree of public (especially local planning authority) involvement is necessary: statutory planners have the legal means, and should have the vision, to reconcile conflicting interests as well as the activities of a wide range of other public landowning bodies. But it must be acknowledged that their relations with farmers are not good. Until they can be improved — by the better training of planners, by the incorporation of those with appropriate skills (in agriculture and estate management) in planning departments, by the greater representation of rural landowners on planning committees, and by the willingness of farmers and planners to bury old hatchets — intermediaries will be needed. In recent experiments, this role has been filled by officers of the Ministry of Agriculture's advisory staff in whom farmers have considerable confidence.[12] But the representation of interest in local environmental management schemes must be wider: it must include not only those owners and managers directly involved, but also those who can be locally accountable to an electorate who will gain or lose from their decisions, as well as those who represent the interests of others outside the locality who will also be affected. In addition to county and district planning authorities, therefore, the relevant national agencies (the Ministry of Agriculture, national landscape and nature conservation agencies and others) must be represented, perhaps even enabled to initiate and execute schemes of rural environmental management, so that piecemeal action is avoided and experience can be pooled.

But administrative change and innovation of this kind will fail if a compartmentalised view of rural resources persists. Some adjustment in the fundamental attitudes of countryside planners and users, and those that must arbitrate in resource decisions, whether between different local authority departments or between different arms of government, will be more important than administrative reshuffling.

Planning and the Rural Environment

The inadequacies we have discussed in countryside planning and in its planners — a failure to understand the variety and complexity of values at stake; a failure to appreciate the growing divorce of many modern activities (especially agriculture) from good resource conservation practice; the lack of vision and of effective means of implementing viable environmental policies, have all emerged earlier in the urban environment. Progress seems to have been much faster in urban planning. Yet many of the lessons of the sixties, often painfully learnt, for rehabilitation rather than total renewal; for more co-ordination of land use and movement; for greater public involvement in decision-making and for a corporate approach to problem-solving are as relevant in the countryside as in the town. Arguably, the greatest benefits for rural planning would come about by ceasing to treat it as a thing apart.

Social and environmental factors make it unrealistic to separate town from country: mobility and the media ensure that communities are no longer easily distinguished by their physical surroundings; pollution respects no boundaries; and visually, with decreasing urban densities and increasing rural industrialisation, the two environments will merge in many more places. There are still clear differences — in the extent of land uses, in the pattern of land ownership and in the dominance of particular 'rural' disciplines such as estate management and the life sciences. Relative neglect, especially of the open countryside, is also a powerful, if temporary, reason for continuing to treat the planning of rural areas as separate, in some measure, from urban planning.

But the two can no longer be treated in isolation. Since the end of the last century the horizons of planners have moved outwards from the house, to include the garden, the neighbourhood and the town in a continuing search for satisfying living and working environments. In this process the nature of planning has changed, it has drawn in those with a new outlook and different skills. It is logical to extend the process and hope that the planning of urban as well as rural environments will gain from the further blending of new interests. Countryside policies need the infusion of more social purpose; those in the town may well benefit from developments in the theory and practice of resource management. Both environments must serve as workshops, but in the long term, that cannot be their only role; the care and re-creation of their fabric, in ways which more people may enjoy, is crucial. In the town we have only just begun to realise how important this is; it would be sad if the countryside disappeared because of our complacent failure to see its problems with similar urgency.

Notes and References

1. Including a renegotiation of the terms of entry during 1974/5.
2. See Chapter 4.
3. Ashworth, G. (1974) Natural Resources and the Future Shape of Britain, *The Planner*, Vol. 60(7), July/August.
4. Population estimates for 2001 have been continually revised (downwards) over the last 10 years. But a slow rate of population growth will still place demands upon rural resources if increasing affluence

and technological innovation continue.
5. See, for example:
    The Ecologist (1972) *A Blueprint for Survival*, Penguin Special, London.
    And also:
    Schumacher, E. F. (1973) *Small is Beautiful*, Blond & Briggs.
    Anderson, M. A. (1975) Land Planning Implications of Increased Food Supplies, *The Planner*, Vol. 61(10).
6. Mellanby, K. (1975) *Can Britain Feed Itself?* The Merlin Press.
7. Weller, J. (1967) *Modern Agriculture and Rural Planning*, Architectural Press. Chapter 1.
    See also: *Architects' Journal* (21 January 1976) Rural Settlement and Landscape Part 3: Recommendations.
    Wibberley, G. (1975) *Rural Resource Development in Britain and Environmental Concern*, Journal of the Agricultural Economics Society, Vol. XXVI, No. 3.
8. See, for example:
    Department of Environment (1972) *Sinews for Survival*, H.M.S.O. which argues for a Standing Advisory Committee of rural interests to develop policies, particularly for the uplands.
    Select Committee on Scottish Affairs (1972) *Land Resource Use in Scotland, Vol. 1* (Report and Proceedings), H.M.S.O. which suggests (for Scotland) a central forum (Land Use Council) to provide guidance and develop ideas on rural affairs supported by a separate Land Use Unit, independent of existing land planning agencies, to provide technical advice to policy-makers.
    Green, R. J. (1971) *Country Planning*, Manchester University Press. Chapter 10 argues for a review of the role of rural regions.
    Committee for Environmental Conservation (1972) *Urban Pressures on the Countryside*, which proposes a Royal Commission on the countryside.
    In 1974, the Department of Environment established a Countryside Review Committee to consider the range of government policies affecting the countryside and identify conflicts between them.
    In 1975, the Environment sub-committee of the House of Commons Expenditure Committee began investigating the workings of the National Parks and Access to the Countryside Act, 1949, and the Countryside Act, 1968.
9. We should at least be looking at the possibilities for modifying British eating habits towards the foods Mellanby (op. cit.) suggests we could produce easily and on less land.
10. Tinker suggests a specialist and executive landscape reconstruction agency:
    Tinker, J. (1974) The End of the English Landscape, *New Scientist*, Vol. 64 (926), 5 December.
11. Kimber, R., Richardson, J. J., Brookes, S. K. and Jordan, G. A. (1974). Parliamentary Questions and the Allocation of Departmental Responsibilities, *Parliamentary Affairs*, Vol. XXVII, No. 3.
12. See, for example, discussion of the Upland Management Experiment in Chapter 9 where officers from the Agricultural Development and Advisory Service were used in the initial stages. But one consequence of recent cuts in government spending is a reduction in the environmental training of advisory officers.

Postscript

The period since the spring of 1976 when this book went to the publishers has seen a welcome increase in research, discussion and comment upon countryside matters. The topic is once more fashionable, enjoying a revival – in words at least – which almost matches the enthusiasm of the later 1960's.[1]

Two of the most significant events have been the successful conclusion of the Upland Management Experiment[2] in the Lake District and official acknowledgement of the importance of this kind of 'area management' for the implementation of environmental policies in the countryside.[3] Similar experimental studies in the Bollin Valley,[4] on the urban fringe of London[5] and in some Heritage Coasts, show that the mechanism has great potential. There now seems to be some way out of the frustrations of the experimental planning work in East Hampshire and elsewhere, where the *methods* of rural plan-making were developed but the means of implementation remained elusive.

The limitations of these pioneer exercises can now be clearly seen: for all their emphasis upon co-operative policymaking, upon the importance of tactical management as well as strategic planning, only bureaucrats were closely involved. The major arbiters of change in the rural environment, especially farmers, were largely excluded from the process, although later studies involved them indirectly. More importantly, plan-making was divorced from implementation; there was no opportunity, as there has been in the area management studies, for policies to be devised and revised in the light of frequent discussions with practising land managers.

In a period of continued economic difficulties and minimal budgets for the luxuries of rural spending, it is encouraging that relatively cheap and inexpensive means have been found of gaining public access and environmental benefits and improving rural goodwill. It is possible that area management projects, following on from the work of the Upland Management Service in the Lake District, could be so widened in scope as to produce a truly 'corporate planning' approach for rural areas, although this would require a great change in the approach of certain rural departments of government.

Encouraging too is the unusually rapid diffusion of ideas developed over the last decade into some spheres of local and central policymaking. A number of recent plans, notably the Hertfordshire and Cheshire Structure Plans and the Dartmoor National Park Plan,[6] show that the general approach to rural planning is changing. The conception of rural problems is more realistic; interrelationships between many components of the countryside are reflected in the composition and consultations of the planning team; methods of plan-preparation are more sophisticated and there is discussion of many means of implementation.

219

If this were not enough, central government has recorded its own process of re-education in rural planning in the first report of the Countryside Review Committee.[7] It is difficult to be accurate and fair in a summary of this attractively written document but the main elements of its own summary are these.

> "The countryside is facing increased pressures [and] an early reassessment of priorities is called for. Present policy is geared towards the achievement of individual goals in the major sectors of rural use and these can conflict. Moreover, national policies [on other matters] such as taxation have significant effects [on the countryside] and other relevant factors and developments lie outside national control. [Therefore,] a sectional approach to the countryside is insufficient. Better inter-Departmental liaison should be developed [with] improvements in coordination on the regional scale. The continued multi-use of land is, and must remain, a central concept. Management measures are the best means of tackling resulting conflicts [and] this depends on the development of a consensus approach. Exploratory, essentially, administrative techniques have the most potential, [as, for example,] monitoring the operation of Section 11 of the 1968 Countryside Act. There may, too, be a case for reviewing the roles of the relevant statutory agencies and their parent Departments. [Finally,] increased expenditure on the countryside will require corresponding savings [elsewhere]."

In its attachment to area management and its suggestion of some government agency restructuring, the report offers a safe and attractive recipe for solving some of the problems of the past ten years. But it is not a document of vision. The problem lies partly in the format of review. This group was the answer to requests for a Royal Commission on the countryside; but a Civil Service Committee, with its partiality for compromise and its unwillingness to rock the establishment boat cannot be expected to generate the kind of ideas about problems or their solution upon which discussion can build. The solutions offered, modern as they are, seem too much like a universal cure-all. The need for new powers of regulation and executive action, for greater public intervention in rural land management, and for more fundamental government restructuring than is implied, have been too lightly dismissed in favour of a method as yet unproven in its replicability or widespread effectiveness. Over much of the lowlands (and even in upland areas such as Exmoor) there is no incentive for private owners to co-operate over land management decisions in the public interest as they have done in those parts of the uplands and the urban fringe where the farming is marginal and the local economy fragile.

But the most dangerous feature of the Countryside Review is its optimism, its complacency about the future. There is no indication of the scale of future problems — especially after the next ten years and the exhaustion of North Sea oil — in, for example, energy generation (with the prospect of a programme dominated by nuclear power stations); in mining (with wholly inadequate proposals for control recommended by the Stevens Committee); in agricultural development on the best land, or in the effects of political decisions on wealth and devolution. For all its enlightened discussion about the importance of planning rural as well as urban areas, the Review accepts that the countryside will be, after all, what is left over after the other programmes of resource exploitation — for food, timber, minerals and aggregates, energy, water, roads — have met their forecast demands.[8] Their practice of planning for the current trend, of increasing demands rather than seeking to reduce them, is not questioned.

In all, the Review is a disturbing document for it masks the real choices. If we maintain present material living standards exactly as we know them, we do so at the expense of accessible and beautiful countryside. With debts of the scale Britain now has we cannot have both, unless, as Mellanby[9] and others have suggested, we modify our habits — in meat-eating, for example. We may prefer to maintain standards, but the sacrifice ought at least to be acknowledged, as it is in other comparable fields of policymaking such as sport or the arts. Both of these, and many other more immediately important branches of social welfare must make do with less money for new developments. But the countryside suffers in a unique way: something irreplaceable is not simply failing to be improved, it is being destroyed. It is like building a national theatre (or a hospital or a school) and not just allowing it to decay, but bulldozing it down.

References

1. Cherry, G. (ed.) (1976) *Rural Planning Problems*, Leonard Hill.
   Gill, C. (ed.) (1976) *The Countryman's Britain*, David & Charles.
   House of Commons Expenditure Committee (1976) *Sixth Report: National Parks and the Countryside*, HMSO.
   MacEwen, M. (ed.) (1976) *Future Landscapes*, Chatto & Windus.
2. Countryside Commission/Lake District Special Planning Board (1976) *The Lake District Upland Management Experiment*, Countryside Commission Publication 93.
   Countryside Commission/Lake District Special Planning Board (1976) *A Study of the Hartsop Valley*, Countryside Commission Publication 92.
3. Countryside Review Committee (1976) *The Countryside – Problems and Policies. A Discussion Paper*, HMSO.
4. Countryside Commission (1976) *The Bollin Valley*, Countryside Commission Publication 97.
5. Hall, A. (1976) Management in the urban fringe, *Countryside Recreation Review*, vol.1.
6. Hertfordshire County Council (1976) *Hertfordshire County Structure Plan Written Statement*.
   Cheshire County Council (1976) *Cheshire County Structure Plan Written Statement*.
   Dartmoor National Park Committee (1976) *National Park Plan*.
7. Countryside Review Committee (1976) Op cit.
8. See, for example, *Land for Agriculture*, Centre for Agricultural Strategy, University of Reading, October 1976.
9. Mellanby, K. (1975) *Can Britain Feed Itself?*, Merlin Press.

Index

URBAN AND REGIONAL PLANNING SERIES

Other Titles in the Series

CHADWICK, G. F.
A Systems View of Planning (Volume 1)

BLUNDEN, W. R.
The Land Use/Transport System (Volume 2)

GOODALL, B.
The Economics of Urban Areas (Volume 3)

LEE, C.
Models in Planning: An Introduction to the Use of Quantitative Models in Planning (Volume 4)

FALUDI, Andreas
A Reader in Planning Theory (Volume 5)

COWLING, T. M. & STEELEY, G. C.
Sub-Regional Planning Studies: An Evaluation (Volume 6)

FALUDI, Andreas
Planning Theory (Volume 7)

SOLESBURY, W.
Policy in Urban Planning: Structure Plans, Programmes and Local Plans (Volume 8)

MOSELEY, M. J.
Growth Centres in Spatial Planning (Volume 9)

LICHFIELD, N. et al.
Evaluation in the Planning Process (Volume 10)

SANT, M. E. C.
Industrial Movement and Regional Development: The British Case (Volume 11)

HART, D. A.
Strategic Planning In London: The Rise and Fall of the Primary Road Network (Volume 12)

STARKIE, D. N. M.
Transportation Planning, Policy and Analysis (Volume 13)

FRIEND, J. K. & JESSOP, W. N.
Local Government and Strategic Choice, 2nd Edition (Volume 14)

RAPOPORT, Amos
Human Aspects of Urban Form (Volume 15)

DARIN-DRABKIN, H.
Land Policy and Urban Growth (Volume 16)

NEEDHAM, D. B.
How Cities Work: An Introduction (Volume 17)

227